Hobbes and the Artifice of Eternity

Thomas Hobbes argues that the fear of violent death is the most reliable passion on which to found political society. His role in shaping the contemporary view of religion and honor in the West is pivotal, yet his ideas are famously riddled with contradictions. In this breakthrough study, McClure finds evidence that Hobbes's apparent inconsistencies are intentional, part of a sophisticated rhetorical strategy meant to make man more afraid of death than he naturally is. Hobbes subtly undermined two of the most powerful manifestations of man's desire for immortality: the religious belief in an afterlife and the secular desire for eternal fame through honor. McClure argues that Hobbes purposefully stirred up controversy, provoking his adversaries into attacking him and unwittingly spreading his message. This study will appeal to scholars of Hobbes, political theorists, historians of early modern political thought and anyone interested in the genesis of modern Western attitudes toward mortality.

Christopher Scott McClure is an independent scholar. His research focuses on the history of Western political thought, particularly the ancient and early modern periods. He has published a variety of articles, most recently in *The Journal of Politics* and *The Review of Politics*.

Hobbes and the Artifice of Eternity

CHRISTOPHER SCOTT McCLURE

CAMBRIDGE
UNIVERSITY PRESS

One Liberty Plaza, 20th Floor, New York NY 10006, USA

Cambridge University Press is part of the University of Cambridge.

It furthers the University's mission by disseminating knowledge in the pursuit of education, learning, and research at the highest international levels of excellence.

www.cambridge.org
Information on this title: www.cambridge.org/9781107153790

© Christopher Scott McClure 2016

This publication is in copyright. Subject to statutory exception and to the provisions of relevant collective licensing agreements, no reproduction of any part may take place without the written permission of Cambridge University Press.

First published 2016

A catalogue record for this publication is available from the British Library.

ISBN 978-1-107-15379-0 Hardback

Cambridge University Press has no responsibility for the persistence or accuracy of URLs for external or third-party Internet Web sites referred to in this publication and does not guarantee that any content on such Web sites is, or will remain, accurate or appropriate.

Contents

Acknowledgments		*page* vii
1	The Desire for Immortality as a Political Problem	1
2	The Effectual Truth of Hobbes's Rhetoric	30
3	*Leviathan* as a Scientific Work of Art	60
4	The Hollow Religion of *Leviathan*	87
5	Hell and Anxiety in Hobbes's *Leviathan*	119
6	War, Madness and Death: The Paradox of Honor in Hobbes's *Leviathan*	147
7	Self-Interest Rightly Understood in *Behemoth*: The Case of General Monck	172
8	The Afterlife of Immortality	200
Bibliography		221
Index		231

Acknowledgments

Most of this book was written during my time as a postdoctoral fellow at Harvard University under the supervision of Harvey Mansfield. I am above all grateful to Professor Mansfield for his encouragement, unwavering support and invaluable suggestions. It was an honor to be in the man's presence for two years.

For their financial support, I would like to thank the Foundation on Constitutional Government and the Jack Miller Center. Also, thanks are due to the *Review of Politics* and the *Journal of Politics* for their kind permission to reprint versions of previously published articles.

For helpful comments and suggestions along the way, I would like to thank John T. Scott, Clifford Orwin, Quentin Skinner, Shalini Satkunanandan, Robert Taylor, Joshua Mitchell, Rory Schacter, Alexander Orwin, Gabriel Bartlett, Joe Hebert, Dustin Sebell, Hannes Kerber, Daniel Kapust and Devin Stauffer.

I could never say enough to express the depth of gratitude to my parents, Kim and Seumas. I would, though, like to thank my mother for holding on to her undergraduate texts of Hobbes, Plato and Machiavelli and for reading the Myth of Er to me as a child. I would like to thank my father for imparting to me an understanding of the importance of law and civilization.

Finally, this book would not have been possible without the support of my wife, Erica. Her eye for details, both large and small, and her stamina in reading and commenting on every draft have made this a much stronger work.

I

The Desire for Immortality as a Political Problem

Hobbes wanted to live a long life. He went out of his way, in his Verse Autobiography and elsewhere, to portray himself as a fearful man. He joked that he was born prematurely when his mother took fright at the approaching Spanish Armada in 1588 and boasted about being "the first of all that fled" to Paris at the outbreak of the English Civil War.[1] This image stuck. In a 1670 attack on *Leviathan*, Thomas Tenison presents Hobbes taking the waters at Buxton Well, "for the old Man being a well-wisher to long life, and knowing that those Waters were comfortable to the Nerves, and very useful towards the prolongation of health."[2]

The caricature that Hobbes promoted of himself as a timorous man was not simply an act. During his lifetime, he assiduously avoided any place rumored to be infected with plague; later in life, he ate no meat other than fish; and played tennis in order to keep fit well into old age.[3] All of this paid off: He lived to be ninety-one years old in an age when the average life expectancy was only about thirty-five, and despite being low born.

Both in life and in popular imagination, Hobbes stood in contrast to most of his contemporaries. All around him were those who courted death for any number of what Hobbes thought were bad reasons. As recounted in *Behemoth*, his history of the English Civil War, ordinary citizens joined

---

[1] Hobbes (1840a, 414). Martinich (1999, 162) also notes in this context that Hobbes was "criticized for leaving, even being called a 'poltroon,' on the grounds that he could have served the royalist forces in some noncombative role, as William Harvey and other soldiers over the age of fifty had."
[2] Tenison (1670, 3).
[3] Martinich (1999).

either the Roundhead or Cavalier armies for the sake of pay and plunder. Far more dangerous, though, were those who fought because of the threat of hellfire and aristocrats, who hoped to make names for themselves. The latter were corrupted, as Hobbes saw it, by the democratic writings of Greek and Roman philosophers. Those who took up arms in pursuit of some form of immortality were the most serious threat to peace and stability.

Hobbes recognized that the desire for immortality, in its various forms, was the greatest obstacle to his proposed political system. The most obvious reason for this was the problem citizens faced when forced to choose between obeying a secular government that threatened them with imprisonment, torture and death, and religious authorities that promised an eternity of agony in hell. Avoiding the latter was clearly the more sensible route. It was also difficult, if not impossible, to convince someone who believed that God had chosen an everlasting life of bliss for him to do anything he thought might jeopardize that destiny. Glory seekers, too, were a perennial threat to peace since they thrived on war and were prepared to kill and often to die for the sake of renown. Hobbes, though, realized that these desires could not be entirely removed, recognizing them as a part of a permanent human nature that would be in constant tension with his system, insofar as the latter rests on a powerful if not absolute fear of death. A major goal, therefore, of Hobbes's political works was weakening or otherwise undermining the two most significant hopes for an afterlife, Christian hope for heaven, as well as the fear of hell, and a desire for immortal honor, and replacing these with a politically salutary desire for longevity. Hobbes wanted to tame, but not eradicate, hopes for eternity. Where there was once certainty about life after death, he sought to leave a deep uncertainty.[4]

What this means is that Hobbes's system, so often noted for its geometric precision, is not a perfect fit with his view of human nature.[5] Just as

---

[4] McGrath (2005, 359) notes that "the doctrine of justification – traditionally regarded as addressing the question of how humanity may establish a transcendent dimension to existence through relating to the divine – is...subverted by the Enlightenment's emphasis upon self-actualisation as the goal of human existence. This has led, both directly and indirectly, to a growing perception that the traditional Christian soteriological agenda is implausible for modernity."

[5] As Johnston puts it, Hobbes "formulated a portrait of man characterized by a systematic opposition between two models. One of these was the model of man as an egoistic, rational being that had underlain his political philosophy from the beginning. The other was a descriptive model of man as an ignorant, superstitious, irrational being" Johnston (1989, 121). I agree with Johnston that Hobbes was engaged in a struggle for

irrational numbers such as pi and the golden ratio reveal the limits of mathematics, but also some of its most fascinating facets, so by examining this dimension of Hobbes's political theory, the desire for immortality which is at the heart of so much human striving, but which can never be entirely rational in the modern sense of the term, we will be able to witness Hobbes's genius at its most subtle.

By approaching Hobbes from this perspective, we will gain not only a deeper understanding of what Hobbes thought he could and could not achieve but also some clarity both about the contemporary approach to mortality in the West and current debates about the nature of liberalism and modernity in general. It is in fact remarkable how closely the tension in Hobbes's system is mirrored in contemporary Western society. About 58 percent of Americans, for example, said that religion was very important in their lives in a 2012 Gallup poll, and 55 percent of respondents claimed that religion could answer all, or most of today's problems. Yet few, if any, wish to die as martyrs for their faiths, and those who do are likely to be branded extremists or fanatics. Similarly, the kind of violence that those in the seventeenth century would have thought necessary for the defense of one's honor, or that of one's family, is today the preserve of street gangs and those on the fringes of society. Even in the armed forces, where the ethos of honor has always been strongest, contemporary observers have noted an increasing aversion to casualties and a decline in the warrior spirit.

The widespread interest in Hobbes over the past few decades stems from the sense that Hobbes stands somehow at the dawn of modernity. Whether because of his impact on liberalism, capitalism, the secular Enlightenment, the scientific view of man and politics, his insistence on the need for powerful government, or all of these, Hobbes is widely recognized as a key figure in the development of the modern world.

Scholars of nearly every stripe, too, have recognized that Hobbes was, in one way or another, a highly rhetorical author. Sometimes this is meant in a straightforward way to mean that Hobbes made use of common rhetorical strategies he would have known of from his early reading of Cicero, Quintilian and others. This is the famous argument of Quentin Skinner, and it would be difficult to deny the presence of such devices in

enlightenment, but, as will become clear, we disagree about the method Hobbes chose. Oakeshott (1991, 245) also speaks about Hobbes's philosophy as the establishment of "true fictions" and claims that "the system of Hobbes's philosophy lies in his conception of the nature of philosophical knowledge, and not in any doctrine about the world."

Leviathan.⁶ There are also those, including Leo Strauss, especially in his later writings on the subject, who see Hobbes as an esoteric author, who wished to conceal his true views from most readers. Still others, beginning with David Johnston, see Hobbes's use of science and theology as part of a single polemical project of cultural transformation. There is some degree of overlap in these views. All of these scholars agree that Hobbes was not simply setting out a scientific view of man, while acknowledging the importance of science to his overall project. I am sympathetic to differing degrees with all of these positions, as well as the thought that Hobbes was instrumental in the development of modernity.

The assumption, explicit or implicit, in these interpretations is that whatever Hobbes's rhetorical strategy, he failed at it. Hobbes's political writings, as is well known, provoked an extraordinarily hostile reaction. Any account of Hobbes's rhetoric must account for this major and unavoidable fact. Hobbes, after all, is famous in large part for his insights into the passions and human nature. If his aim was to win over his audience through the clever use of rhetorical devices, would his total failure in this regard not detract from his reputation as a great political philosopher? Would we not be justified in claiming that Hobbes badly misjudged the passions and concerns of those among whom he lived?

My central claim about Hobbes's rhetorical strategy is that he intentionally provoked his readers into attacking him in order to subtly induce them to draw conclusions that Hobbes could not state openly and to increase the influence of his work through notoriety generated by controversy. This rhetorical strategy is closely intertwined with the specific aims of Hobbes's political works. The particular aim that I am concerned with in this book is that of instilling grave doubts about the possibility of achieving any kind of immortality. This was a goal Hobbes could not state openly. Nor could he have been successful in this aim through anything other than an indirect method.

So, while I am in agreement that Hobbes had a great impact on modernity, I also want to stress another dimension of this impact that is not often mentioned: Hobbes's contribution to the sense of malaise that many critics of modernity have identified. Fred Dallmayr, a rare exception, has argued that there is a deep affinity between Hobbes's view of life and that of existentialist thinkers such as Camus, Sartre and Merleau-Ponty.⁷ For Hobbes, according

---

⁶ Skinner (1996).
⁷ Dallmayr (1969, 615–40). Other scholars who do not explicitly draw attention to these affinities nevertheless speak of Hobbes as depicting man alone in a disordered universe,

to Dallmayr, life is endlessly restless and the world disenchanted; Hobbes is quite close to Camus, who writes, "[i]n a universe suddenly divested of illusion and lights, man feels an alien, a stranger. His exile is without remedy since he is deprived of the memory of a lost home or the hope of a promised land."[8] Hobbes's view, Dallmayr goes on, "must appear dry and uninspiring: his terse sentences never soar to the heights of eternal vistas or awesome revelations. His starting point – life and its continuous affirmation – is almost offensively mundane."[9] Part of my argument is that this anxiety about the fact of mortality is not an unintended consequence but a necessary, political one that Hobbes, at least, has built into his system. One of the requirements of peaceful politics, for Hobbes, is that citizens have more or less disquiet minds.

THE DISQUIET MIND OF THE HOBBESIAN CITIZEN

The Cambridge Platonist Robert Cudworth, in one of many polemics attacking the religious thought of *Leviathan* in the decades after its publication, accuses Hobbes of being the latest inheritor of the atomistic and Epicurean brand of ancient atheism embodied in the poem *De Rerum Natura* by Lucretius.[10] Like Hobbes, Lucretius taught that men's beliefs about the gods originated in their fear of nature's unexplained flux and its inscrutable effect on their lives. This supposedly elementary fear, Cudworth claimed, tended, "to the great *Disquiet* of mens own Lives, and the *Terrour of their Minds*" and "cannot be accounted other than a kind of *Crazedness* or *Distraction*."[11] For atheists such as Hobbes and Lucretius, he goes on, "it is all one as if they should affirm the Generality of mankind, to be Frighted out of their Wits, or Crazed and Distemper'd in their Brains: none but a few Atheists, who being undaunted and undismaied have escaped this *Panick Terrour*, remaining *Sober* and in their *Right Senses*."[12] This, in fact, is not

---

unable to understand or really relate to others. Thus, Flathman: "By denying the humanly knowable divine, natural or rational order posited by his main theological and philosophical opponents, by claiming to liberate human beings to devise an order of their own making and liking, Hobbes cast humankind into an abyss of self- and mutual unintelligibility" Flathman (1993, 5).

[8] Dallmayr (1969, 620).
[9] Dallmayr (1969, 625).
[10] Cudworth (1678). For the charge of Hobbes's Epicureanism, see also Dowell (1683, 11).
[11] Cudworth (1678, 658).
[12] Cudworth (1678, 658). In an early letter to Hobbes, Sorbrière also implied that Hobbes was dispelling religious superstition as Lucretius had. Hobbes (2007, 122) and Malcolm's note (2002, 123).

a bad characterization of *De Rerum Natura*, where Lucretius maintains that men "are often held in suspense with affrighted wits – happenings which abase their spirits through fear of the gods, keeping them crushed to the earth, because their ignorance of causes compels them to refer events to the dominion of the gods, and to yield to them the place of kings."[13] Once men understand the principles and laws of nature, however, Lucretius promises "tranquil peace of spirit."[14]

Unlike Lucretius, though, for Hobbes even those who understand the origins of religion and the laws of physics are driven by a "perpetuall and restlesse desire of Power after power."[15] No one can remain satisfied with his current condition, and everyone is thus forced to "assure for ever, the way of his future desire."[16] There is no trace in Hobbes's political philosophy of the "*animi tranquilla pace*" Lucretius speaks of.[17] What accounts for this different view of the possibility of human happiness between Lucretius and Hobbes? We find a clue if we follow Cudworth further in his attack on Hobbes's atheism. Against the "*Sottish Stupidity*" of Hobbes and other atheists, Cudworth claims, there is indeed a "*Religious Fear* of God," but this has nothing to do with fear for one's worldly fate, since no true believer is concerned with what happens to him here on earth.[18] In fact, it is atheists like Hobbes who are subjected to the vicissitudes of fortune and acknowledge "no other Good, but what belongs to the *Animal Life only*," who are "*Timourous* and *Fearful*."[19] In Hobbes's case, this is obvious from the central place of fear in his political philosophy. The fundamental error atheists make, according to Cudworth, is that they believe they are freeing themselves from a wrathful, spiteful and ultimately malicious god, or gods, when in fact, all, "*agree in this, that God is to be praised, as one who is Good and Benign.*"[20] Cudworth acknowledges that this may be a difficult claim to prove, and indeed, it fails as an indictment of Lucretius, for whom the real gods are so benign that they do not concern themselves in the slightest with man's fate. This was an improvement over pagan gods, "rolling great billows of wrath," and meting out everlasting punishment after death.[21]

---

[13] Lucretius (1992, 497 (sections 6.51–5)). See also (1992, 15 (section 1.146)).
[14] Lucretius (1992, 499).
[15] Hobbes (2012, 150).
[16] Hobbes (2012, 150).
[17] Lucretius (1992, 498).
[18] Cudworth (1678, 658–9).
[19] Cudworth (1678, 659).
[20] Cudworth (1678, 659).
[21] Lucretius (1992, 499, 13).

One who doubted the truth about Christianity in Hobbes's time would not only be free of the fear of eternal hellfire but would also have lost the possibility of immortality in heaven and a savior who cared for him as a father. This, as Cudworth suspected, could be deeply unsettling. What is odd about Hobbes's work is that, despite never admitting to being an atheist, he seems to embrace almost with enthusiasm the great disquiet of mind that Cudworth claims is the result of atheism. In *Leviathan*, his darkest work, Hobbes goes to great lengths to emphasize the absence, or at least great distance of God from man, the precarious nature of human life, and the fragility of civilization. Hell seems less real, but so does heaven.

Hobbes, though, in an apparent paradox, wants above all to release man from fear. What is "worst of all" in the state of nature is not only the danger of violent death, but the perpetual fear that pervades it.[22] But the constant fear of physical harm and insecurity of property are not the same as the restless anxiety that will underlie the lives of at least some in the Hobbesian state. Hobbes does not expect the citizens of his state to be atheists, but he does expect many to experience the disquiet Cudworth claims is the consequence of atheism. It is as if the anxiety of the Christian for the next world that Cudworth describes had been transferred to this world. Hobbes, though, was not reverting to a pagan worldview: The essentially negative Christian view of life on earth is retained, at least in the background, in the Leviathan.

As mentioned, this sentiment is stronger in *Leviathan* than in his earlier works. In both the *Elements of Law* and *Leviathan*, Hobbes claims that man's appetites can never be satisfied and that there is no greatest good. In the *Elements*, though, we find a discussion of the pleasures and joys of both body and mind, which has dropped out in *Leviathan* in favor of a startling assertion of the futility of the pursuit of happiness: The desire for power after power "ceaseth only in Death."[23] In de-emphasizing the importance of pleasures available to mortal creatures and sharpening his focus on the grasping nature of life and the finality of death, Hobbes moves further from anything recognizably Epicurean.[24] All human endeavor can be reduced to a desire for power, of which we can never have enough. Mankind is engaged in a race from which individuals drop out once they die, but which never ends while they are alive, and which can

---

[22] Hobbes (2012, 192).
[23] Hobbes (2012, 150). Cf. Hobbes (1999, 46–7).
[24] *Pace* Strauss (2011, 65–7).

never be won. The prospect of escaping this race through some form of transcendence or immortality has also dimmed in *Leviathan*. The Christian vision of the afterlife seems less believable. The traditional idea that one could win immortality through great deeds in war and politics has been undermined as well. Even the idea that one could win everlasting honor through wisdom, which we find in the *Elements*, has been left out in *Leviathan*.

This is not an accidental development in Hobbes's works. Hobbes intentionally subdues all forms of the hope for immortality and promotes instead a vague sense of anxiety at the loss of this hope. This is an essential part of his project. Clarendon, perhaps the greatest contemporary reader and critic of *Leviathan*, descried something of this strategy when, in discussing Hobbes's very strange thoughts on hell, he speaks of the "comfort that is in the uncertainty" of hell's whereabouts or even its existence.[25] Hell is not as frightening, but, Clarendon notes, Hobbes also makes "the joies of Heaven more indifferent."[26]

The uncertainty about what happens after death makes one uneasy, but there is a certain comfort in being relieved from constant terror at the prospect of eternal damnation. Hobbes repeatedly stresses that damnation is a worse fate than death. If one was certain to be damned for some action, then, by the same logic through which Hobbes allows for resistance against those who seek to kill the body, he would also have to acknowledge a right to resist those who can imperil the soul. Widespread atheism was not a realistic option for Hobbes, for whom the seeds of religion "can never be so abolished out of humane nature, but that new Religions may againe be made to spring out of them."[27] If it was impossible, as I will argue it was, to make men believe that breaking the law would result in damnation, a fundamental uncertainty about the afterlife was essential to a stable regime. One's mortal life becomes more important in light of this uncertainty, and because of this, men become more politically pliant. What critics such as Cudworth and Clarendon failed to see was that Hobbes's real goal was changing how men thought about death. Nor did they see the extent to which they were playing into Hobbes's plan with their attacks.

It is sometimes said that Hobbes was a rhetorical failure because of the black reputation he gained among his contemporaries, earning nicknames

---

[25] Hyde, Earl of Clarendon (1676, 223).
[26] Hyde, Earl of Clarendon (1676, 219).
[27] Hobbes (2012, 180).

such as the Monster of Malmesbury and the Agent of Hell. The theology and the depiction of human nature in *Leviathan* could not easily be dismissed and were deeply unsettling. In fact, though, Hobbes realized that notoriety acquired through controversy was the surest means of achieving widespread influence. An early scholar of Hobbes's reception, Sterling Lamprecht, argued that at the hands of his critics, Hobbes became a caricature in large part because of his "remarkable gift for trenchant utterance and a glee in exploiting this gift to the irritation of his opponents."[28] Lamprecht and others have interpreted the creation of the Hobbist caricature as something Hobbes did not want and had no control over. One of the main arguments of this book, however, is that Hobbes was fully aware of how his works would be read and that he therefore knew he would become a caricature and welcomed this outcome. He was, in fact, a rhetorical genius. Hobbes, who claimed that the universities of his day were like Trojan horses importing destabilizing Greek philosophy into society, understood the insidious course language and thought could take. He wanted his own works taught in the universities, and despite his apparent hubris, his wish has been fulfilled – a wish that not incidentally conferred on Hobbes his own immortality.[29]

As noted, Hobbes wanted to alter how men thought about their lives here on earth, and this went hand in hand with undermining traditional hopes for immortality. The entire philosophical system Hobbes lays out in his political works, as we shall see in greater detail in the following chapters, is part of this rhetorical strategy.

PRESCRIPTION, NOT DESCRIPTION

The political system Hobbes built was meant to be impervious to destruction except from external threat and was therefore, he claimed, a mortal god. He claims, moreover, that previous regimes failed not because of man as the matter but as the maker of them. In other words, he seems to imply that he will take man as he is and place him in a new system that will account for his deficiencies; the Leviathan, then, appears to have the virtue of neither requiring the inculcation of virtue nor a degree of piety or

---

[28] Lamprecht (1940, 34). Quoted in Parkin (2007, 3).
[29] Martinich (1999, 338) notes that when John Fell, dean of Christ Church, tried to besmirch Hobbes's reputation by altering the celebratory biography of him being prepared for a history of Oxford, Hobbes retorted that his reputation "took wing a long time ago and has soared so far that it cannot be called back."

patriotism that is not ordinarily seen in man. While it is true that Hobbes's Leviathan does not rely on the kind or degree of civic virtue that would have satisfied Cato the Elder, neither does Hobbes simply take man as he finds him. He takes man as the matter in the sense that man is always driven by appetites and aversions, but he does not in any way want to leave the targets of those appetites and aversions as he found them.

For what must Hobbes have thought of those appetites and aversions when he walked through cities whose most impressive buildings were cathedrals, when the most intense political controversies of his time were about the right path to heaven, when he saw so many men fight and die in battle as a matter of course? He spent much of his life attached to one of the most important aristocratic families in England, the male line of which, all named William Cavendish, has persisted from the sixteenth century until today. Hobbes's earliest memories, according to his Verse Autobiography, were of the Malmesbury monastery, and the monuments to Athelstan, first king of all England, which stood in his hometown.[30] For a large number of Hobbes's contemporaries, the aversion to death was weaker than the appetite for immortality.

Hobbes, though, would claim in his political works, and especially in *De Cive*, that the fear of death is impossible to overcome. In *Leviathan* he says that it is the most reliable passion on which to found the civil state. This, though, was Hobbes's goal, not his starting point. When he speaks about the great power of the fear of death, and its usefulness in creating a stable regime, he is prescribing how men should think about death, not how they did think about it in his time.

In the natural state, Hobbes makes it clear that many, in fact, the majority, of men are willing to kill at the slightest provocation. And yet, from this situation, according to Hobbes's prescriptive system, the commonwealth arises. One scholar, explaining the transition from the natural to the political state, describes the mechanism thus, "[i]n the absence of a binding arbiter, disputes surrounding reputation escalate into mortal combat. However, in these battles, combatants experience one passion, fear of violent death, which pierces inflated egos, prompts rational deliberation, and inclines men to contract."[31] This description, which seems to accord with the explicit system Hobbes sets out, puts into sharp relief the fact that Hobbes seems to have skipped a step. If men care more about their reputations than their lives, at which point during the mortal combat

---

[30] Hobbes (1994c, liv).
[31] Cooper (2007, 520).

they have engaged in to protect those reputations does the fear of death pierce their egos? This scenario, of course, is implausible. What we see here are, in fact, two distinct periods: one in which men are willing to kill and die for reputation, and another in which men no longer feel compelled to do so, and thus fear death more than did their predecessors.

A careful reading reveals that Hobbes was fully aware of the inefficacy of the fear of death, and that there are numerous exceptions to this supposedly inescapable passion. The claim, moreover, that the fear of death could not be overcome was out of step with several of his philosophical forebears. Francis Bacon, for example, claims that "there is no passion in the mind of man so weak, but it mates and masters the fear of death ... Revenge triumphs over death; Love slights it; Honour aspireth to it; Grief flieth to it."[32] Montaigne tells us that "all the wisdom and argument in the world eventually come down to one conclusion; which is to teach us not to be afraid of dying," and he recommends that we "deprive death of its strangeness; let us frequent it, let us get used to it; let us have nothing more often in mind than death."[33] Montaigne's, of course, is the view of a philosopher urging his readers to do that which does not come easily, and in this he is following a long line of philosophic thought, through Plato and the Stoics. Hobbes broke with this tradition.

What is remarkable about Hobbes is that he does not urge us to get used to death, and to have it always in mind. He manifestly does not want to deprive it of its strangeness.[34] In order for death to remain the most reliable passion on which to create a stable political system, death must in fact remain strange – something that we ought not dwell on. Hobbes certainly does not agree with Calvin, the theologian many claim he follows most closely, who advises Christians to "ardently long for death, and constantly meditate upon it, and in comparison with future immortality, let us despise life, and, on account of the bondage of sin, long to renounce it whenever it shall so please the Lord."[35] Hobbes, as we shall see, in fact wants us to fear death more than we otherwise might. In order

---

[32] Bacon (2002a, 6).
[33] Montaigne (2003, 89, 96).
[34] This corresponds to a general unwillingness to think about death in the modern West, according to Philippe Ariès: "What today we call the good death, the beautiful death, corresponds exactly to what used to be the accursed death ... the death that gives no warning. 'He died tonight in his sleep: He just didn't wake up. It was the best possible way to die.'" Ariès (1991, 587).
[35] Calvin (2008, 462, 467). Calvin's thought is consistent with Ecclesiastes (KJV) 7:1, "the day of death is better than the day of one's birth," and Philippians 1:21 "to die is gain," to cite just two examples.

for his system to work, his citizens must calculate that extending their lives here on earth is a safer bet than any form of transcendence. Longevity had to become the priority. The fear of death had to become an unacknowledged civic virtue.

A corollary of this new way of thinking about death is that the desire for commodious living becomes a higher priority than it was. Acquiring wealth becomes not only a way to help stave off death and insulate the individual against unpleasant circumstances, but a legitimate way to channel the tamed desire for mundane honor. While later philosophers, perhaps most importantly Montesquieu, Adam Smith and Kant, believed that commerce and prosperity would make states more peaceful, this view overlooks the extent to which the new emphasis on longevity Hobbes describes would contribute to this. It may not be the spread of commerce and commodious living that leads to peace so much as adopting the view that self-preservation is mankind's top priority. Increased commerce can be seen as part of the increased desire for commodious living, and this shift in focus in turn should be seen at least in part as the result of the fact that hopes for immortality in an afterlife or through fame have been undermined.

With the advancement of medical science that began to flourish in Hobbes's time, longevity became more and more attainable, eclipsing, for increasing numbers, concern with everlasting glory or everlasting life in heaven. The potential to ward off death for as long as possible became one of the dreams of political philosophy. John Stuart Mill, for example, was able to exclaim, "[s]urely one of the most certain fruits to be expected hereafter from the progress of knowledge and good sense will be that nobody, unless killed by accident, will quit life without having completed the allotted term of three-score and ten."[36] If Hobbes's goal was to divert our attention from death and to focus it on living for as long as possible (what I take Mill to mean by "good sense" earlier), the goal has been achieved. Indeed, a common criticism of modernity is precisely that we avoid thinking seriously about death and that death has become too strange to contemplate.[37] This was not, though, a necessary corollary of the advances in medical science.[38]

---

[36] Mill (1910, 382).
[37] A recurrent theme in Tolstoy's short stories, for example, is the inability of the bourgeois man to grapple with this question, in contrast with the simple pious peasants who see death all the time, and for whom it is not nearly as dreadful. For two good examples, see Tolstoy (2004).
[38] For one perspective on the relationship among Islam, science and, immortality, see Iqbal (2012) and my "Reconstructing Islam in a Post-Metaphysical Age; Muhammad Iqbal's Interpretation of Immortality," in Hillier and Koshul (2015, 142–166).

Hobbes, among others, was responsible for challenging the metaphysical framework that held the Christian world together. This process, which could be said to have culminated in Kant's *Critique of Pure Reason*, was necessary for the toleration and freedom that characterizes modern societies. But some experience this development as a sense of loss or disenchantment. The most perceptive of those who critique modernity on this count often focus specifically on the issue of death. We can mention in this regard Heidegger, and any number of existentialist thinkers. Hobbes, thus, offers a more complex and subtle vision of modernity, one that fits with our own experience of the modern world.

THUCYDIDES, LEVIATHAN AND THE PROBLEM OF PRIDE

Ioannis Evrigenis finds in Thucydides's descriptions of the plague and the civil war at Corcyra a model for Hobbes's images of anarchy in the state of nature. In discussing these dire episodes in Thucydides, he claims that "[t]he commodious living that had made Athens the envy of the whole world in Pericles' assessment gave way to a breakdown of commitments so fundamental that individuals began to live as though they were alone in a universe that was about to come to an end."[39] The focus of Evrigenis here on the nexus between commodious living and anarchy is clearly Hobbesian. What strikes most readers, and what we must suppose struck Hobbes, though, was not this contrast between comfort and society, on the one hand, and isolation, on the other, but that between the vision of bodiless, painless immortal glory offered by Pericles in his funeral oration and the gruesome physical death of those who perished from the plague. The promise of immortality Pericles offers in Thucydides is just too glaring for Hobbes not to have noticed. The sheer number of characters in the work who are driven by this desire alone would be hard to overlook: Pericles, Nicias, Brasidas, Alcibiades, to name a few. Evrigenis is no doubt correct that Hobbes wants to emphasize the contrast between anarchy and commodious living, but Hobbes's neglect of any direct confrontation with the longing for immortality in Thucydides calls for some comment. In fact, Hobbes wants to obscure the lure of promises of the sort Pericles makes and to refocus his readers' attention on the commodious living Evrigenis points to.[40]

---
[39] Evrigenis (2014, 191).
[40] Closer to my own view is Peter Ahrensdorf (2000), who recognizes Hobbes's concern with the longing for immortality. But where Ahrensdorf argues that the fear of especially

14   *The Desire for Immortality as a Political Problem*

The desire for immortality is a permanent part of human nature, according to Hobbes, but it manifests itself in a wide variety of ways and levels of intensity. Hobbes would have been able to observe this in Thucydides, whose work he translated into English and published in 1629. Thucydides maintained that human nature would always remain the same. At the same time, he observed great variations and alterations in the way Hellenes thought about honor, glory and the gods. But where Thucydides merely observed these transformations, I contend that Hobbes was actively engaged in effecting one. One of the lessons Hobbes learned from Thucydides was that the existence of a permanent human nature did not preclude a certain degree of mutability: Man's passions may remain the same but their objects could be altered by external circumstances. A brief contrast between Thucydides and Hobbes will make this clearer.

The Leviathan Hobbes sketches is not the object of its citizens' deep affection. Pericles, though, urges Athenians to fall in love with Athens.[41] For Pericles, "becoming enamoured" of Athens made perfect sense since, as he says in the funeral oration as translated by Hobbes,

having everyone given his body to the commonwealth, they receive in place thereof an undecaying commendation and a most remarkable sepulchre not wherein they are buried so much as wherein their glory is laid up upon all occasion … to be remembered forever. For to famous men all the earth is a sepulchre; and their virtues shall be testified not only by the inscription in stone at home but by an unwritten record of the mind, which more than any monument will remain with everyone forever.[42]

Athenians, then, should "be forward to encounter the dangers of war" and even for "death, which is without sense" (ἀναίσθητος can also be translated as unfelt).[43]

As we shall see in greater detail in Chapter 6, this is quite different from what Hobbes expects from most soldiers in war. What is striking here for our purposes is that Pericles promises that the soldier who dies in battle will be remembered not only by Athens, but also by the whole world.[44]

---

violent death can distract man from these longings, my argument is that Hobbes had a much more complex strategy for undermining, rather than distracting from, those hopes.
[41] Thucydides (1989, 113).
[42] Thucydides (1989, 113).
[43] Thucydides (1989, 114).
[44] More recently the psychologist Otto Rank claimed that "Every group, however small or great, has, as such, an 'individual' impulse for eternalization, which manifests itself in the

For a Spartan, it was enough to be honored by Sparta, but for one living in Periclean Athens, the horizon was greater. Athens, according to Pericles, is a perfect vehicle for immortality, one that fully justifies any sacrifice. In fact, the soldier who dies for Athens does not make any sacrifice at all. For sacrifice means giving something up, and the soldier depicted in the funeral oration really has nothing to lose and everything to gain. Athens indeed is so perfect a means to immortality that the gods, whom Pericles scarcely mentions, no longer have any role to play in one's fate after death. Athens is enough.

Thucydides, though, famously juxtaposes the funeral oration with his vivid description of the plague. The most important part of that description, though, is not the horrible physical effects it had on the Athenians, and indeed on Thucydides himself, but the "dejection of mind," which was "the greatest misery of all."[45] This dejection was due to the feeling that death was imminent and unavoidable. Once the Athenians felt they had nothing to look forward to, they fell into "great licentiousness," and indulged in whatever conduced to immediate pleasure. The closeness of death so corroded the underpinnings of Athenian life that, "men grew careless both of holy and profane things alike."[46] They ignored funeral rites, and buried their family and friends, who had often been left to die alone, wherever they could, sometimes throwing them on the funeral pyres of others. Likewise, no one was willing to put any effort into "any action of honour ... because they thought it uncertain whether they should die or not before they achieve it. But what any man knew to be delightful and to be profitable to pleasure, that was made both profitable and honourable."[47]

We see here first how a change in the type of death one expects can, according to Thucydides, radically alter one's fundamental orientation toward honor, pleasure, family and the law. A whole society can, in this stark contrast, be transformed from one in which citizens disregard bodily pain and throw themselves headlong into the breach, to one where such nobility no longer makes sense because of the uncertainty of the reward.

---

creation of and care for national, religious, and artistic heroes ... the individual paves the way for this collective eternity impulse," quoted in Becker (1997, 149). As Ernest Becker, in the same context says about this "natural expansion of the creature," "The urge to immortality is not a simple reflex of the death-anxiety but a reaching out by one's whole being toward life," Becker (1997, 152-3).

[45] Thucydides (1989, 117).
[46] Thucydides (1989, 118).
[47] Thucydides (1989, 119).

Nobility for Thucydides, as for Hobbes, has to make sense. That is, there must be some payoff. The Athens of the funeral oration, though admittedly an ideal, can elicit the ultimate sacrifice of its citizens because it can promise them so much. The plague-ridden city can promise nothing, and so elicits nothing. The man who dies of plague does not join, in the erotic fashion Pericles suggests, with the more permanent, transcendent entity that is Athens. He cannot even expect his family to be with him when he dies, or for a proper marker for his grave, and so vanishes without a trace. For someone in this predicament, noble actions not only seem unprofitable, they appear foolish.

This juxtaposition also underlines the instability of what Pericles describes in his oration. Athens' peak, or the peak of any great civilization like classical Greece, is fragile and short-lived. For Hobbes, as perhaps for Thucydides, this was decisive. As Orwin puts it, "Thucydides shows us that the chasms that yawn beneath us in politics are deeper than the peaks that beckon us are high. No regime that he shows us approaches the heights limned by Pericles: not Athens, not any other. The evils of anarchy, on the other hand, prove only too real and near at hand."[48] Glory was too unreliable to serve as the foundation of a lasting state.

The instability of this vision of Athens stems, as readers of Thucydides know, not only from its susceptibility to natural disasters, but also from the fact that this kind of city praises virtues that can, when taken to an extreme, threaten the city's stability. The Greek *poleis* paradoxically demanded a high degree of conformity and devotion to the city, but also aimed at creating extraordinary individuals who stood above the norm. Athens cultivates citizens whose desire for glory is so powerful that it can destabilize and even destroy the city. Alcibiades, the clear example of this, in effect turns Pericles's vision on its head by deciding that instead of becoming part of immortal Athens, he would force Athens to be a means to his own immortality. It was precisely this kind of self-interested citizen that Hobbes feared: one who thought nothing of leading his country into turmoil, and even destruction, for the sake of his own immortal fame. And immortality was manifestly what Alcibiades wanted.

The psychological state of Athenians suffering from the plague, as described earlier, in fact, is closer to what Hobbes wants insofar as those living under the shadow of a painful and unremembered death seek only immediate pleasure, or what Hobbes and Locke would call commodious

---

[48] Orwin (1997, 183).

living.⁴⁹ The main difference, though, being that in a Hobbesian state, there is enough stability to make it worth the citizen's while to obey the law. The total despair that enveloped Athens during the plague could be almost as destabilizing as the acts of those driven by the prospect of immortal glory gained through martial valor. The transgressions of those afflicted with the plague were characterized by a lack of ambition because of their short time horizon, or, in other words, the impossibility of accomplishing anything very important before dying. Part of the explanation for the behavior of the Athenians living in the shadow of the plague is their feeling that the gods had already passed judgment on them: "Neither the fear of the gods nor laws of men," in the rendition Hobbes gives of this episode, "awed any man, not the former because they concluded it was alike to worship or not worship from seeing that alike they all perished ... they thought there was now over their heads some far greater judgment decreed against them before which fell they thought to enjoy some little part of their lives."⁵⁰

This judgment of the gods, in fact, justified the Athenians' pleasure seeking. If their fate had already been decreed, they might as well enjoy themselves while they were here. Hobbes had to find some middle way between the politically destabilizing guarantee of transcendence and the destabilizing dejection of mind caused by the certainty of annihilation. As we shall see throughout this book, Hobbes aimed to keep his citizens in a state of limbo between these two poles. Hobbes wanted citizens to indulge in the pursuit of commodious living within the bounds of law. They could enjoy themselves and make long-term plans, but most would not attempt to achieve greatness in their lifetimes. This golden mean, so to speak, also implies a degree of incertitude regarding the existence of God and religious visions of the afterlife.

The civil war in Corcyra, another episode Hobbes must have studied carefully, also demonstrates the speed with which a society can change what it looks up to and how its members live. Civil war is, for Hobbes, worse than international war, and the description we find in Thucydides of such a war is perhaps the most memorable in the Western canon. Here again we find the meaning of honor altered, since "[t]he received value of names imposed for signification of things was changed into arbitrary."⁵¹

---

[49] Hobbes was in fact held responsible for a perceived outbreak of libertinism after the Restoration. See Mintz (1962, 134ff.).
[50] Thucydides (1989, 119).
[51] Thucydides (1989, 204).

Whereas in the funeral oration dying was a worthwhile sacrifice, and during the plague simply nonsense, during civil war, "[a] furious suddenness was reputed a point of valour" and "he that could outstrip another in the doing of an evil act or that could persuade another thereto that never meant it was commended."[52] And, striking some themes that would become familiar in Hobbes's political works, during civil war, "[t]o be revenged was in more request than never to have received injury. And for oaths (when any were) of reconcilement, being administered in the present for necessity, were of force to such as had otherwise no power, but upon opportunity, he that first durst thought his revenge sweeter by the trust than if he had taken the open way."[53] Unlike the plague, which saw Athenians transgressing traditions and indulging in pleasant peccadilloes, the civil wars in Hellas elicited a competition so intense that the desire to kill and take revenge eclipsed any concern for self-preservation, a concern that was equated with cowardice.

Thucydides, like Hobbes after him, recognized that these dramatic fluctuations in how men think about life, death and honor stemmed partly from the circumstances into which they had been thrown and partly from a latent desire for power. As Thucydides puts it,

And many and heinous things happened in the cities through this sedition, which though they have been before and shall ever be as long as human nature is the same, yet they are more calm and of different kinds according to the several conjunctures. For in peace and prosperity as well cities as private men are better minded because they be not plunged into necessity of doing anything against their will.[54]

And further, "[t]he cause of all this is desire of rule out of avarice and ambition, and the zeal of contention from those two proceeding."[55] Hobbes similarly claims that men naturally love dominion over others, but also suggests that given the right circumstances, a commonwealth can be peaceful and law abiding.

Hobbes, though, not content to simply observe these turnings, presented his views on human nature in a way calculated to persuade his readers of the futility of reaching for more than a long peaceful life. There are clear and often noted similarities between the description of the civil war in Corcyra and Hobbes's description of the state of nature in

---

[52] Thucydides (1989, 205).
[53] Thucydides (1989, 204), cf. Hobbes (1999, 52), on the sweetness of revenge.
[54] Thucydides (1989, 204).
[55] Thucydides (1989, 205).

Leviathan. In both the state of nature and in the Corcyrean conflict, men have, under pressure of necessity, been forced into a war of all against all, in which striking first is the best strategy. The most dangerous kinds of men in the state of nature, and the ones Hobbes most wants to eliminate, are the ones who fight for glory, since these will kill, "for trifles, as a word, a smile, a different opinion, and any other signe of undervalue, either direct or in their Persons or by reflecxion in their Kindred, their Friends, their Nation, their Profession, or their Name."[56] We notice here that what Pericles praised so highly, fighting for the sake of one's nation (or perhaps family or tribe, since Hobbes is speaking of a pre-political situation), is for Hobbes a trifle.

In fact, it is striking that in Hobbes's political writings there is virtually no trace of the vision Pericles articulates in his funeral oration. With very rare exception, which I will discuss in Chapter 6, glory seekers, as described by Hobbes, are never making the kind of rational calculation about immortality that Pericles proposes. They are always destabilizing, dangerous, and, as I will show, crazy. Hobbes is able to present glory seekers this way by showing them primarily in the context of the state of nature. That is, a state in which there is no lasting political or social structure that can perpetuate their fame and that they can, as Pericles urged, join with in erotic union. This vision, with which Hobbes was clearly aquatinted, is necessarily absent from his work. He never openly confronts the possibility of achieving immortality in this way, but rather dismisses it indirectly as a fool's game.

Instead of a brilliant, shining Athens whose glory will last for all time, then, Hobbes proposes the Leviathan, which may be colorless by comparison, but which is nevertheless impervious to internal decay, and is therefore called by Hobbes a mortal god. The Leviathan state is built to survive not as "an unwritten record of the mind, which more than any monument will remain with everyone forever," but as that which, "might be secured, at least, from perishing by internall diseases."[57] There may be a real unity of wills in this commonwealth, but there is nothing transcendent about it. It is a space in which individuals can live long lives, not a vehicle for immortality. If threatened with destruction, citizens are not bound by patriotism to die fighting for the homeland, or their king, but should change allegiance to whichever power can best protect them.

---

[56] Hobbes (2012, 192).
[57] Hobbes (2012, 498).

Beyond the absence of the state as a vehicle for immortality in Hobbes's vision, there is also no transcendent standard of justice to which one might attach oneself. We can see this, for example, in the way Hobbes alludes to Thucydides in the tenth chapter of *Leviathan*. In Thucydides there is a historical progression in the idea of justice. In the early part of the work, known as the archaeology, Thucydides says that in earlier times there was no stigma of injustice attached to piracy, but in fact, a certain honor in it. Hobbes paraphrases this section of Thucydides in more than one place as evidence that there is no standard of justice beyond positive law. In *Leviathan* he says that "amongst men, till there were constituted great Commonwealths, it was thought no dishonour to be a Pyrate, or a High-way Theefe; but rather a lawfull Trade."[58] In the Hobbes translation, the likely source of this sentiment, thievery, is said to be "a matter at that time nowhere in disgrace but rather carrying with it something of glory [δόξης μᾶλλον]."[59] The absence of an independent standard of justice is essential to Hobbes's political theory because citizens could appeal to such a standard in order to determine that their sovereign was acting unjustly and rebel. Natural law, for Hobbes, is a matter of reason, and reason dictates that one should always obey the law. There is, however, nothing transcendent about justice for Hobbes.

In Thucydides, though, justice has an independent and expanding existence. One of the great themes in Thucydides is the discovery of ever-broader notions of justice, progress that results in universal metaphysical standards; something that Hobbes wants to undermine. Once cities are established, for Thucydides, they tend to equate justice with their own good. For Sparta, justice is what is good for Sparta. Hence the ominous question posed to the Plateans after their surrender to the Spartans: "whether they had done to the Lacedaemonians and their confederates in this war any good service."[60] The Athens of Thucydides, by contrast, is depicted as a city with a broader world view than her insular and xenophobic rival, Sparta. At least some Athenians were able to understand the perspective of the Mytilenians who revolted against Athens, and prevent their wholesale slaughter. Those Spartans who do taste something of this wider horizon – Pausanias and Brasidas are the key examples – lose all concern for Sparta and are overcome with self-serving ambition.

---

[58] Hobbes (2012, 142).
[59] Thucydides (1989, 4).
[60] Thucydides (1989, 186).

We have seen that for Pericles, the stage of Athenian glory was the whole world. This broad scope is connected with an awareness of a more universal understanding of justice. In a speech warning the Spartans against going to war with Athens, envoys from Athens claim that the Athenians deserve their empire not just because of their greater power, but also because of their greater justice. As they say of themselves, "[t]hose men are worthy of commendation who following the natural inclination of man in desiring rule over others are juster than for their own power they need. And therefore if another had our power, we think it would best make appear our own moderation."[61]

Here the idea of justice as something beyond self-interest is the reason, the envoys say, "that our city deserveth reputation."[62] It is in large part this superior justice that leads Pericles to say, in Hobbes's not entirely accurate translation, "we have opened unto us by our courage all seas and lands and set up eternal monuments on all sides both of the evil we have done to our enemies and the good we have done to our friends."[63] As Grene notes in his edition of the Hobbes translation, Thucydides says only, "eternal memories of *both good deeds and ill.*" Hobbes has added the classic definition of justice, and made Athenian justice the subject of eternal monuments.

This nascent idea of universal justice is not dissimilar from the theory of universal natural law that we find in Thomas Aquinas, and which was connected to the universal scope of Christianity. Hobbes wants to break down the universality of both and to rein justice back in behind the walls of the state. In order to do so, he has not only to undermine the reigning theology of his time, but as we will see in Chapter 3, also challenge the very possibility of metaphysics as conceived by the ancients.

In trying to achieve immortality through honor, justice or piety, one is seeking to escape death through entirely conventional or artificial means, according to Hobbes. For him, the Bible is far more a man-made than divine artifact, honor is relative and therefore not grounded in any reality, and metaphysics is a fiction derived from errors of language and logic. Man's desire for immortality is part of his nature, but the paths he has created to achieve it are mere artifice. The Leviathan, too, is artificial. Because it imitates the natural man, it also wants immortality. Joining this

---

[61] Thucydides (1989, 45).
[62] Thucydides (1989, 42).
[63] Thucydides (1989, 112).

mortal god may be the best that man can do. Leviathan can confer longevity but not eternity.

PRIDE, DEATH AND IMMORTALITY

Hobbes does not explicitly attack the desire for eternity as the primary obstacle to his proposed political system; instead, he claims that pride is the greatest obstacle.[64] In this section, I want to introduce a theme that will be developed over the course of this book. This is the complex relationship between pride, the fear of death and the desire for immortality, and how all of these fit and do not fit into Hobbes's system. Hobbes sets up an opposition between the fear of death and pride that obscures or abstracts from the full spectrum of ways in which the fear of death and pride can manifest themselves. In particular, this opposition downplays the danger of the desire for immortality by treating it as more susceptible to manipulation through the fear of death than I argue Hobbes thought it really is. Hobbes does not try to cut off the roots of the most dangerous forms of pride by instilling the fear of death directly, but by cutting off the traditional paths to immortality, and thus lowering the heights to which one's pride might aspire.

Pride is a general and significant problem for Hobbes. It leads to violent conflict in the state of nature and makes individuals unwilling to submit to political authorities in civil society. The root of this problem is that everyone believes that everyone else should regard him as he regards himself. It is a problem of the ego vis-à-vis others. It is also a temporal problem: In order to satisfy this kind of pride, one must be able to exert power over others through reputation money, and other means.[65] As he puts it in

[64] Johnston explains this clear omission as follows: "The possibility that men *in general* might *not* fear death as the greatest of evils is neither raised explicitly nor hinted at in [*Leviathan*]. Presumably, Hobbes did not regard it as a sufficiently likely possibility to merit serious discussion," Johnston (1986, 94). As will become clear, I do not accept this explanation.

[65] Riches, reputation, knowledge, are all manifestations of a desire for worldly power. Hobbes often speaks as though what we want from God is not immortality, but worldly success. When he says, for example in *De Homine* (Hobbes 1998a, 75), "Thus we cultivate the land so that it may be more fruitful for us; we worship powerful men for the sake of the power and protection that may accrue to us; so also we worship God, that we may have His favour for ourselves," he leaves the substance of God's favor indeterminate, but there is at least the suggestion that what we want from God is the same as what we want from powerful men, rather than eternal bliss. Further in the same chapter, 77, Hobbes claims prayer and thanksgiving are good because the former signifies that "all future goods that are to be hoped for come from God," and the latter shows that "we

The Elements, "GLORY, or internal gloriation of the mind, is that passion which proceedeth from the imagination or conception of our own power, above the power of him that contendeth with us ... and this passion, by them whom it displeaseth, is called pride."[66] Hobbes repeatedly stresses this competitive dimension of pride. As is well known, Hobbes claims that the antidote to this kind of pride is the fear of death. Michael Oakeshott, for example, claims that "[h]uman life is ... tension between pride and fear."[67]

If pride is a matter of exerting power over others, and is necessarily competitive, then death is the worst fate because it brings the competition to a close, and in fact should be regarded as a defeat. Oakeshott, again, describes the situation thus:

Fear ... is not merely being anxious lest the next pleasure escape him, but dread of falling behind in the race and thus being denied felicity ... with men the chief fear (before which all others are of little account) is fear of the other competitors in the race ... the ultimate fear in man is the dread of violent (or untimely) death at the hands of another man: for this is dishonour, the emblem of all human failure.[68]

The thought that there is a nexus between pride and the fear of death, and that death at the hands of another man represents the ultimate failure, and therefore the ultimate evil, is one Hobbes clearly wanted to impart to his readers. In *The Elements of Law* he compares the life of man to a race, in which "[c]ontinually to be out-gone is misery. Continually to out-go the next before is felicity. And to forsake the course is to die."[69] If Hobbes is correct, pride can be overcome by armed agents of the state and the threat of physical punishment. To be more precise, it is not the case that the fear of death overcomes pride here, but that a particular kind of pride compels one to avoid death. Hobbes's system relies on this kind of competitive, longevity-seeking pride.

---

believe that all past goods were given to us by God." The goods of the future here are equated with the goods we have received in the past. There is no mention of the greatest good we hope God will grant. Hobbes often speaks of the Christian god as if he were more like the god of the Old Testament, or the pagan gods, who delivered only worldly goods such as rain or victory.

[66] Hobbes (1999, 50).
[67] Oakeshott (1991, 302).
[68] Oakeshott (1991, 302). Johnston (1986, 36), makes a similar statement about the relationship between vanity and the fear of death. Leo Strauss (2011, 111) also claims that "as vanity is the power which dazzles, the diametrically opposed passion, fear, is the power which enlightens man."
[69] Hobbes (1999, 60).

There is, though, a distinction between the desire to live longer than our peers, or to avoid being killed by them, and a desire to live forever, regardless of the fate of others. For Hobbes, as Ahrensdorf points out, "[p]recisely because [men] long to be free from fear, and hence from the very possibility of evil and death, humans long not only to preserve themselves but to do so 'for ever.' Humans establish the state and subject themselves to it 'for their perpetuall, and not temporary, security.'"[70] Man does not only want to live longer than his peers, he wants to live forever if he can.

This desire is a permanent consequence of human psychology and does not relate to the fate or status of others. Man, as described in the eleventh and twelfth chapters of *Leviathan*, has a concern for his fate before the formation of civil society that leads him to seek out the causes of the effects he sees, but there is no indication that this concern is rooted in his desire to outdo others. This search for causes, which Hobbes calls the seed of religion, induces fear in man for his own fate. He invents stories about imagined causes, and tells them to others, but he also believes them himself: "so that Ignorance it selfe without Malice, is able to make a man both to believe lyes, and tell them; and sometimes also to invent them."[71] The fact that he believes these lies, and tells them to others without malice, implies that his primary fear is for his own fate alone. Tracing further the roots of religion, Hobbes says that "it is impossible for a man, who continually endeavoureth to secure himselfe against the evil he feares, and procure the good he desireth, not to be in a perpetuall solicitude of the time to come," and, "[t]his perpetuall feare, alwayes accompanying mankind in the ignorance of causes, as it were in the Dark, must needs have for object something. And therefore when there is nothing to be seen, there is nothing to accuse either of their good, or evill fortune, but some *Power* or Agent *Invisible*."[72] The roots of religion, to reiterate, are in man's concern for himself apart from any kind of competition with others. The Hobbesian man would want to live as long as he could, and forever if possible, even if he lived alone on a desert island.[73] "The object of man's desire," for Hobbes, "is not to enjoy once onely, and

---

[70] Ahrensdorf (2000, 584), Hobbes (2012, xix, 248; see *De Cive* 1.15).
[71] Hobbes (2012, 160).
[72] Hobbes (2012, 164–6).
[73] Of course, one could object correctly that for Hobbes, such a life might not be worth living since it is devoid of any comforts. The point still holds, though, that as long as there is a path available to continue to live comfortably, man will take it, and he will continue to take it perpetually if he can. This is a basic premise of Hobbes's psychology.

for one instant of time; but to assure for ever, the way of his future desire."[74] Hobbesian man fears not only violent death at the hands of another, but also annihilation itself.

This noncompetitive and unlimited desire for self-preservation makes man prone to hopes for various kinds of immortality that are not so easily controlled by, or put into the service of, the fear of death. Hobbes in *Leviathan* famously denies that there is any "such *Finis ultimus* (utmost ayme,) nor *Summum Bonum* (greatest Good,) as is spoken of in the Books of the old Morall Philosophers."[75] This is because for Hobbes, there is no limit to man's search for felicity. This is a specific denial of Augustine's claim that "*aeternam vitam esse summum bonum* [eternal life is the greatest good]."[76] Once immortality in heaven as a definite and finite goal seems out of reach or impossible, the only remaining goods, for Hobbes, are limitless. This is why the search for power, in all its manifestations, for Hobbes as it was for Machiavelli, is endless.[77] Self-preservation, of course, is an indefinite goal. Hobbes later acknowledges that which Christians most want is the attainment of the kingdom of God, which, Hobbes says, "is taken most commonly for Eternall Felicity, after this life, in the Highest Heaven, which they also call the Kingdome of Glory."[78] One could make the argument that pride is somehow involved in this search for eternal life. Tertullian, for example, spoke of the joy and feeling of superiority those in heaven would experience watching the suffering of the damned. The attainment of eternal life, though, comes to light here as an absolute and final good that one seeks as a consequence of the perpetual search for felicity. This desire, in its Christian context, as we will see, is extremely dangerous for Hobbes. This desire also exists outside of the "fear-pride" nexus that Oakeshott and others identify.

---

[74] Hobbes (2012, 150).
[75] Hobbes (2012, 150).
[76] Augustine (2003, 852).
[77] This transformation is a fundamental shift from the Aristotelian view of a teleological nature, to the non-teleological view we find in Hobbes. As Spragens (1973, 102) puts it in contrasting Aristotle and Hobbes,

> The new face of nature is not that of something which possesses an inherent tendency toward growth and fulfillment, but rather something which merely persists in its motion without end. The new world of nature is not a cause of order but rather the absence of order. The whole is not prior to the parts, but the parts are the realities and the wholes merely works of artifice.

> One way of understanding my argument is as the application of this insight to the transformation in how man viewed death and immortality before and after this shift.

[78] Hobbes (2012, 634).

It leads individuals to martyrdom, and to fight against overwhelming odds for the sake of their immortal souls.

The issue of pride for glory seekers is more complex, but operates along the same lines. The most dangerous glory seekers, though, for example, Alexander, did not seek reputation only because of the temporal advantages it conferred. The ultimate satisfaction of one's pride is knowing that one will be remembered forever. This kind of desire, again, the most dangerous desire politically, cannot be defeated through the fear of death. Dying heroically is often, in fact, an essential part of satisfying one's pride. This desire for immortality is an extension of the desire for preservation. It relies on others, but it would be too simple to see this desire as simply a matter of competition and not a desire for an absolute good. Pericles portrayed death in battle for Athens as a straight exchange of temporal life for immortal glory. The appeal here cannot only be the satisfaction of outdoing one's neighbor. Again, at the extreme – and it is the extreme that Hobbes most worries about – the fear of death does not subdue pride. Rather, pride subdues the fear of death.

We see here that there are two types of pride at work in Hobbes's thought, and two corresponding attitudes toward death. On the one hand, there is a desire to outdo others that Hobbes likens to a race, which results ideally in a very powerful fear of violent death. On the other, there is a desire for immortality that is not so directly bound to the fate of others, and which cannot be overcome, or put into the service of the fear of death. The former desire could only take hold once the latter had been radically undermined. When Hobbes claims that his Leviathan will be lord over the sons of pride, he is consciously offering a simplified ideal that his political philosophy is trying to achieve.

Scholars, including Ahrensdorf, argue that Hobbes is engaged in a project of Enlightenment. I agree with this, but it is important to define precisely what Hobbes thought such enlightenment entailed. I disagree with Johnston, for example, who argues that for Hobbes, "the irrationality which seemed to characterize human behavior in the present was neither an essential nor a permanent feature of human nature," and that Hobbes's political theory would ultimately render man more rational and enlightened.[79] For Hobbes, according to Johnston, "[t]he seeds of superstition and irrationality, he suggests in *Leviathan*, lie deeply imbedded in human nature," but can still be uprooted.[80] What Hobbes actually says,

---

[79] Johnston (1986, 121–2).
[80] Johnston (1986, 125).

though, in the passage Johnston alludes to, is not only that the seeds of religion are deeply embedded, but that they "can never be so abolished."[81] For Hobbes, "the fault is not in men, as they are the *Matter*; but as they are the *Makers*."[82] Man will not change in the manner Johnston suggests; the matter will remain the same, but will be placed in different circumstances. The lure of immortality will always be a possibility for man, and Hobbes's project does not entail seeing that possibility as irrational, but as impossible, or extremely unlikely. The distinction here is important. Man will continue to respond to the same stimuli when enlightened as he did when unenlightened. The fear of death can only take hold when the paths to immortality appear to have been closed. If immortality were a viable option, it would be irrational for Hobbesian man not to pursue it.

For Ahrensdorf, "[t]he purpose of enlightenment is to make human beings who are secure feel insecure, so that they may properly appreciate their security and thereby continue to be secure."[83] This process requires man to constantly be aware of the threat of anarchy and the natural state lurking beneath the commonwealth. I will argue in Chapter 6 that Hobbes has a more complex understanding of fear than Ahrensdorf suggests here, and that the Hobbesian citizen need not feel perpetually insecure. Even more important than making man aware of the dangers of anarchy, though, is the need for disenchantment; as long as man has reasonable hopes for immortality, the threat of falling into the state of nature is not the worst fate. Violent death in an anarchic situation is far less dire than eternal torment, or the loss of everlasting bliss. We need only recall that during the Renaissance and before, Christians were constantly reminded through innumerable works of art depicting the saints that dying a horrible and violent death was a means to transcendence, and something true Christians should both valorize and aspire to.[84] Similarly, for those who have a reasonable expectation of being remembered forever, it is not violent death that poses the greatest threat, but the fate of Ozymandias. Until these hopes for transcendence were broken, visions of the state of

---

[81] Hobbes (2012, 180). In fairness, Johnston does quote this passage shortly after, but his interpretation seems to imply a lack of permanence for the problem that Hobbes clearly claims for it.

[82] Hobbes (2012, 498).

[83] Ahrensdorf (2000, 582-3).

[84] Two very common examples are Saint Peter the Martyr, who is generally shown with a cleaver in his head or knife in his chest or back, and Saint Sebastian who is always riddled with arrows.

nature could not have the effect that Ahrensdorf, Evrigenis, Johnston and others claim. The kind of education that will suppress the desire for immortality, then, must take a more subtle route. The real education Hobbes offers consists in challenging deeply held cultural beliefs in order to make men fear death more than they had but without ever doing so explicitly.

By claiming that the greatest threat to political stability is pride that can be subdued by the fear of death, and intentionally overlooking the danger posed by the desire for immortality, Hobbes is able to present what he regards as an insoluble problem as soluble. It is one of the brilliant achievements of his rhetoric that he was able to recast the desire for transcendence as an irrational pathology that can be controlled by the police. Hobbes knew, though, that by nature men would always yearn for immortality, and that his system offered such a truncated prospect of eternity that they would in some instances chafe against it. He understood that man was driven far less by the fear of death than by the desire for immortality, and that the latter was not simply a reaction against the former. What Pericles offers in his oration is much more than simply staving off death indefinitely. What he offered was closer to deification. No degree of longevity could make up for this loss.

In the following chapter I set out my argument about Hobbes's rhetorical strategy and his manipulation of his readers' passions as well as his attempt to inculcate his teaching through insinuation. I also discuss his complicated relationship with Aristotle, and especially his *Rhetoric*. In Chapter 3, I focus on Hobbes's creative use of science for political purposes in *De Corpore* and the rhetorical use of a scientific system in his political works. Chapters 4 and 5 deal with Hobbes's theology. I focus more closely in Chapter 4 on the reactions of Hobbes's critics, and especially Clarendon's to his religious teaching, and how these reactions in fact furthered Hobbes's project. I also discuss the oddly circular nature of many of Hobbes's arguments here. Chapter 5 focuses more narrowly on Hobbes's bizarre interpretation of hell, which was one of, if not the most controversial aspects of *Leviathan*. In Chapter 6 I outline the intentional incoherence Hobbes sets up regarding soldiers, who Hobbes expects to fight and die, despite there apparently being no reason to do so according to his system. In Chapter 7 I argue that *Behemoth* is Hobbes's attempt to promote what, according to him, is a more rational form of self-interest, especially in the person of General Monck. Hobbes juxtaposes this to the often incoherent mix of short-sightedness and irrational longing for immortality among his contemporaries. In the conclusion I offer some reflection on the relation between Hobbes's undermining of the longing for immortality and more recent concern with equality, dignity and disenchantment.

2

The Effectual Truth of Hobbes's Rhetoric

> *gainst my Leviathan*
> *They rail, which made it read by many a man,*
> *And did confirm't the more; tis hoped by me,*
> *That it will last to all eternity.*
> – Verse Autobiography

It is not rational to expect human beings to be rational. This key insight is the starting point for understanding Hobbes's rhetorical strategy, which was directed far less at his readers' reason than at their passions. It is through this rhetorical strategy that Hobbes ultimately expected to undermine hopes for immortality and replace these with a desire for longevity. It is generally recognized today that *Leviathan* is a highly rhetorical work precisely because it aims not only to present logical arguments, but also to persuade by means other than logic. As I mentioned in the previous chapter, a general problem with interpretations of Hobbes's rhetoric is that they do not take into account the fact that, by any reasonable standard, he was a rhetorical failure.

David Johnston is correct when he says that for Hobbes, "it was less important to demonstrate the truth of his political doctrines than to drive those doctrines into the minds of his readers, to express them in language that would leave a deep and lasting impression upon them."[1] The question is what precisely those doctrines are, and how exactly Hobbes hoped to drive them into his readers' minds. On the whole, scholars who focus on Hobbes's rhetoric presume that what Hobbes was trying to convince his

---

[1] Johnston (1986, 90). I disagree with the mechanism Hobbes adopted, but agree with the goal here. More recently, Hoekstra (2006), has echoed this sentiment. See also Miller (2011, 205).

readers of is fairly straightforward, and they differ mostly about his methods. There are those, such as Quentin Skinner, who argue that Hobbes was rhetorical because he deployed classical rhetorical devices in his work.[2] On these readings, Hobbes simply thought that these devices would persuade his readers and make his theories more acceptable. Another group of scholars tries to specify the relationship between Hobbes's humanism and his science, arguing that Hobbes's science was itself a rhetorical tool (Kahn, Strauss), or that Hobbes's science was a part of his humanism and that there is no need to draw such a sharp line between the two (Miller).[3] There are also those who emphasize Hobbes's use of images, a method he learned from Thucydides, as a tool to persuade (Ahrensdorf, Evrigenis).[4]

These theories are not necessarily mutually exclusive, and there is some overlap between them. Evrigenis argues, for example, that Hobbes used many different methods to convince his readers of the horrors of the state of nature, because he was trying to convince many different kinds of readers.[5] All of these approaches, though, take for granted that in one way or another, Hobbes hoped to charm his readers and to draw them in; they all assume that Hobbes wanted his readers to agree with him.[6] This assumption is highly problematic given the actual reception of Hobbes's work.

In this chapter, and over the course of this book, I want to challenge two of the key assumptions that inform much recent scholarship: that what Hobbes wanted to convince his readers of was simply the explicit

---

[2] Skinner (1996, 6): "I employ the word [rhetoric] in the way that Hobbes himself would have understood it. I use it, that is, to describe a distinctive set of linguistic techniques ... derived from the rhetorical doctrines of *inventio, dispositio* and *elocutio*, the three principle *elementa* in classical and Renaissance theories of written eloquence."

[3] Kahn (1985); Strauss (1963); Miller (2011).

[4] Ahrensdorf (2000); Evrigenis (2014).

[5] Evrigenis (2014, 21).

[6] Evrigenis (2014, 120), for example, argues that Hobbes wanted his readers to believe themselves to be involved in something of a conspiracy with Hobbes. Evrigenis thus says that "Hobbes's manner of proceeding [in *De Cive*] allows the reader to walk away from his portrayals of the disobedience thinking that nothing therein applies to him – the reader is a reasonable interlocutor." Evrigenis does not, though, consider the possibility – which was in fact a reality – that most readers considered themselves superior to Hobbes as well. Another recent statement on this issue comes from Noel Malcolm's Introduction to his edition of Hobbes (2012). There (19), he asks why Hobbes made "various changes to his political and philosophical theory? The most obvious answer is that he was doing what philosophers normally do when they re-state their views: trying to render them more consistent, more compelling, and less vulnerable to objections." Certainly on the latter score, Hobbes could hardly have done a worse job.

arguments he sets out, and that he hoped his readers would agree with him overtly. My own approach has the virtue of accounting for the fact that Hobbes provoked a near universally hostile response. This widespread omission is a severe problem for any interpretation of Hobbes that claims, explicitly or implicitly, that Hobbes had a profound insight into human nature and that he was somehow a master rhetorician.

Skinner says the following about modern scholars such as Martinich who think that Hobbes was sincere in his political works and not being rhetorical: "While assuring themselves that there are no hidden codes to ensnare them, they have, I think, become ensnared in exactly the way that Hobbes intended."[7] The assumption on Skinner's part is that Hobbes used rhetorical devices in order to conceal what he really thought and hoped that his readers would take him seriously and at face value. About Hobbes's hostile contemporaries, Skinner asks, "whether they may not have been nearer the mark than those modern and literal-minded interpreters who have concentrated on what Hobbes *says* about such topics as the Christian mysteries without paying any attention to his tone and manner of saying it."[8] For Skinner, Hobbes was a rhetorical failure among his own contemporaries, who saw through his rhetoric, but is a rhetorical success among certain literal-minded scholars of our own time. In particular, Skinner implies that Hobbes wanted to appear to his contemporaries as a sincere Christian and wanted his rhetorical ridiculing of Christianity to go mostly unnoticed. What effect Hobbes would have hoped for with this method is not clear. In fact, it is those who saw through the rhetorical codes, well-known to Hobbes's contemporaries, who were ensnared in the way Hobbes intended.[9] Those who read Hobbes literally are, and have always been, a very small minority, and they are doubly mistaken; first because they do not read Hobbes with the critical eye Hobbes expected from his readers, and secondly, because they do not foresee that Hobbes foresaw such a critical reading.

---

[7] Skinner (1996, 14).
[8] Skinner (1996, 14).
[9] Skinner's own presentation of Hobbes's use of rhetoric lends itself well to my interpretation, despite his intention. To take just one example, Skinner notes that Hobbes often uses *elocutio* to reinforce his points. He uses language such as, "It is self-evident," "all men agree on this," and it is "universally agreed on" to bolster arguments that are not at all self-evident or universally agreed on. Hobbes, moreover, was attacked for this hyperbolic language by Wallis, who says that Hobbes can, "by a *Manifestum est*, save him the trouble of attempting a Demonstration" (quoted in Skinner 1996, 382). Skinner, however, does not consider that Hobbes made these provocative statements precisely in order to provoke.

Hobbes was indeed highly rhetorical, but he did not expect to convince his readers by coaxing them into agreement with his explicit arguments. His goal was to enrage those who thought of themselves as sophisticated readers, and thus provoke them into attacking, and thus propagating, his thought. This provocation was, in a sense, a form of flattery, because the impetus for these attacks was an irresistible feeling of intellectual superiority on the part of Hobbes's critics. Hobbes, in short, engaged in a masterful manipulation of the passions of his readers. This manipulation was also an ingenious use of the lessons Hobbes learned from Aristotle's *Rhetoric*.

We know that Hobbes, despite his apparent antipathy towards Aristotle, thought his teaching on the passions in his *Rhetoric* was "rare."[10] He made several digests of these passages over the course of many years. In his *Rhetoric*, Aristotle tells the prospective orator that "[p]raise and counsels have a common aspect" and that "if you desire to suggest, look what you would praise."[11] If a teacher wants a student, for instance, to pay close attention to the details of a text, praising him for doing so, even if he has done a mediocre job, will in fact encourage him to be more assiduous in the future. Praise can, in this way, be used as a subtle means to influence someone's behavior. A crude example would be praising someone's intelligence in conjunction with a suggestion: A smart person like you wouldn't do a thing like that. As any careful observer of human beings knows, this strategy can take on a variety of forms, and need not involve direct praise. Many are impressed by, or take seriously, what those they look up to are impressed by or take seriously. They often laugh at what those they respect laugh at, without quite knowing why.

Perhaps the main advantage of this indirect strategy is that it does not require a fully worked out rational argument. Similarly, ridiculing someone can be a quick way to dismiss him without having to having to provide a lengthy set of logical reasons. College professors know that they can generally get students to laugh at things the students probably do not fully understand. Those in the class who laugh at the joke are, by implication, smart enough to get it, and, therefore on the same cerebral plane as the speaker. A professor also knows that speaking with reverence about a certain author primes students to feel the same reverence. Indirect suggestions of this kind are often also the only means of persuasion, since, as Aristotle puts it, "in dealing with certain persons, even if we

---

[10] Aubrey (1898, 357).
[11] Aristotle (2006, 101–3).

possessed the most accurate scientific knowledge, we should not find it easy to persuade them by the employment of such knowledge. For scientific discourse is concerned with instruction, but in the case of such persons instruction is impossible."[12]

We see a similar distinction between Hobbes's more popular works such as *Leviathan*, and more thoroughly scientific works such as *De Corpore*. Hobbes, in *De Corpore*, offers a rarefied depiction of philosophy, which, he says, "professedly rejects not only the paint and false colours of language, but even the very ornaments and graces of the same; and the first grounds of all science are not only not beautiful, but poor, arid, and, in appearance, deformed."[13] *De Corpore*, he goes on to say, was written for the "few, who are delighted with truth and strength of reason in all things."[14] And indeed, *De Corpore* has never been as widely read as Hobbes's political works. On the whole, it is less rhetorical, and pitched at a narrower scientific audience. *Leviathan* and *De Cive*, on the other hand, were meant to have a broad impact. The goal was to convince more than a few.

It is in order to have such a broad impact that Hobbes used a complex form of the rhetoric of indirect suggestion that I have described above. His political works, and *Leviathan* in particular, are not primarily scientific. This implies that his political theory is not a science in any simple sense. The doctrine he sets out, he claims, can only be demonstrated by introspection, not syllogistic reasoning. There are powerful arguments in these works, but for our purposes, we must consider them as attempts to manipulate the passions.

Interpreting *Leviathan* has always been a troublesome task. Whatever Hobbes meant, there has always been a very widespread sense that he was being intentionally slippery, and this has always aroused suspicion. As Martel puts it, "not many books have generated as much controversy – nor as many competing claims as to the meaning of a book as does *Leviathan*." Indeed, he goes on, "it seems there is something else going on in this book, something that is not merely an accident or confusion about interpretation. There is a particular quality to the ambiguity of this text that gives more than enough ammunition for the complaints of [his critics]."[15] Hobbes provided this ammunition in order to achieve a specific effect.

---

[12] Aristotle (2006, Loeb 11).
[13] Hobbes (1839, 2).
[14] Hobbes (1839, 2).
[15] Martel (2007, 7). Although I cannot wholeheartedly accept Martel's reading of Hobbes as a radical democrat, I am sympathetic to his suggestion that Hobbes's rhetoric undermines authority. On my reading, though, this is done not simply to subvert authority as

It is not so much the truth of his doctrines, but their effect that Hobbes is interested in. One piece of evidence in support of this claim is that this is how Hobbes approached the history of theology. In *Behemoth*, when the speaker "B" challenges the plausibility of transubstantiation, "A" responds as follows:

> I am now in a narration, not a disputation; and therefore I would have you consider at this time nothing else, but what effect this doctrine would work upon kings and their subjects in relation to the clergy, who only were able of a piece of bread to make our Saviour's body, and thereby at the hour of death to save their souls.[16]

Whether or not transubstantiation made sense was not the point. What mattered was that Christians believed it, and it had the very specific effect of making priests appear more powerful than kings. In his dispute with Cardinal Bellarmine about the temporal authority of the pope, furthermore, Hobbes says the following:

> Before I come to consider the arguments by which he would prove this Doctrine, it will not be amiss to lay open the Consequences of it; that Princes and States, that have the Civill Sovereignty in their severall Common-wealths, may bethink themselves whether it bee convenient for them [Latin: "safe for them to grant"], and conducing to the good of their Subjects, of whom they are to give an account at the day of Judgment, to admit the same.[17]

The suggestion here is that the truth of Bellarmine's arguments may well be less important than their consequences. In his own writings, Hobbes is aware of the effect his doctrines will have on his readers and consciously shaping that effect was his goal.

Peace, not truth, was the highest goal for Hobbes. "*True* and *False*" for Hobbes, after all, "are attributes of Speech, not of things. And where Speech is not, there is neither *Truth* nor *Falsehood*."[18] And because politics, according to Hobbes, aims at peace, "Doctrine repugnant to Peace, can no more be True, than Peace and Concord can be against the Law of Nature."[19] To make this unusual claim more concrete, if one claimed that the sovereign was a cruel tyrant and that cruel tyrants ought to be overthrown, one would not be telling the truth for Hobbes

such, as Martel has it, but for a specific political purpose. On the ambiguity of Hobbes's rhetoric, see also Prokhovnik (1991).

[16] Hobbes (1990, 15).
[17] Hobbes (2012, 910).
[18] Hobbes (2012, 54).
[19] Hobbes (2012, 272).

because it would be destabilizing. The commonwealth was established to preserve the lives of its members, and any doctrine that prevents it from fulfilling that goal is false. This is why the sovereign must exercise strict censorship. Hobbes is aware that he is using the term "truth" here loosely. He warns that "disobedience may be punished in them, that against the Laws teach even true Philosophy."[20] Hobbes claims later in *A Dialogue Between a Philosopher and a Student of the Common Laws of England* that the emperor Constantine "caused this Confession [the Nicene Creed] to be made, not for the regard of Truth of Doctrine, but for the preserving of the Peace."[21] Hobbes too, in his political theory, is more concerned with establishing peace than revealing the truth about human nature.

ARISTOTLE'S DANGEROUS REVERIES

That Hobbes expected such a transformative role for his works is supported by his definition of philosophy, the aim of which is *"to bee able to produce, as far as matter, and humane force permit, such Effects, as humane life requireth."*[22] For "[t]he end of knowledge is power," and "the scope of all speculation is the performing of some action, or thing to be done."[23] His chief criticism of the political and moral philosophy of the ancients, and Aristotle in particular, is that it was at best useless "having increased nothing but words," and at worst dangerous, since "they make the Rules of *Good*, and *Bad*, by their own *Liking*, and *Disliking*: By which means, in so great a diversity of tastes, there is nothing generally agreed on; but every one doth (as far as he dares) whatsoever seemeth good in his owne eyes, to the subversion of the Common-wealth."[24]

When Hobbes criticizes Aristotle he tends to dismiss his political teaching as idiosyncratic rather than as the product of bad reasoning. This is most apparent in the twenty-first chapter of *Leviathan*, where Hobbes claims that Aristotle's love of democracy was rooted in the fact that he

---

[20] Hobbes (2012, 1102). See also what Hobbes says (2012, 574) in chapter 31 about his aim to "convert this Truth of Speculation, into Utility of Practice," and his comment in the Review and Conclusion (1139): "But in this time, that men call not onely for Peace, but also for Truth, to offer such Doctrines as I think True, and that manifestly tend to Peace and Loyalty, to the consideration of those that are yet in deliberation, is no more, but to offer New Wine, to bee put into New Cask."
[21] Hobbes (1997, 127).
[22] Hobbes (2012, 1052).
[23] Hobbes (1839, 7).
[24] Hobbes (1839, 9); Hobbes (2012, 1058–60).

lived in one. The Athenians were taught that they were free "to keep them from desire of changing their government" rather than from the "Principles of Nature."[25] Aristotle simply continued and reinforced this tradition, as did Cicero and others. Note here that the Athenians were convinced of this teaching because it had been taught, not because it made sense. Hobbes thought it was possible, in other words, to convince a whole population of an erroneous doctrine by the simple fact that it had been taught to them. At least in Hobbes's telling, the superiority of democracy was accepted without any arguments worthy of the name. This opinion about democracy persisted across the centuries through habit: "And by reading of these Greek, and Latine Authors, men from their childhood have gotten a habit (under a false shew of Liberty,) of favouring tumults, and of licentious controlling the actions of their Soveraigns."[26]

"The naturall Philosophy of those Schools," Hobbes concludes, "was rather a Dream than Science."[27] Aristotle's philosophy, moreover, and especially his *Metaphysics* was open to abuse by later theologians who concocted for the use of the universities something Hobbes called "Aristotelity."[28] One way of summing up Hobbes's fundamental criticism of Aristotle, even though he never says so in so many words, is that Aristotle was blind to the actual effect his philosophy would have outside the realm of philosophical speculation. His philosophy was ambiguous and therefore open to abuses he could not predict (in fairness, Hobbes had the examples of Plato and Aristotle from which to learn what effect philosophic thought could have on the wider world).

The political science Hobbes sets out, by contrast, will be practical and unambiguous. This, at least, is the most obvious conclusion to be drawn from his criticism of Aristotle. Hobbes offers a clear, scientifically based, plan that can be adopted in the real world, while Aristotle offered a series of arguments for and against various regimes that anyone could adopt and a vague sketch of a best regime that could never be implemented. There is no doubting the power of the logical arguments Hobbes sets out for his political system. Much of the power of his work, though, derives from the transformative influence it had and has on his readers' passions. Hobbes did not think that rational persuasion was the best means of effecting the change he had in mind.

---

[25] Hobbes (2012, 334).
[26] Hobbes (2012, 334).
[27] Hobbes (2012, 1058).
[28] Hobbes (2012, 1074).

Aristotle's *Politics* is "repugnant to Government" because its author simply did not know what he was talking about.[29] There has been progress in geometry, which has resulted in advances in navigation, architecture, geography, etc., but none in politics: "What, then, can be imagined to be the cause that the writings of those men have increased science, and the writings of these have increased nothing but words, saving that the former were written by men that knew, and the latter by such as knew not, the doctrine they taught only for ostentation of their wit and eloquence?"[30] Political science aims at establishing peace and stability in actual communities, and because Aristotle did not understand this, he has no legitimate claim to be a political philosopher, according to Hobbes. Sensible people understand that peace and stability trump all other considerations. The fact that Aristotle did not see this severely undermines his standing as an authority on politics. One of the more foolish suggestions Aristotle makes is that the law should rule rather than men. Hobbes, though, will not be fooled: "What man," he asks, "that has his naturall Senses, though he can neither write nor read, does not find himself governed by them he fears, and beleeves can kill or hurt him when he obeyeth not? [O]r that beleeves the Law can hurt him; that is, Words and Paper, without the Hands, and Swords of men?"[31] Hobbes does not bother to provide the context for Aristotle's assertion, which is an argument about the perpetual political struggle between the many and the few, and the obstacle that human passion poses to fair and equitable political arrangements.[32] Hobbes does not do so because he wants to emphasize the role that fear and the threat of physical violence play in promoting stability. Individuals, Hobbes implies here, are really driven by men with swords, not abstract ideas about the law. Any discussion of the sovereignty of the laws would give citizens the wrong idea about their own place in the regime and about what kind of claims they could make against perceived injustices. Not to mention the affinity between the notion that the laws should rule and the Old Testament notion that the Law is sacred and therefore superior to the commands of any earthly ruler. Hobbes downplays, and in fact does not even consider, the fact that for

---

[29] Hobbes (2012, 1060).
[30] Hobbes (1839, 9). Cf. Bacon (1989, 8): "[T]hat wisdom which we have derived principally from the Greeks is but like the boyhood of knowledge, and has the characteristic property of boys: it can talk, but it cannot generate; for it is fruitful of controversies but barren of works."
[31] Hobbes (2012, 1096).
[32] Aristotle (1984, 100).

Aristotle, politics is about constant deliberation among individuals and different classes of individuals who all want liberty. This sort of deliberation has no place in Hobbes's system.

It would be an understatement to say that Hobbes is not giving Aristotle a fair hearing, and it is unlikely that Hobbes really held such an obtuse attitude. It would not, though, have served Hobbes's purpose to give Aristotle a fair hearing. For example, because Hobbes wanted to promote longevity as a worthy goal, he does not enter into a direct conversation with Aristotle on what would likely be his main objection on this point: That the political community comes into being "for the sake of living," but "it exists for the sake of living well."[33] Hobbes offers an indirect response to this in *De Cive*, where he explains what he takes to be a misunderstanding of the term "liberty," and offers the disquieting suggestion that the difference between life as a citizen and life as a slave is like the difference between a prisoner in a large prison and a prisoner in a small prison: "Every man has more or less *liberty* as he has more or less space in which to move; so that a man kept in a large jail has more *liberty* than a man kept in a small jail." As consolation, Hobbes allows that free citizens "perform more honourable services in commonwealth and family, and enjoy more luxuries."[34] We can note in passing that these luxuries seem to be worldly goods, rather than the renown that honor seekers usually want. The desire for liberty is a potential threat to the efficacy of the fear of death, one that we shall see is connected to a desire for transcendence. Engaging in an extended exegesis of Aristotle's text on this point, Hobbes understood, would only draw his readers' attention back to Aristotle, and Hobbes wanted their undivided attention. He wanted his readers to think about, and argue about, his own doctrine as a means of instilling in them his own perspective. To that end, he resorts to name-calling and ridicule rather than engagement with Aristotle as well as Scholastics such as Thomas Aquinas and Duns Scotus.

Beyond ridicule, Hobbes lays the blame for the religious and civil warfare of his time at Aristotle's feet: "So, whence have arisen those civil wars about religion in Germany, France and England, if not from

---

[33] Aristotle (1984, 37). Hobbes, to the best of my knowledge, uses the term "living well" only in *On Man*, to describe man's emergence from the state of nature. What Aristotle calls "living," Hobbes calls "living well." See Hobbes (1998a, 39–40).

[34] Hobbes (2004, 111).

the philosophy, ethics, and politics of Aristotle, and of those Romans who followed Aristotle?"[35]

It should be clear from this why Hobbes thought dismissing Aristotle by calling his thought repugnant, ignorant and absurd was a safer strategy than writing an extended critique of his works. By engaging directly with Aristotle, Hobbes would only encourage more reading of Aristotle. This same reasoning can be applied to the Scholastic thinkers. These latter authors disagreed among themselves, and, from Hobbes's point of view, were digging themselves into a deeper, darker, hole with each subsequent book. Teachers are capable to instilling opinions in their readers and auditors because they are teachers, and these opinions stick, potentially for centuries, through the force of habit. Hobbes did not want his readers to spend any more time with Aristotle or Thomas Aquinas. He wanted as many people as possible reading his own works, and being taught his doctrine. The best way to accomplish this was to make himself, and not Aristotle, the center of attention. In this, he was singularly successful. Hobbes did not write any book length attacks on Aristotle, but there were dozens of book length attacks on Hobbes in the decades after *Leviathan's* publication.

The philosophy of Aristotle and the Scholasticism of the universities turned out to be so dangerous that they had to be rejected in their entirety. The assumption underlying all of this is that peace is an absolute good. Hobbes asserts that "all men agree on this, that Peace is Good."[36] It is not obvious that everyone would agree that it is the highest good. Hobbes, though, implies that peace is trump. He makes no explicit argument for this position, but expects, rather, that the rationalist garb of his political system and the general tone of his political works will make it seem as though peace is indeed self-evidently the most important thing.

FRAMING THE MIND

Hobbes presents his political teaching in *Leviathan* and *De Cive* as a science, built upon clear definitions that, once added together, draw us inexorably to accept the logic behind Leviathan's absolute power. The fundamental starting point of his argument is his teaching on the passions, which is presented in scientific form. In this section, I will argue that Hobbes's argument is indeed scientific, but not primarily because he

---

[35] Hobbes (2012, 1095). Malcolm's translation.
[36] Hobbes (2012, 242).

expects his readers to accept his definitions and classifications, but because he is manipulating his readers on the basis of his scientific understanding of the passions. Hobbes does indeed think that men are driven by appetites and aversions, and that their wills can be shaped on the basis of a clear understanding of these, but his actual view of the range of appetites is more complex than his overt presentation would suggest. A fundamental component of his rhetorical strategy involves indirectly altering the way his audience thinks about death and immortality.

To state briefly and in simplified form what I will expand on below, Hobbes's indirect attempt to frame the mind relies on the following strategy. Hobbes argues that because men are "X," we need political system "Y." Hobbes makes an argument that men are "X" and then proceeds to argue the necessity of "Y." Hobbes, though, does not openly state that for men to be "X," "Z" must also be true. That is, they must fear death more than Hobbes thinks they actually do, and they must not want to achieve immortality as strongly as they actually do. His argument is somewhat like an enthymeme, a type of argument Aristotle discusses at great length in the *Rhetoric*, in which one of the premises of the argument is not openly stated. Throughout the arguments for X and Y, Hobbes is indirectly trying to convince his readers of Z, which is, in fact, the *sine qua non* of his entire argument.

Hobbes's rhetoric, then, makes use of the scientific account of the passions which he simultaneously presents in his political works. That is, he is not only describing how the passions work, but presenting his argument in such a way as to play on the very passions he is describing. Hobbes understood, and various scholars have noted, that the scientific form of his argument was a powerful part of his rhetoric. Geometry, he claims, was the only real science, since it begins with clear and precise definitions. Hobbes faults all previous authors for failing to begin their arguments with such definitions and thus falling into absurdity.[37] By contrast, he offers such a set of definitions when discussing the passions in chapter 6 of *Leviathan*, and so proceeds scientifically.

For Hobbes, though, not many had the capacity to understand science in general. "Very few," he says, have "that skill of proceeding upon generall, and infallible rules, called Science ... and but in few things."[38] We have seen above that Hobbes thinks that philosophy is in fact too arid and unattractive for most, and that in writing *De Corpore*, he thought he

---

[37] Hobbes (2012, 68).
[38] Hobbes (2012, 188).

might do well, "to take this pains for the sake even of those few."[39] In speaking of the few who could grasp natural science, Hobbes likely had in mind those who could understand Galileo's *Discourse on the Two World-Systems*, probably the most important scientific treatise of Hobbes's time. The average intended reader of *Leviathan* was not one of these few. This again is evidence that the scientific pretense of *Leviathan* is just that. We find a precedent for this in Hobbes's presentation of the rhetorical strategy of the scholastics in *Behemoth*. Hobbes, almost certainly disingenuously, has the character "A" say that the schoolmen had "leanrt the trick of imposing what they list upon their readers, and declining the force of true reason by verbal forks; I mean distinctions that signify nothing, but serve only to astonish the multitude of ignorant men."[40]

De Corpore was the first part of Hobbes's philosophical system, which culminated in *De Cive*. It makes sense, then, that Hobbes thought that the few who could understand *De Corpore* would also be able to grasp the political science of *De Cive*. I will question this assumption more closely below, but for now we can note that *De Cive* was always much more widely read than *De Corpore*, or the second part of his system, *De Homine*. It was also the most widely read of Hobbes's works in the non-English speaking world. *Leviathan*, though, was also meant for a wider audience. Apart from the language in which it was originally published, *Leviathan* is self-contained and filled with the most dramatic language and imagery of all his philosophical works. The logic of *Leviathan*, though, also appears to rest on clear definitions, which begin from man's most basic faculties and capacities and builds to an absolute sovereign.

Paradoxically, though, the proof that Hobbes is correct about human nature and the need for the political structure he proposes in *Leviathan* does not stem from the logical reasoning behind a set of syllogisms, such as we find in his geometric proofs in *De Corpore*, but in the introspection of his readers. As he says in the introduction: "When I have set down my own reading orderly, and perspicuoulsy, the pains left another, will be onely to consider, if he also find not the same in himself. For this kind of Doctrine admitteth no other Demonstration."[41] This should be the first hint that what Hobbes offers here is not science in any ordinary sense of the term.

---

[39] Hobbes (1839, 2).
[40] Hobbes (1990, 41).
[41] Hobbes (2012, 20).

Indeed, as noted above, he claims that understanding the nature of mankind, "is hard to do, harder than to learn any Language or Science."[42] This statement in fact brings Hobbes much closer to the view of Aristotle, who famously noted the difference between demonstrable sciences like mathematics and geometry and non-demonstrable sciences, such as politics and rhetoric. This statement also contradicts Hobbes's warning about the reader who, "takes up conclusions on the trust of Authors, and doth not fetch them from the first Items in every Reckoning (which are significations of names settled by definitions), loses his labour; and does not know any thing, but onely beleeveth."[43]

When Hobbes describes the impact the work had many years later, he says that it had "framed the minds of a thousand gentlemen."[44] It would be unfair to put too much weight on this statement, but it is significant that he speaks of his influence in terms of framing minds rather than demonstration or proof. To frame a person's mind is, for Hobbes, to shape his will. For example, Hobbes says in another context: "nor does an Unrighteous man, lose his character, for such Actions, as he does, or forbears to do, for feare: because his Will is not framed by the Justice, but by the apparent benefit of what he is to do."[45] In *The Elements of Law*, moreover, he says, "For he that cannot of right be punished, cannot of right be resisted; and he that cannot of right be resisted, hath coercive power over all the rest, and thereby can frame and govern their actions at his pleasure."[46] He also speaks of the opinions of pagans regarding good and evil being "framed" by their vivid imaginations.[47] Will, which for Hobbes is simply the "last Appetite," can be shaped in various ways, and the sovereign's chief duty is to "conforme the wills of them all" through terror.[48] The will is in fact framed by all manner of appetite and aversion. When Hobbes speaks of his *Leviathan* framing the minds of one thousand gentlemen, he does not imply that he has convinced them through the logic of his reasoning, but that he has shaped their wills through the manipulation of their passions.

---

[42] Hobbes (2012, 20).
[43] Hobbes (2012, 66).
[44] Parkin (2007, 95).
[45] Hobbes (2012, 226).
[46] Hobbes (1999, 117–18).
[47] Hobbes (2012, 622).
[48] Hobbes (2012, 260).

SECRETLY INSTRUCTING THE READER

The passion Hobbes claims he is most worried about is pride. It is especially man's pride that has, "compelled him to submit himselfe to Government."[49] The Leviathan is meant to be, "a king over all the children of pride" (Job 41:34). The pride of glory seekers in the state of nature is the chief cause of the war of all against all. It is not, though, only those who resort to violence for the sake of glory who are susceptible to pride. In the opening of *De Cive*, Hobbes says that there is something about civil science, in particular, that makes those who have it, or think they have it, extremely proud:

> What most contributes to its dignity is that those who think they possess it or are in a position where they ought to possess it, are so very pleased with themselves for the semblance of it which they do possess, that they will gladly allow specialists in the other sciences to be considered intelligent, learned and erudite, and to be called so, but they never want them to be called Statesmen. Because of the preeminence of this political expertise they believe the term should be reserved to themselves ... almost everyone is delighted to have even a false semblance of it.[50]

Even Hobbes, who we must assume grasped the full implications of his own doctrine, claims to be affected: "I am a man that love my own opinions, and think all true I say."[51]

Pride is so widespread, especially among those who aspire to political philosophy, those who would be most interested in *De Cive* and *Leviathan*, that it would have been an egregious error on Hobbes's part to write his political works without taking this fact into consideration. If his goal was to frame the minds of readers of varying levels of intelligence, appealing to their passions would be the only rational choice. Hobbes indicts the sort of pride that leads to conflict, but he must do so in a way that flatters the pride of his readers. This, Hobbes thought, was the surest way to draw them in, and to propagate his vision of a new political and social order. In so doing, Hobbes was following Aristotle's suggestion about successful rhetoric: "The emotions are all those affections which cause men to change their opinion in regard to their judgements, and are accompanied by pleasure and pain."[52]

---

[49] Hobbes (2012, 496).
[50] Hobbes (1998b, 8).
[51] Hobbes (2012, 6).
[52] Aristotle (2006, 173).

Hobbes tells us,

> I recover some hope, that one time or other, this writing of mine, may fall into the hands of a Soveraign, who will consider it himselfe (for it is short, and I think clear,) without the help of any interested, or envious Interpreter; and by the exercise of entire Soveraignty, in protecting the Publique teaching of it, convert this Truth of Speculation, into the Utility of Practice.[53]

He did not, though, think that there were any interpreters who were disinterested and free of envy any more than he thought his book was short and clear.

By the time he wrote *Leviathan*, two things were certain: the book would be read, and it would be controversial. Through his earlier political and scientific works, Hobbes had gained a reputation for himself among philosophers, scientists, theologians and political figures that guaranteed that he would have an audience, even if not always an approving one. There is also little doubt that he knew what kind of response the work would generate. He knew that *De Cive* would be a, "political theory which offends the opinions of almost everyone," even before the work had been widely circulated.[54] In anticipation of the publication of *De Homine*, Hobbes says that, "though by the contumelies and petty injuries of some unskillful men, I know already, by experience, how much greater thanks will be due than paid me, for telling the truth of what men are."[55] Hobbes, in other words, knew that men would not be flattered by his unflattering depiction of them. As he put it in his translation of Thucydides, "it is hard for any man to love that counsel which maketh him love himself less."[56] Hobbes knew he was offending the pride of his readers, and he knew just how deep human pride ran. Martinich, in his biography of Hobbes, says that one of the exam questions Hobbes may have had to answer was, "Whether anyone thinks that he is stupid."[57] In the thirteenth chapter of *Leviathan* he raises this very issue in claiming that, "such is the nature of men, that howsoever they may acknowledge many others to be more witty, or more eloquent, or more learned; Yet they will hardly believe there be many so wise as themselves . . . But this proveth rather that men are in that point equall, then unequall."[58] At the very least, Hobbes

---

[53] Hobbes (2012, 574).
[54] Hobbes (2007, 157).
[55] Hobbes (1839, xii).
[56] Thucydides (1989, 572).
[57] Martinich (1999, 12).
[58] Hobbes (2012, 188).

says, they are "contented with their share."⁵⁹ Telling men "what they are," he knew, was not the way to win friends.

Evrigenis claims that Hobbes "seeks to recreate for his reader, in political terms, his own experience with Euclid by bringing the reader to the point of accepting his propositions no matter how improbable they might seem, all the while feeling as though he had done so on his own."⁶⁰ This is partially correct, but overlooks the degree of antagonism that is characteristic of readers of such works; an antagonism Hobbes clearly wanted to provoke, and which he did in fact provoke. Hobbes wanted his reader to think he had come to his own conclusion, but in opposition to what Hobbes said, not in collusion with him. Evrigenis, thus, reads Hobbes too literally when he claims that Hobbes's "private appeal to the reader to reconsider *nosce teipsum* is the first step of that process, in which *capitato benevolentiae* is the result of flattery."⁶¹

We can see that this was Hobbes's goal in part by examining the early reception to *Leviathan*. On the whole, early readers were perplexed by the work and found it difficult to understand. Jon Parkin, who has done some of the best recent work in this area, notes that, "Hobbes's unusual combination of ideas presented in such a politically ambivalent manner could simultaneously delight and appal audiences on all sides of the political and religious spectrum."⁶² Hobbes pulled his readers in by ensuring that there was something that would appeal to members of every important political and religious stripe. He simultaneously repulsed every group by incorporating elements he knew would be offensive to each. Speaking of the reception of his work in his Latin autobiography, written in the third person, Hobbes says, "Poised as it were in equilibrium between friends and enemies, his doctrines were neither whole-heartedly accepted, nor yet oppressed."⁶³ Even before the publication of *De Cive*, Hobbes understood that the educated would not like everything he had to say, and that the book would elicit a mixed response from many. As he writes to Sorbrière before the work was printed: "Nor accordingly, if it can be prevented, should the printer be allowed to get judgements on the

---

⁵⁹ Hobbes (2012, 188).
⁶⁰ Evrigenis (2014, 242).
⁶¹ Evrigenis (2014, 242).
⁶² Parkin (2007, 101).
⁶³ Quoted in Parkin (2007, 355). I thus agree with Parkin (2007, 10), that Hobbes often employed a "deliberate ambiguity," but am less sanguine that Hobbes, "was ultimately associated with a surprising range of positions, in ways that he could not control, and mostly to his detriment."

book's importance from people who, in his own opinion, he considers to be learned men. Then you must beware of those who approve most of it but disapprove of the rest."[64] A common reaction to the jumbled quality of *Leviathan* is summed up by Henry Hammond's comment that is was "a farrago of all the maddest divinity that ever was read."[65] Brian Duppa as well had the following to say: "And yet as in the man, so there ar [sic] strange mixtures in the book; many things said so well that I could embrace him for it, and many thing so wildly and unchristianly, that I can scarce have so much charity for him, as to think he was ever Christian."[66] Hobbes set himself up as a lightning rod, and sure enough, before long intellectuals were lining up by the dozen to land a blow.

In terms of politics, Hobbes was attacked by Royalists and republicans alike, with the consequence that neither side was able to use his arguments to bolster their positions. His absolutism was tainted by his theory of all government resting on the consent of the governed, and his theory of consent was marred by his absolutism. As a political teaching, Hobbes's works satisfied no one. The obscurity of Hobbes's political position meant that there was a great deal of debate about what exactly he was trying to say. The fact that *Leviathan* and *De Cive* could generate extended responses and commentaries from figures such as Robert Filmer cemented their reputation as essential reading, and ensured that they would be prominent enough to reach the canonical status they now occupy.

Part of the power of Hobbes's confusing assortment of positions lay in his eloquence. Mintz notes that, "Harrington, who could find nothing to admire in Hobbes's politics, was nevertheless moved to compliment him extravagantly as one who 'is and will in all future ages be accounted the best writer at this day in the world.'"[67] Hobbes's good prose in fact put his readers on guard. The Archbishop Tenison decries the fact that Hobbes insinuates himself, "by the handsomeness of his style, into the mindes of such whose Fancie leadeth their Judgements: and to say truth to an Enemy, he may with some Reason, pretend to *Mastery*, in that Language."[68] John Dowel, moreover, worries that "he had so fine a Pen, that by the clearness, and propriety of his Style, and exactness of his method, he gain'd more Proselytes than by his Principles."[69] As Mintz

---

[64] Hobbes (2007, 127). Malcolm translation.
[65] Quoted in Parkin (2007, 102).
[66] Quoted in Parkin (2007, 99).
[67] Mintz (1962, 20).
[68] Tenison (1670, A4).
[69] Dowell (1683, iii).

notes, "In almost all the attacks on Hobbes there is an undercurrent of resentment against the general excellence of his style. It was almost as if the critics were saying that it was unfair of Hobbes to be so wrong and yet to write so well – unfair, and moreover, dangerous."[70] What could be more noble than warning impressionable youth against the dangerous charms of the Monster of Malmesbury?

This is in fact not too distant from the criticism Hobbes himself levels at the political writings of the ancients. Those who learned Greek and Latin, Hobbes says, "became acquainted with the democratical principles of Aristotle and Cicero, and from the love of their eloquence fell in love with their politics."[71] Although Hobbes may be the first to call Aristotle's *Politics* eloquent and lovable, he no doubt refers here to the emotional force of the arguments Aristotle puts forward on behalf of the demos. Whether it is fair to read Aristotle as simply a champion of democracy, Hobbes recognized that the arguments of Aristotle and Cicero were accepted primarily on the basis of emotion, not the reason that both authors vaunted. Hobbes uses a parallel strategy, and there are no doubt many eloquent passages in his works. His charm and wit, though, gained him more notoriety than dedicated converts.

In addition to *Leviathan*'s literary charm, the deep ambiguity of the work drove Hobbes's most determined critics to reveal the truth about its darker implications. As Parkin says, "Hobbes's critics were particularly concerned about this stealthy approach, given that [Hobbes's] orthodox premises could mislead readers into a positive evaluation of his ideas. Clarendon noted that Hobbes's heterodoxy was concealed beneath quotable and innocuous phrases."[72] Hobbes was, Clarendon complained, pulling the wool over his readers' minds:

The novelty and pleasantness of the Expressions, the reputation of the Gentleman for parts and Learning, with his confidence in Conversation, and especially the humor and inclination of the Time to all kind of Paradoxes, have too much prevail'd with many of great Wit and Faculties, without reading their context, or observation of the consequences, to believe his Propositions to be more innocent or less mischievous, then upon a more deliberate perusal they will find them to be; and the love of his person and company, have rendered the iniquity of his Principles less discernable.[73]

---

[70] Mintz (1962, 37).
[71] Hobbes (1990, 43).
[72] Parkin (2007, 15).
[73] Hyde, Earl of Clarendon (1676, iv–v).

It was, paradoxically, by provoking such a negative response that Hobbes was able to flatter the pride of his audience and disseminate his ideas. Hobbes does not flatter his readers by praising them directly. No intelligent reader would fall for such a strategy. He understood that those who aspire to be a part of the intelligentsia, perhaps even more than the average person, are only really pleased by their own achievements and discoveries. We have seen above that Hobbes admits to this tendency in himself. He understood that readers are much more keen to display their own intelligence than they are to be taught by others. Men, "will hardly believe there be many so wise as themselves," he proclaimed in the midst of an argument about the general equality of intelligence among human beings.[74] An insight, of course, that puts us one step ahead of the common man. When accused of being morose and peevish with those who disagreed with him, Hobbes, speaking of himself in the third person, said the following: "When vain and ignorant young scholars, unknown to him before, come to him on purpose to argue with him, and to extort applause for their foolish opinions; and, missing of their end, fall into indiscreet and uncivil expressions, and he then appear not very well contented: it is not his *morosity*, but their *vanity* that should be blamed."[75] His description of meeting with various Oxford scientists on his return to England in 1651 is also instructive: "divers persons that professed to love philosophy and mathematics, came to see me: and some of them to let me see them, and hear and applaud what they applauded in themselves."[76]

This was the cast of mind of those Hobbes wanted to influence, and his surest bet was to allow them to applaud themselves for what they discovered in his text. Hobbes knew that readers loved nothing better than refutation, since this was the best way to demonstrate their own brilliance. And what could be better than refuting one who seemed as arrogant as Hobbes did?[77] One who referred to his critics as "flies" that he expected to "transfix" with his pen?[78] As he says of the reasons for his translations of Homer late in life: "Why publish it? Because I thought it might take off my adversaries from showing their folly upon my more

---

[74] Hobbes (2012, 188).
[75] Hobbes (1840a, 439).
[76] Quoted in Parkin (2007, 117).
[77] See Cooper (2007) for a discussion of Hobbes's arrogance. While Cooper argues that Hobbes was not, in fact, arrogant, it makes more sense to see his arrogance as insincere and as an important part of his rhetorical strategy.
[78] Hobbes (1998a, 36).

serious writings, and set them upon my verses to show their wisdom."⁷⁹ In other words, he thought his adversaries had spent enough time demonstrating their wisdom by attacking his political works, and he wanted to set them a new task. By this time, Hobbes was secure in the knowledge that *Leviathan* would be part of the canon, that it would "last to all eternity," but it was, more than anything, the controversy he consciously stirred up that put it there.⁸⁰

Anger, Aristotle notes in his *Rhetoric*, is always tinged with pleasure "due to the hope of revenge to come."⁸¹ Refutation, which is often a kind of revenge, also tends to be pleasant. Hobbes admits to indulging in this pleasure himself when defending what he knows to be his own strange ideas. Speaking of spending his time in Rouen discoursing with various people, he says that, "I serue when I can be matched as a gladiator. My odde opinions are bayted. But I am contented wTH it, as beleeuing I haue still the better, when a new man is sett vpon me; that knowes not my paradoxes, but is full of his owne doctrine, there is something in the disputation not unpleasant."⁸² It was this often angry pleasure of his adversaries that Hobbes was manipulating in order to "secretly instruct the reader" as he says Thucydides had.⁸³ What he relied on was the exultant joy his reviewers would experience in proving they were more clever than Thomas Hobbes.

Hobbes in proceeding this way was leading his accusers down a road he knew they would find irresistible. This was, Hobbes writes in *Behemoth*, the way Biblical scholars operated. It is "pride," the character "A" says, that leads the learned to propound what they think are new interpretations of the Bible, "not before thought on by others."⁸⁴ These scholars, "take delight in finding out the meaning of the most hard texts, or in thinking they have found it, in case it be new and not found out by others." "These," "B" goes on to say, "and the like points are the study of the curious, and the cause of all our late mischief."⁸⁵ The scholastics, in other words, could not help but attack each other, and strive to propose ever more creative interpretations, and ever finer distinctions in their quest

---

⁷⁹ Quoted in Mintz (1962, 19).
⁸⁰ Hobbes (1994c, lx).
⁸¹ Aristotle (2006, 173).
⁸² Hobbes (2007, 124).
⁸³ Thucydides (1989, 577).
⁸⁴ Hobbes (1990, 53).
⁸⁵ Hobbes (1990, 55).

for intellectual dominance. Hobbes consciously harnessed this hermeneutic impulse to promote his own project.

The mission of authors such as Ross, Cudworth and Clarendon was to reveal the truth about Hobbes. Thomas Tenison describes his work as an effort to, "expose this insolent and pernicious Writer, to shew unto my Countrymen that weakness of head, and venome of mouth, which is in the Philosopher, who hath rather seduc'd and poyson'd their imaginations, than conquer'd their Reason."[86]

Hobbes was attacked for his view of man as a psychological egoist, his theory of the state of nature and his materialism. The most blistering attacks, though, were not aimed at what Hobbes said explicitly, but what many took to be the hidden implications of these aspects of his work. Critics saw in these implications Hobbes's unstated intentions, and they never tired of announcing these to the reading public. Judging from the degree of fury in these attacks, which sometimes devolved into the scatological, there was obviously a great deal of pleasure involved in exposing the Devil's Secretary. John Wallis, a professor of geometry, provides a typical example:

> Who does not see that thereby you not only deny (and not just in words) angels and immortal souls, but the great and good God himself; and if you were not wary of the laws (which to you is the highest "rule of honouring and worshipping God") you would profess this openly. And however much you may mention God and the Holy Scriptures now and again (although I do not recall your mentioning the immortal soul), it is nevertheless to be doubted whether you do this ironically for the sake of appearance rather than seriously and from conviction.[87]

Filmer, in another typical line of attack, claims that the real intention behind Hobbes's emphasis on self-preservation is depriving the king of his prerogative to make war. If citizens are not obliged to put their lives at risk, "then a sovereign may be denied the benefit of making war, and be unable to defend his people – and so the end of government be frustrated."[88] These detractors felt that they had been so successful in demolishing Hobbes's arguments and exposing the real nature of his teaching that in 1658 Bramhall could proclaim that in his *The Catching of Leviathan* he was merely throwing "on two or three spadefuls of earth towards the final interment of his pernicious principles and other

---

[86] Tenison (1670, 2).
[87] Quoted in Parkin (2007, 152).
[88] Quoted in Parkin (2007, 110).

mushroom errors."[89] In fact, though, the attacks on Hobbes were only just getting started in 1658.

Despite, or perhaps because of these efforts, "Hobbism" seems to have been popular with university students for decades after. Or at least this was the worry. Parkin claims that "Hobbes's paradoxical work and the problems that it raised, undoubtedly did influence the minds of those university-educated individuals who were forming their views in the 1650s and early 1660s, but for all the critics' nightmares, there were very few publicly confessed disciples of *Leviathan*."[90] Be that as it may, the nightmares were still real. Mintz notes that the universities, "instituted a number of repressive measures designed to protect the young and impressionable 'sophister' from Hobbist influence," and the dean of Christ Church College, Oxford, "was also instrumental in having the *Leviathan* and *De Cive* formally banned by university decree in 1683 and publicly burnt."[91] Daniel Scargill, a student who was expelled from Cambridge University for being a Hobbist, said in his recantation:

I have lived in great licentiousness ... boasting myself insolently, corrupting others by my pernicious principles, to the Dishonour of God, the Reproach of the University, the Scandal of Christianity, and the just offence of mankind ... having contributed what my profane wit could devise, or my foul mouth express, to instill it into others, to confirm them therein ... that there is a desirable glory in being, and being reputed an Atheist: which I implied when I expressly affirmed that I gloried to be an *Hobbist* and an Atheist.[92]

Bishop Vesey claimed in 1677, moreover, that Hobbes's doctrines, "have had so great a share in the debauchery of his Generation, that a good Christian can hardly hear his name without saying o his prayers."[93]

What is most noteworthy here is that the young, in fact, embraced the very dark implications that Hobbes's more experienced critics had pointed out, namely his atheism. This means that it was especially what Clarendon and others had warned about, and which Hobbes never says explicitly, that at least some students found most attractive. What Clarendon and others seemed to fear was that readers would adopt Hobbes's political doctrine in order to bolster, say, a Royalist or republican political position, or that they would buy into his theology, and

---

[89] Quoted in Parkin (2007, 191).
[90] Parkin (2007, 245).
[91] Mintz (1962, 50). On Hobbes's influence over the young, see also Parkin (2007, 120–1).
[92] Mintz (1962, 51).
[93] Quoted in Mintz (1962, 57).

would thereby inadvertently insinuate the poison of Hobbes's atheism, his attack on the immortality of the soul, and his debunking of the worth of honor, into society as a whole. This did not happen, and, given what Hobbes must have known was the Janus-like quality of his political teaching, was very unlikely to happen. Instead, Hobbes's teaching was influential precisely on the basis of those aspects of the work that his critics thought were deeply hidden, and which they announced to the world. Their proclamations about Hobbes's hidden intention very probably helped to propagate Hobbes's teaching more than anything else. If he had openly argued for the positions that his critics accuse him of holding, he would not have been taken seriously in the first place. His works would have been rejected outright. By clothing his most dangerous ideas in a translucent facade, Hobbes allowed his critics to connect the dots he had laid out for them, and to present major points of his argument for him with more power and volume than he ever could have.

Hobbes was able to yoke his critics into spelling out implications of his work which he could not easily have stated openly. Hobbes's attack on the immortality of the soul, and his undermining of notions of the worth of everlasting honor had been proclaimed by his adversaries and embraced by a new generation. Macauley's famous statement on this is that, "Hobbism soon became an almost essential part of the character of the fine gentleman," because it, "degraded religion into a mere affair of state."[94] Whether Hobbes had a direct role in this or not is difficult, and probably impossible, to say. But given his pride in framing the minds of gentlemen, it is clear that this was the outcome he hoped for. Older notions of aristocratic honor as well as more traditional ideas about religion were on the wane. No one had embraced Hobbes as an authority on politics, at least in any straightforward way. No one has explicitly attempted to institute a Hobbesian state. There were, and are, no Hobbesians the way there are Lockeans. His vision of man as a fearful creature that was potentially dangerous enough to require absolute rule, however, has continued to gain in influence from Hobbes's time to our own. At the core of this vision is the assumption of a very powerful fear of death in man.

---

[94] Quoted in Mintz (1962, 137).

INCREASING THE FEAR OF DEATH

In the culture of Hobbes's time, death was not something one should fear. Very often the opposite sentiment was in vogue. The following song, written by John Dowland, a very well-known lutanist and songwriter from whom Hobbes apparently took lute lessons, is just one example of the melancholia that was popular in the sixteenth and seventeenth centuries:

> Me, me and none but me, dart home, O gentle Death,
> And quickly, for I draw too long this idle breath.
> O how I long till I may fly to heav'n above,
> Unto my faithful, unto my faithful beloved turtle dove.
>
> Like to the silver swan, before my death I sing,
> And yet alive my fatal knell I help to ring.
> Still I desire from earth and earthly joys to fly,
> He never happy liv'd, never happy liv'd that cannot love to die.[95]

The love of death Dowland speaks of is, to put it mildly, incompatible with an inescapable fear of death. The thought that man is afraid of death above all else, though, is a necessary corollary to a worldview in which there is no immortality of the soul, and no sense in striving to leave a reputation for great deeds to posterity. Without any reasonable hopes for any kind of transcendence, life here on earth matters much more. And while Hobbes's detractors proclaimed the implications of Hobbes's thought for traditional conceptions of immortality, they did not see clearly that a more intense fear of death and a far greater concern for living a long comfortable life would be a further consequence. This very real corollary was a major hidden goal of Hobbes's teaching that was not seen by his critics. Hobbes must have expected that he would be attacked for his theology and that no one would accept it. The more subtle but essential teaching that man should be more afraid of death than he is, though, he hoped would insinuate itself surreptitiously into the culture. Many have indeed been persuaded that for Hobbes, death is the *summum naturæ malum*.[96]

---

[95] I owe the insight about Hobbes's lute lessons to Quentin Skinner who mentioned that he found a large bill at Chatsworth for these lessons.

[96] Hobbes (2004, 75). See also Strauss (1963, 16): "death – being the *summum malum*, while there is no *summum bonum* – is the only absolute standard by reference to which man may coherently order his life." Also, Oakeshott (1991, 253) claims that "it may be observed that death, the involuntary cessation of desire and the pursuit of which is the end of desire, is the thing of all others the most hateful: it is the *summum malum*." See also

Increasing the Fear of Death

The Earl of Clarendon, for example, whose attack on Hobbes we will consider at greater length in Chapter 4, notes that

> the example of *Socrates*, who scorned to redeem his life by the least trespass against truth or ingenuity; or the Precepts and Judgments of *Seneca*, will be of no force with him... What would *Seneca* have thought or said of any corrupt way for the prolongation of life, if he had known anything of the obligations of Christianity, when only upon the strength of natural reason, he could so much undervalue it... What shall we say, when a Heathen Philosopher valued life only as it was a way to somewhat more precious, tho he could not comprehend it; and when a Christian Philosopher, who pretends to have a full prospect of all that is most precious, will redeem his life at the price of disclaiming to have any share in it?[97]

Clarendon sees that Hobbes's theology would lead one to be more concerned with life here on earth than the prospect of immortality in heaven, but he attributes this to Hobbes's corruption and baseness. He does not consider the possibility that Hobbes wanted to make longevity man's highest goal as a response to the political instability of his time. He did not consider that for Hobbes, Christianity itself was a problem precisely because it focused men's minds too much on another world.

What Hobbes's ultimate intentions were according to his seventeenth-century critics is not entirely clear. In the religious realm, Hobbes seemed to be deeply heretical and probably an atheist, and his goal was therefore seen to be promoting heresy and atheism. He was simply arguing, as forcefully as the law would allow, for the elimination of Christianity as usually understood and its replacement with some kind of ritualistic civil religion. In politics he was, according to his attackers, driven by a narrow and unrealistic view of human nature and a perverse understanding of the basis of sovereignty and meaning of liberty. The possibility that Hobbes did not expect his theology to be taken seriously is rarely considered, and the possibility that these arguments were all a means to a deeper intended effect was not seen.[98] No critic thought that by exposing what he saw as Hobbes's heretical teachings, he was in fact doing exactly what Hobbes hoped his critics would do.

The most important carrier of this teaching in Hobbes's work is the rationalist political system Hobbes draws out in *De Cive* and *Leviathan*.

Berns (1987, 399), Ahrensdorf (2000, 582), Martinich (1992, 267) and Evrigenis (2014, 139).

[97] Hyde, Earl of Clarendon (1676, 292–3).

[98] An important exception was Hyde, Earl of Clarendon (1676), whose *A Brief View* I will consider at length in chapter 4.

Mintz notes that Hobbes's critics, especially the Cambridge Platonists, were obliged to use his methods in their attempts to attack him:

> they tried to refute Hobbes with Hobbes's own weapon, logical analysis ... The positive outlook of More and Cudworth was anti-rational, at least insofar as rationalism was understood by Hobbes; but when they argued explicitly against Hobbes they argued on his own ground, and thus gave further testimony of the growing importance which rationalism assumed in English thought during the latter part of the seventeenth century.[99]

It was very difficult to prove the existence of a spiritual realm using this method, and this made Hobbes's arguments appear all the stronger. Consequently, this kind of logical rationalism was also amenable to promoting what Hobbes would claim was an inescapable fear of death. Depicting man as a kind of machine that operates only on the material plane and wants above all to continue to exist was a powerful way to encourage the thought that premature death was the worst possible fate and that dying for the sake of anything non-material was the result of delusion. Rationalism was a perfect tool for this strategy and was, in fact, Hobbes's most powerful rhetorical innovation. In constructing a logical system that builds a political theory on the basis of a rational account of man's appetites and aversions, Hobbes began a tradition that is still alive in the twenty-first century. This method itself presupposed the rationality of self-preservation and the irrationality of striving for immortality, a striving that had been a fundamental assumption of all previous Christian and pre-Christian thought.

Grasping the peculiar character of Hobbes's rhetoric helps to explain the diversity of interpretations of his strategy. Bryan Garsten, for example, is somewhat of an outlier in recent Hobbes scholarship for taking more seriously than some the fact that Hobbes claims to be an avowed enemy of rhetoric even in *Leviathan*.[100] For Garsten, Hobbes did indeed use rhetoric but he did so in order to convince his readers not to resort to rhetoric ever again. This is the rhetoric to end all rhetoric: "Hobbes used rhetoric to persuade citizens to seek a politics immune from controversy and thereby to eliminate the need for the art of controversy."[101]

---

[99] Mintz (1962, 83). Cf. Martinich (1999, 259), "One of the oddities of the early criticisms of *Leviathan* is that some of them unwittingly used Hobbes's own doctrines with the intention of criticizing him."

[100] *Pace* of course Skinner's well-known theory of Hobbes's initial championing of science and gradual realization that the truth needs eloquence to make itself heard (Skinner, 1996).

[101] Garsten (2006, 54).

There is a kernel of truth to this position. I agree with Garsten's claim that Hobbes wanted to sow doubt in his readers' minds and "introduce into the human psyche a dramatic disunity."[102] I also agree with his claim that Hobbes's readers were meant to find unity in the opinions of the sovereign. Garsten, though, understands this process too literally. Hobbes knew that human beings were perennially contentious creatures, dominated by conflicting passions, and would remain so. Their agreement with the sovereign would not be the overt act Garsten and others suggest it to be. They would not experience their agreement with the sovereign as an arrival in a safe harbor after being tossed on a sea of doubt and confusion. Rather, Hobbes's rhetoric would render certain topics off-limits to controversy. Those influenced by Hobbes would redirect their contentiousness elsewhere. They would, for example, argue about the best means of living commodiously instead of the surest means of avoiding hell. This approach also implies that what Hobbes means by the term "sovereign" must be understood more broadly than is usually done. I return to this theme in the concluding chapter.

THE SMILING MONSTER OF MALMESBURY

Hobbes did have admirers. He was regularly peppered with hyperbolic praise from two Frenchmen, Francois Peleau and Francois du Verdus. The former, for example, exclaimed that he "should rather have one Hobbes than three thousand Socrates," while the latter wrote that he is "the only person to have given us a true system of metaphysics, and the only one to have settled, in a few words, all the scholastic controversies – all the while following [his] own course, without being diverted into quibbling disputes."[103] Even these admirers, though, found it difficult to swallow Hobbes's ideas about human nature and theology. Du Verdus, who authored French translations of *De Cive* and several other of Hobbes's works, struggled with his arguments about biblical history, and complained, "It strikes me as a very forced explanation that the verb 'to be' should mean 'to signify'; and I see no likelihood that anyone will grant it to you, unless you put forward similar passages from Holy

---

[102] Garsten (2006, 53).
[103] Francois Peleau to Hobbes, 18/28 May 1656, Hobbes (2007, 291); Francois du Verdus 13/23 December 1655, Hobbes (2007, 227). Du Verdus would later advise Hobbes, when he did engage in quibbling disputes about squaring the circle, "if you have not found the solution, do not hurl yourself against the problem anymore." Hobbes (2007, 413).

Scripture in which the copula 'is' means 'signifies.'"[104] Peleau, moreover, doubted that man was as asocial as Hobbes's state of nature theory suggested, adding that Hobbes's "definition of honour is not valid: if it were true that we only honour those whom we think powerful, and whose power we esteem, it would follow that we would honour people more or less according to whether we had more or less hope or fear."[105] In other words, even those best-disposed to him pinpointed the odd and potentially inflammatory character of Hobbes's statements about theology and honor, the two topics most directly related to Hobbes's thinking about the possibility of immortality.[106]

As I have argued in this chapter, and will argue throughout the remainder of this book, we have every reason to believe that Hobbes was fully aware of the effect he would have on his readers. He knew which parts of his works his contemporaries would find most disturbing and he worked hard, especially in *Leviathan*, to disturb them in precisely the right way.

Hobbes knew that the legacy of a philosopher is mainly in the hands of those who do not have the capacity to grasp all of the complexities of his teaching. Aristotle, Hobbes writes, had come down to him as "Aristotelity," which had little to do with the philosopher's speculations. Why not, Hobbes must have thought, take control of this legacy by assuming that it would not be the most careful readers who would define what he really meant? If a philosopher's main effect on the world turns out to be primarily a caricature of his philosophy, why not consciously manipulate that caricature?

Hobbes had a potential model for this approach in the figure of Machiavelli, whose most lasting effect on the world derives not from sifting through the complexities of his interpretation of Livy, but what we would call his amoral realism and what his contemporaries would have called his glorification of evil. The effectual truth of Machiavelli's teaching was the transformative effect wrought by the surface impression of his works, a surface impression that he very likely wanted to

---

[104] Hobbes (2007, 325–6).
[105] Hobbes (2007, 309).
[106] Noel Malcolm (2012, 160) points out that de Cardonnel, a highly sympathetic reader of Hobbes (2012), balked when it came to some of the theological positions in the third part of that work: "Against Hobbe's idiosyncratic account of the 'eternal torments' of the reprobate (on p.345), he wrote: 'This is hard to be understood.' And against Hobbes's suggestion (on p.348) that 'perhaps there may be place left after the Resurrection for the Repentance of some sinners': 'Bold conjecture.'"

The Smiling Monster of Malmesbury 59

create.[107] Machiavelli is the main character in many of his works, overtly or not, and it seems more than likely that he thought carefully about how he was going to appear to later generations. Machiavelli's fate was to become a character on the stages of English theatres. Hobbes may well have seen Christopher Marlowe's *The Jew of Malta*, in which Machiavel states that "such as love me, guard me from their tongues."[108]

Could Thomas Hobbes, who was called the Monster of Malmesbury during his own lifetime, see himself as a character on some future stage?[109] The answer is undoubtedly, yes. Hobbes must have seen that Machiavelli was far more influential through notoriety than others had been through more gentle approaches. In a letter to his friend Sorbrière, who had written a treatise against doctors bleeding their patients too often, Hobbes offers the following insight: The treatise, "will help many people, but it will not be without inconvenience to yourself. You will become a perpetual object of hatred to the doctors, just as I am (because of my political theory [*propter Politica mea*]) to the theologians. The kingdom of truth is not of this world, but the next."[110]

From this point of view, Hobbes was singularly able to overcome the power of pride by wilfully sacrificing his reputation for the sake of having what he viewed as a positive effect on the world. Cultivating a bad reputation also requires a much greater degree of courage than we sometimes recognize in Hobbes. Although it is not easy to trace direct lines of impact or influence when speaking of philosophers, it is very likely that Hobbes wanted future generations to think about religion, honor, life, death and immortality in the way that they in fact do. This was the effectual truth of his philosophy. And we can be sure that he smiled at the prospect.

---

[107] Kahn (1994) has argued that critics of Machiavelli's *Prince* often inadvertently reproduced his language, much in the manner that Mintz, as quoted above, says that Hobbes's critics emulated him even while attacking him.
[108] Marlowe (1997, 17).
[109] For an interesting argument about the connection between Hobbes and Machiavelli's influence on stage villains in Restoration England, see Teeter (1936, 140–69), who speaks of "rebels, usurpers, tyrants, and Machiavellians bedeck them-selves with finery stolen from the Leviathan and rant Florentine a la Malmesbury" (154).
[110] Hobbes (2007, 448).

3

Leviathan as a Scientific Work of Art

Hobbes famously claimed that civil philosophy was, "no older ... than my own book *De Cive*."[1] He knew this was a provocative claim and admits that he made it to fan the flames of the fire he had started: "I say it provoked, and that my detractors may know how little they have wrought upon me."[2] This is an example of the provocative rhetoric sketched in the previous chapter: Hobbes here explicitly claims that he intends to annoy his many critics, and also that he is not bothered by their criticism. From this statement, we see that Hobbes thought his claims about the scientific nature of his work would rile his readers. His science itself, in particular in *De Corpore*, I argue in this chapter, was also calculated for effect, and, specifically, was meant to dislodge the metaphysical framework that supported the paths to immortality. *De Corpore*, although published later than *De Cive*, was meant to be the foundation of Hobbes's system, and equally indisputable.[3] It is ostensibly a work about the nature of body, or the material world, beginning with logic and syllogisms, moving through various mathematical and geometrical concepts and ending with Hobbes's thoughts on the heavens and gravity. Hobbes clearly had a genuine interest in natural philosophy and mathematics, but political philosophy was his primary concern, and it decisively shaped the presentation of his science in *De Corpore*. The context of *De Corpore* is political, and specifically the relation between politics and metaphysics, and its approach is creative rather than strictly logical. As such, *De Corpore* is

[1] Hobbes (1839, ix).
[2] Hobbes (1839, ix).
[3] On Hobbes's high hopes for the solidity of his system, see Hobbes (2007, 133).

of critical importance for understanding Hobbes's underlying goal of undercutting man's innate hopes for immortality and it clarifies exactly what is at stake in his overtly political works. This will become clear through a close reading of the *De Corpore*'s opening passages.

THE ART OF HOBBES'S SCIENCE: DE CORPORE

Scholars tend to read Hobbes's political works as a sincere attempt to be scientific, and *De Corpore* as a seamless part, or foundation, of his system, or they think of the political works as highly rhetorical, with either a false facade of scientific language or a very loose and inconsistent use of science, and of *De Corpore* as quite a separate and sincere endeavor at the advancement of science.[4] In both cases, in other words, they tend to see *De Corpore* as work of science. There are also scholars who come much closer to my own view that *De Corpore*, in fact, is just as much a part of what we could call Hobbes's culture critique as I have been arguing his political works are.[5] Yves Charles Zarka, in discussing the discontinuity between Hobbes's science and political theory, notes, "A natural body, which is material, and a body politic, which is artificial, could never work according to principles of the same kind. Hobbes's political theory has nothing to do with the physics of the state: It concerns institutions, and its sources and implications are quite unlike those of a physical theory."[6] Zarka's claim is that Hobbes's metaphysics does not provide a foundation for his political theory: They are separate endeavors that have separate logics. The presumption here is that, ideally, a philosopher's metaphysics should be the foundation of his political theory, as seems to have been the case for Aristotle, for example. Part of what I want to argue in this chapter, though, is that, in fact, for Hobbes, there is a relationship

---

[4] Gauthier (1969, 3), for example, arguing for unity in Hobbes's thought, claims that "[h]ad Hobbes succeeded in his grand design for a unified science, questions of morals and politics would be treated in purely synthetic manner, by derivation from the supreme relations or principles established through an analysis of body." Kavka (1986, 447), on the other hand, claims that "Hobbes's moral and political theory is essentially independent of his materialist-determinist metaphysics."

[5] On this score, I am in agreement with the premise (despite important differences) with Johnston who sees Hobbes's philosophy as a unity, aimed at "a transformation in the popular culture of his contemporaries": "Hobbes came to the conclusion that both theology and metaphysics were of direct political importance, that political consequences flowed from the widespread adoption of certain theological and even metaphysical views" (Johnston 1986, xx, xix).

[6] Zarka (1996, 76).

between first philosophy and political theory, but that his first philosophy is bounded by his political theory, not the other way around. Since, as Zarka goes on to note, "The distinction made by Hobbes between the merely conditional knowledge we have of natural things and the certain knowledge we have of things we made adds to the discontinuity between the concepts of first philosophy and those of politics," it was both more logical and more prudent for Hobbes to circumscribe what counts as first philosophy by the boundaries of political theory.[7] Since the absolute truth about nature cannot be known, and since there may be several valid interpretations of observed phenomena, there is no reason the exposition of first philosophy need include doctrines or ideas that pose a danger to stable politics.[8] Indeed, as Sorell puts it, Hobbes's "politics had an independent claim to be a science, indeed a better claim to be a science than physics."[9] Given that, it makes more sense to look to Hobbes's political science for guidance to his physics and metaphysics, not the other way around. *De Corpore* was less successful in the sense that it was not as widely read as *Leviathan* or *De Cive*, but it does shed important light on Hobbes's overall strategy in using science as a rhetorical tool.

David Johnston, among others, has noticed that there is a discrepancy between Hobbes's science and his empirical observations. Of particular importance for my project is his claim that "Hobbes was perfectly aware that people sometimes face death willingly. Yet he shows no sign of believing that this fact undermines his contention that men must by their nature seek to avoid death."[10] Johnston also rejects the suggestion that those instances in which Hobbes acknowledges the weakness of the fear of death are simply exceptions, and his view of science conditional. "It would be a mistake," he goes on, "to assume that he meant science is conditional upon the possibility of falsification by experiment or experience," since "Hobbes took almost no interest in the possibility of

---

[7] Zarka (1996, 76).

[8] As James (1949, 13) says, "Hobbes is less concerned to discover the methods of God in creation than to satisfy the rational requirements of the human mind; and whether in fact we know the real cause or another but equally intelligible cause, is immaterial to the results for human happiness. It is less reality than intelligibility that Hobbes looks for." Hobbes, in other words, might not have been surprised by Kuhn's (1996) theory of paradigm shifts in the history of science. Hobbes, though, was engaged in a conscious attempt at such a paradigm shift for political reasons. Spragens (1973, 42ff.), also sees a similarity between what Hobbes is doing with the Aristotelian foundation of his time and Kuhn's idea of a paradigm shift.

[9] Sorell (1986, 4).

[10] Johnston (1986, 51).

experimental falsification or verification, even in physical science."[11] Hobbes's science, for Johnston, as for many other scholars, is absolute, and rests on the logical consistency of interrelated propositions. Because of this, the discrepancy noted above does not pose a fatal problem to Hobbes's scientific model: "The propositions of science, as Hobbes conceives them, are absolutely not to be confused with empirical hypotheses."[12]

For Johnston, Hobbes's science, like geometry, was grounded in experience, but not necessarily bound by it. The advantage of this kind of science is that, again like geometry, "it can be used to control and change reality."[13] Just as the concept of a straight line can be used to make objects in the real world straighter, so Hobbes's science can be used to correct certain problems with political society. This is in general correct. Johnston, though, does not consider that Hobbes's science is a rhetorical tool as well as a model. Since Johnston does not see that Hobbes was attacking the desire for immortality and did not believe the fear of death to be the most rational or powerful impulse, he is able to make the following suggestion:

Hobbes may have thought that this capacity for reason to mislead accounts for the extraordinary extent to which some people diverge from the way to their own preservation, the end that nature prescribes to every man. Even the fact that some men prefer to sacrifice life itself in order to avoid humiliation or the possibility of eternal damnation could be construed as one of the absurd results of the human ability to misreckon in spectacular fashion.[14]

For Johnston, self-sacrifice is best explained as an instance of simple miscalculation, or irrationality. He does not consider the possibility that Hobbes devised his scientific model precisely in order to alter the way individuals think about death and the possibility of immortality. Johnston thus recognizes to some extent the polemical nature of Hobbes's science, but he does not recognize just how polemical it is. After all, if hellfire were real, avoiding it at all cost could not possibly be a miscalculation. Dying in order to avoid hell can only appear as an absurd misreckoning if grave doubts have been raised about its reality. Johnston does not consider that for Hobbes, self-sacrifice was not at all

---

[11] Johnston (1986, 51).
[12] Johnston (1986, 52).
[13] Johnston (1986, 53).
[14] Johnston (1986, 56).

irrational, and that undermining the desire for immortality was a major goal of his scientific model.[15]

In the dedication to the Earl of Devonshire, Hobbes says that he wrote *De Corpore* in order to establish "the true foundations of natural philosophy."[16] He set himself the task of establishing this foundation, though, because for want of it "we have all suffered much damage lately."[17] More specifically, he claimed that the "*pernicious philosophy*" of the past "hath raised an infinite number of controversies in the Christian world concerning religion, and from those controversies, wars."[18] Hobbes thus makes it quite clear that *De Corpore* was motivated by political concerns. The connection between a lack of true metaphysical foundations and the religious warfare of the seventeenth century, though, is not immediately clear. The most obvious plane on which to solve the problem of religious warfare is that of theology, or perhaps political philosophy. Hobbes, of course, addressed these both in *De Cive*, as he tells us in this dedicatory epistle. He claims to have "long since reduced all power ecclesiastical and civil by strong argument of reason, without repugnance to God's word, to one and the same sovereign authority."[19]

What, then, is the role of natural philosophy as opposed to theology or political thought, in fomenting religious wars? This is an especially important question given the context Hobbes places himself in with regard to other philosophers of his time. Hobbes traces the history of modern natural science from Copernicus, Galileo and Harvey, to Kepler, Gassendi and Mersenne.[20] As great as these men were, Hobbes implies, they failed to address the foundation of science itself. In other words, they failed to directly tackle the problem of metaphysics. Until this fundamental problem is addressed, there would be no peace. This was not because Hobbes thought that politics, theology and metaphysics should be separate endeavors, and their respective boundaries had to be established, but

---

[15] I do not, therefore, accept Johnston's claim that the discrepancy between Hobbes's science and observed reality "posed no obstacle" to the usefulness of Hobbes's theory "as long as they remained relatively small," Johnston (1986, 94). In fact, as I argue throughout this work, this discrepancy is the crucial problem; even if the number of individuals who do not fear death sufficiently is small, they are nevertheless the most dangerous and destabilizing.
[16] Hobbes (1839, xi).
[17] Hobbes (1839, xiv).
[18] Hobbes (1839, x).
[19] Hobbes (1839, xi).
[20] Hobbes (1839, viii–ix).

because natural science, metaphysics and theology all had to be circumscribed by political considerations.

The context of *De Corpore*, then, is the danger unbridled metaphysical speculation poses to politics. After discussing the scientific achievements of his contemporaries and near contemporaries, Hobbes steps back and traces the course of ancient philosophy: "There walked in old Greece a certain phantasm, for superficial gravity, though full within of fraud and filth, a little like philosophy."[21] These quasi-philosophers of Greece taught, "instead of wisdom, nothing but to dispute, and, neglecting the laws, to determine every question according to their own fancies."[22] This was only a minor irritation until

[t]he first doctors of the Church, next the Apostles, born in those times, whilst they endeavoured to defend the Christian faith against the Gentiles by natural reason, began also to make use of philosophy, and with the decrees of Holy Scripture to mingle the sentences of heathen philosophers; and first some harmless ones of Plato, but afterwards also many foolish and false ones out of the physics and metaphysics of Aristotle; and bringing in the enemies, betrayed unto them the citadel of Christianity. From that time, instead of the worship of God, there entered a thing called school divinity, walking on one foot firmly, which is the Holy Scripture, but halted on the other rotten foot, which the Apostle Paul called vain, and might have called pernicious philosophy.[23]

In the epistle, Hobbes likens school teaching to the Greek monster Empusa, "a ghost that changed shapes, having one brazen leg, but the other was the leg of an ass."[24] Hobbes's goal in *De Corpore* is "to fright and drive away this metaphysical *Empusa*; not by skirmish, but by letting in the light upon her."[25] The ostensible goal, then, of *De Corpore* is the establishment of a new foundation of science that will purify Christianity of its accretions of Greek philosophy. Philosophy is to be separated from theology, since "[i]t excludes the doctrine of *angels*, and all such things as are thought to be neither bodies nor properties of bodies ... It excludes such knowledge as is acquired by Divine inspiration, or revelation, as not derived to us by reason, but by Divine grace in an instant, and, as it were,

---

[21] Hobbes (1839, ix).
[22] We might be tempted here to think of the sophists who appear in Plato's dialogues, such as Callicles and Thrasymachus, as opposed to "real" philosophers. Hobbes, though, seems to paint Plato and Aristotle with the same brush.
[23] Hobbes (1839, x).
[24] Hobbes (1839, x). In fact, in Aristophanes (2005, line 300), Empusa is said to have one bronze leg, and one leg of dung. Hobbes indicates by his reference to the comic poet that those who teach school divinity are *pleni scati*.
[25] Hobbes (1839, x).

by some sense supernatural."[26] This separation, which I will argue is in fact a subsumption, will open the path to peace and allow for the same kind of progress in politics that others had achieved in astronomy and biology.

In a more concrete sense, though, and despite his protestations about the division between philosophy and theology, Hobbes is implicitly launching an assault on the possibility that there can be an immaterial soul, let alone an immortal soul. In fact, Henry More's attacks on Hobbes in *The immortality of the soul* (1659) were a response to *De Corpore*.[27] In terms familiar to readers of chapter 46 of *Leviathan*, Hobbes blames the misunderstanding of abstract speech for the widespread belief in spirits in Greece. Abstract words, as well as the copulative verb, conjure concepts in the mind that many mistake for actual entities. "They speak of accidents, as if they might be separated from all bodies. And from hence proceed the gross errors of writers of metaphysics ... they think also that quantity may be without body and body without quantity"[28] This error is the root of belief in ghosts, and, by implication, of the traditional understanding of the soul and a spiritual realm. Although Hobbes does not spell out the consequences of his attempt to eliminate such incoherent speech in *De Corpore*, he does do so in *Leviathan*, where he says his purpose is "that men may no longer suffer themselves to be abused, by them, that by this doctrine of *Separated Essences*, built on the Vain Philosophy of Aristotle, would fright them into Obeying the Laws of their Countrey, with empty names; as men fright Birds from the Corn with an empty doublet, a hat, and a crooked stick."[29] By circumscribing philosophy within the bounds of what can be stated with absolute certainty by propositions of the sort Hobbes describes in the first chapters of *De Corpore*, he effectively closes off the possibility of any plausible argument for the existence of a spiritual realm, the independent existence of natural law, or any standard of justice.[30]

---

[26] Hobbes (1839, 10–11).
[27] Parkin (2007, 134).
[28] Hobbes (1839, 33–4).
[29] Hobbes (2012, 1082).
[30] This seems to have been readily recognized by contemporaries. Francois Verdu, an admirer of Hobbes who made a French translation of *De Corpore* (1839) relates that when explaining to others that "it is not possible to be a philosopher without also being a geometer. At that, I have seen these people take fright immediately, thinking that a geometrical philosophy (the true philosophy, in other words) tends to overturn the most important truths." Hobbes (2007, 224).

Given his ambition in *De Corpore* to dislodge the metaphysical foundations of Western thought in order to radically transform politics, religion and philosophy, it is surprising that Hobbes claims, as he does also in other works, that natural science is harmless, and something to be pursued for intellectual enjoyment alone. In the opening of *Leviathan*, Hobbes anticipates that the work will be offensive. We have also seen that he knew *De Cive* would offend nearly everyone who read it. By contrast, he ends *Leviathan* by claiming that he will turn from offensive doctrine of the artificial body, Leviathan, to the pleasing speculation of natural bodies (*De Corpore*) which had been interrupted by the civil war: "For such Truth, as opposeth no man profit, nor pleasure, is to all men welcome."[31] Earlier in the work as well, he had suggested that the study of lines and figures is not disputed by the sword because "it crosses no mans ambition, profit, or lust."[32] In *The Elements of Law* as well, he claims that "to this day was it never heard of, that there was any controversy concerning any conclusion in this subject."[33] If, however, it was "interest of men that have dominion, That The Three Angles Of A Triangle Should Be Equall To Two Angles Of A Square; that doctrine should have been, if not disputed, yet by the burning of all books of Geometry, suppressed, as farre as he whom it concerned was able." In moving on to his strictly scientific work, he was engaging in a topic, "without any offensive novelty."[34]

These claims about the innocuous nature of mathematics as compared with the contentiousness of political thought are jarring, especially in *De Corpore*, where he mentions almost in the same breath figures such as Copernicus and Galileo, the latter of which had been called before an inquisitor in 1632, and whom Hobbes may have met in person. It could not have escaped Hobbes's notice that these mens' speculations on mathematics and geometry were seen as quite offensive to a certain group of men who had a very great dominion.

One of the striking features of *De Corpore* is precisely this double presentation of philosophy as something harmless to be pursued for enjoyment, as well as something of the utmost seriousness that exposes one to the greatest danger because of its political ramifications. By exploring this paradox more closely we will see that Hobbes is arguing

---

[31] Hobbes (2012, 1141).
[32] Hobbes (2012, 158).
[33] Hobbes (1999, 74).
[34] Hobbes (1839, vii).

that natural philosophy can be pursued productively and safely in a non-metaphysical, mainly synthetic mode. Natural philosophy, that is, should retain a healthy degree of skepticism about the true nature of the natural world. Hobbes is speaking to two audiences at once. For readers such as Ralph Bathurst, Hobbes's natural science is inoffensive, and, as Bathurst says, *De Corpore* is a work "in whose argument no man's *Diana* will be brought into question."[35] To another audience, he indicates the ultimately political context of his natural science, and his attempt to contain its inquiries within a certain arena.

We can begin to see this from an examination of what can only be described as a very odd epistle to the reader in *De Corpore*. Here, Hobbes makes clear in the first line that he is not speaking of inanities such as "philosophers' stones, nor that which is found in the metaphysical codes."[36] The implication here is that the metaphysical thought of his age was just as ridiculous as a substance that can turn lead to gold or make men immortal. The philosophy he is going to present, rather, is "the child of the world and your own mind," because it involves observing the world and "bringing back a true report" of it.[37] Hobbes makes it clear that his own method is only presented as a suggestion: "[A]nd if it like you, you may use the same; for a I do but propound, not commend to you anything of mine."[38]

Hobbes goes on to describe philosophy in terms of both art and religion. Philosophy "is within yourself; perhaps not fashioned yet, but like the world its father, as it was in the beginning, a thing confused."[39] The reader's potential for philosophy here is likened to the world described in Genesis: "[I]n the beginning ... the earth was without form and void."[40] Rather than urging the reader to cultivate his mind in order to understand the true nature of the world, Hobbes says the following: "Do, therefore, as the statuaries do, who, by hewing off that which is superfluous, do not make but find the image."[41] The comparison of the philosopher with a sculptor is striking. The sculptor may claim to have found an image inside the stone, but this is at least as much an act of

---

[35] Hobbes (2007, 180). Bathurst here refers to Paul's trouble with image makers in Ephesus as recounted in Acts 19:24–8.
[36] Hobbes (1839, xiii).
[37] Hobbes (1839, xiii).
[38] Hobbes (1839, xiv).
[39] Hobbes (1839, xiii).
[40] Hobbes (1839, xiii).
[41] Hobbes (1839, xiii).

creation as it is of discovery. Hobbes here is urging the potential philosopher to see his own creative understanding of the world as a discovery of the truth. This is an especially jarring sentiment in a work that purports to be a strict set of demonstrations of the nature of the material world. He is urging his many potential readers to create their own synthetic vision of the world, which may or may not agree with his presentation, or the visions of any other reader.

In the following sentence, Hobbes deepens this unexpectedly poetic view of philosophy. "Or," he urges, "imitate the creation: if you will be a philosopher in good earnest, let your reason move upon the deep of your own cogitations and experience; those things that lie in confusion must be set asunder, distinguished, and every one stamped with its own name and set in order; that is to say, your method must resemble the creation."[42] There is again an unmistakable evocation of Genesis here: "[A]nd darkness was upon the face of the deep. And the Spirit of God moved upon the face of the waters" (1:2, KJV). Like *Leviathan*, *De Corpore* opens with the idea of an artistic creation. But, Hobbes wants his reader to see himself more than as an artist, as a god in the act of creating a world, as well as Adam who first named all the creatures of the earth.

One should be attracted to philosophy in part because "we have all suffered much damage lately" but also because philosophers, like the wealthy, love to "behold and contemplate their own wisdom."[43] This is an obvious appeal to pride, which is followed by a description of the "pleasure it is to the mind of man to be ravished in the vigorous and perpetual embraces of the most beauteous world."[44] The final exhortation to philosophy is that it is a good way to "fill up your time."[45]

In stark contrast to this depiction of philosophy, Hobbes says in the first chapter of *De Corpore*, in a passage already quoted above, that "Philosophy professedly rejects not only the paint and false colours of language, but even the very ornaments and graces of the same: and the first grounds of all science are not only not beautiful, but poor, arid, and in appearance, deformed."[46] It is remotely possible that Hobbes was simply describing the joys of the accomplished philosopher when addressing the reader, while here he is speaking only of the difficult first steps. But the

---

[42] Hobbes (1839, xiii).
[43] Hobbes (1839, xiv).
[44] Hobbes (1839, xiv).
[45] Hobbes (1839, xiv).
[46] Hobbes (1839, 2).

purpose he assigns philosophy in the first chapters of *De Corpore* is also quite different from what he says in the dedication to the reader. Rather than a pleasant pastime that flatters one's pride, philosophy is practical and very difficult:

> The *end* or *scope* of philosophy is, that we may make use to our benefit of effects formerly seen; or that, by application of bodies to one another, we may produce the like effects of those we conceive in our mind ... for the commodity of human life. For the inward glory and triumph of mind that a man may have for the mastering of some difficult or doubtful matter, or for the discovery of some hidden truth, is not worth so much pains as the study of Philosophy requires.[47]

"The end of knowledge," Hobbes says, "is power."[48]

We can reconcile these two views of philosophy by interpreting Hobbes's presentation of philosophy as a private and harmless endeavor as being itself a practical, hoped for, effect of his own philosophy. Hobbes is engaged in a project that involves profoundly altering the way man thinks about politics, religion and immortality for the sake of peace.[49] This circumscribing of philosophy is a part of that project. The errors of Aristotle and Plato stemmed from the fact that "they take for principles those opinions which are already vulgarly received."[50] Hobbes, though, wants to instill new opinions: "I am not ignorant of how hard a thing it is to weed out of man's minds such inveterate opinions as have taken root there, and been confirmed in them by the authority of the most eloquent writers."[51]

We have seen that the primary goal of *De Corpore* is to scare away the Empusa metaphysics. As long as there was an agreement, explicit or tacit, that it was not possible to come to any concrete conclusions about metaphysical matters that would create an authority beyond the state,

---

[47] Hobbes (1839, 7).
[48] Hobbes (1839, 7).
[49] By grasping this, we can overcome one of the conundrums that has perplexed scholars of Hobbes. Namely, that Hobbes seems to have a very specific goal in mind, political stability, but he does not seem to offer a set of practical policy proposals to achieve this goal. Thus, Vaughan (2002, 32) says that "Hobbes had practical intentions for his political philosophy," but "we are still left with the question of what they might be. We know that they were not institutional and we also know that they must somehow lead to civil peace." Vaughan goes on to propose that Hobbes wanted to affect change on the level of education, and I am in agreement, but he overlooks the extent to which Hobbes's education had as one of its primary aims the undermining of traditional ideas of the paths to immortality. One of the practical aims of his philosophy was to make most scientific speculation appear politically harmless.
[50] Hobbes (1999, 75).
[51] Hobbes (1839, 2).

individuals could think what they wished, and philosophers could continue to improve life through reasoning about cause and effect. In juxtaposing the image of philosophy as a creative endeavor that was both beautiful and a good way to fill one's leisure hours, as he had as a younger man contributing to the *Horae Subsecivae*, with that of philosophy as the only effective way to end war and improve life, Hobbes is in fact pointing to the best strategy with which to forestall any future abuses of philosophy. In the future, Hobbes may have hoped, everyone will have his own personal philosophy. On matters of fact, so-called (an issue I will return to below), we must agree. On foundational issues, though, we must remain agnostic and admit that we do not, in fact, know any better than anyone else.

For Hobbes, the foundations of science were always built on assumptions that could not be verified. Better, he thought, to make those assumptions such as would conduce to peace. This naturally begs the question as to why Hobbes thought peace was good. For my purposes in this chapter, though, I want to show that Hobbes thought these assumptions about the foundations of science were in fact malleable.

First, Hobbes thought that true philosophy had to begin with precise definitions. Once these had been set out, they could be added and subtracted, just as figures are in geometry, which is also founded on precise definitions. Part of the problem here is how Hobbes derived his definitions. We saw above that Hobbes criticized Plato and Aristotle for beginning with the everyday definitions that were already accepted by their society. While we might expect him for this reason to offer us a wall of neologisms as we might find in Heidegger, Hobbes in fact proceeds by modifying definitions that are already accepted in order to shift the argument in his favor. We will see several examples as this along the way, but even the casual reader of *Leviathan* must note that Hobbes's definitions of terms such as liberty and virtue are meant to challenge accepted understandings and shift his readers' perception. In other words, his definitions are clearly rhetorical. This tendency was noted and attacked by Hobbes's scientific adversaries. John Wallis, for example, noted that

[f]or Mr. Hobs is very dexterous in confuting others by putting a new sense on their words rehearsed by himself: different from what the words signify with other Men. And therefore if you shall have occasion to speak of Chalk, He'll tell you that by Chalk he means Cheese: and then if he can prove that what you say of Chalk is not true of Cheese, he reckons himself to have gotten a great victory.[52]

---

[52] Shapin and Schaffer (1989, 118).

In this specific case, Wallis is attacking Hobbes for his definition of air in the course of his debates with Boyle about the latter's air pump. These debates are particularly instructive. One of Hobbes's chief complaints about the new mode of experimental science, as recounted in Shapin and Schaffer's *Leviathan and the Air Pump*, is that Boyle had made many unstated assumptions in drawing conclusions from his experiments. In particular, Boyle had made certain assumptions about the elasticity and composition of air. Because he did not have a completely worked out system, Boyle was open to the possibility that there could be several equally valid explanations for what was observed during the experiments with the air pump. Hobbes, moreover, thought that Boyle and the Royal Society in general relied too heavily on sense experience, which Hobbes thought to be inherently faulty, as we saw in the first section of this chapter.

By not self-consciously beginning with the establishment of foundational matters, Boyle was not engaged in philosophy at all, and in fact was on a dangerous path that could lead to a renewed belief in spirits, according to Hobbes. In *Leviathan*, as Shapin and Schaffer point out, "Hobbes took away vacuum on definitional, historical, and ultimately political grounds. The vacuism Hobbes attacked was not merely absurd and wrong, as it was in his physical texts; it was *dangerous*. Speech of a vacuum was associated with cultural resources that had been illegitimately used to subvert proper authority in the state."[53] The political grounds were in fact primary both in *Leviathan* and *De Corpore*, as we have seen.[54] For Hobbes it was politically essential to begin with the assumption that reasoning about metaphysics, as traditionally conceived, was impossible. Since it was not possible to arrive at any incontestable definitions or conclusions about notions like "vacuum," it made more sense to err on the side of political caution. Ultimate causes and the true nature of the universe had to remain forever shrouded in mystery if the authority of the state was to be preserved.

In *De Corpore* Hobbes sets out the framework within which individuals can derive their own ideas and their own definitions. Despite the very certain terms in which Hobbes couches his science, the work also contains caveats that allow for a certain flexibility:

Seeing there may be many who will not like this my definition of philosophy, and will say, that, from the liberty which a man may take of so defining as seems best to himself, he may conclude any thing from any thing ... yet, lest in this point there

---

[53] Shapin and Schaffer (1989, 91).
[54] Hobbes's friend Sorbrière (2007, 436–8), was skeptical of Hobbes's theory of a plenism.

should be any cause of dispute betwixt me and them, I here undertake no more than to deliver the elements of that science by which the effects of anything may be found out from the known generation of the same, or contrarily, the generation from effects; to the end that they who search after other philosophy, may be admonished to seek it from other principles.[55]

As long as it was possible to know anything certain about foundational matters, citizens could be certain that there were more important things than life here on earth. The foundations of Hobbes's philosophy are built in such a way that no certainty can ever be found. Everyone can have his own ideas about heaven, hell, the nature of justice and honor, but no one can point to anything certain about any of these, the way they can point to men with swords.

There is thus in Hobbes's philosophy, both political and scientific, a dimension that can appear confusing or contradictory. On one hand, he seems to advocate the need for rigid agreement among all citizens on matters of theology, justice, and rights, among other things. On the other hand, there is a less-well noted artistic, or creative element in his philosophy that would seem to promote a great deal of disagreement among citizens. Miller, for example, notes that Hobbes wants us to "imitate God *as a creator*. We use philosophy to turn ourselves into creators. Instead of remaking what God has made, we make what we wish. We become more dignified by creating something original, not something that merely emulates a thing created by someone else."[56] Flathman similarly emphasizes what he sees as Hobbes's promotion of creative individual autonomy.[57] For both Miller and Flathman, this degree of creativity is possible because of the essentially unknowable nature of the universe. Hobbes, though, seems to be promoting a degree of disagreement that would pose a challenge to the "reall Unitie" that the sovereign is supposed to impose for the sake of political stability.[58]

At least one scholar has criticized Hobbes precisely because of this apparent contradiction. Dungey claims that

Hobbes's materialism creates a diffusion of perspectives, words, and definitions that undermine the foundation upon which the rules of civil life must be built. Following Hobbes's materialist anthropology step by step, a kaleidoscope of images, words, and definitions seems more likely than agreement about images

---

[55] Hobbes (1839, 12).
[56] Miller (2011, 50).
[57] Flathman (1993).
[58] Hobbes (2012, 260).

and words, consent about procedures, and contract concerning public meaning and peace. If human beings are unable to establish a shared foundation of perspectives, words, and definitions, then no commonwealth is possible.[59]

Dungey's critique is useful because he misunderstands Hobbes in a particularly helpful way. His starting point is the claim that "Hobbes intends to produce a unified philosophical system linking his materialist account of our senses, imagination, and passions to his moral and political theory."[60] It is because Dungey is committed to the idea that Hobbes's philosophy was united in this way that he sees the disagreement Hobbes's theory promotes as so problematic. He takes Hobbes too literally and does not recognize the destructive goal of *De Corpore* on the issue of metaphysics. In fact, Hobbes wants us to recognize that there are clear boundaries between what we can and cannot know. This is a point that Richard Tuck takes great pains to explain; Hobbes's skepticism, like that of Descartes and Mersenne, is not total. Rather, there are things we cannot know, but also things that we can have knowledge of because of the nature of our sense perceptions.[61]

One of the most important things Hobbes wants us to agree on is precisely that there are things we simply cannot know. It is on the basis of this fundamental agreement that we can have non-destabilizing disagreement. Dungey is correct that Hobbes promotes disagreement, but he does not recognize that this disagreement is founded on a deeper foundation of agreement. In fact, it may be the case that a plethora of groundless and divergent opinions on a given subject will only reinforce the perception that it is impossible to arrive at certain knowledge about that subject. This is, I am arguing, precisely Hobbes's goal when it comes to inquiries into man's fate after death.[62]

---

[59] Dungey (2008, 219).
[60] Dungey (2008, 191).
[61] See for example, Tuck (1993, 292ff.).
[62] It is important to realize just how striking a claim Hobbes was making when challenging the immortality of the soul and implying that we cannot know anything for certain about it. As Tuck (1993, 329) notes,

> We must distinguish Hobbes's position on this matter from previous arguments about the immortality of the soul, for it was a distinctive and (to contemporaries) far more alarming claim than the earlier theories. The conventional view was, of course, that all men possess an immortal soul which is capable of experiencing both the pleasures of heaven and the torments of hell, and that human reason unaided by revelation can arrive at knowledge of this immortality.

THE SCIENTIFIC ABSTRACTION OF THE HOBBESIAN MUSHROOM MAN

In the opening lines from the Introduction of *Leviathan*, Hobbes states,

> Nature (the art whereby God hath made and governes the world) is by the art of man, as in many other things, so in this also imitated, that it can make an Artificiall Animal ... Art goes yet further, imitating that Rationall and most excellent worke of Nature, Man. For by Art is created that great LEVIATHAN called a COMMON-WEALTH, or STATE (in latine CIVITAS) which is but an Artificiall Man; though of greater stature and strength than the Naturall, for whose protection and defence it was intended; and in which, the Soveraignty is an Artificiall Soul, as giving life and motion to the whole body.[63]

What is remarkable about this passage is not only its eloquence but the fact that it encapsulates Hobbes's strategy of using his scientific method to further his rhetorical goal. Or, more accurately, this passage exemplifies the complex way in which Hobbes blurs the line between science and rhetoric to further his primary goal, which is political. God created the world by means of nature, but we have only the dimmest grasp of God and nature. From what we do know of man, we can imitate him to create the commonwealth. The state is a work of art built on a model that is not fully understood. The advantage of this approach is that Hobbes can abstract from, or ignore, certain problematic aspects of man. The state exists to preserve the life of its constituent members and nothing more. Man, by implication, wants from the state above all safety. There is no higher purpose; no desire for immortality that can be satisfied through the state. The artificial soul of the state, like the natural soul of man, expires and vanishes once the motion and life of the body ends. This vision of an artificial man is both an incomplete imitation of natural man, but also Hobbes's goal.

I thus do not accept Miller's claim that

> [w]hen Hobbes suggests that the heart is but a spring, his efforts are not so much a matter of reductionism as they are a proclamation of equivalency between divine and human creation. God may make a heart, but we may make a spring – and that is all we need to do. In the face of his remarkable prospect, the goal of knowing the world as it really is becomes less important.[64]

The problem here is that if we do not know the world as it really is, we are not in a position to judge whether what we have created is the

---

[63] Hobbes (2012, 16).
[64] Miller (2011, 53).

equivalent of what God has created. This becomes especially problematic when we consider that what Christians traditionally want most from God is salvation, and eternal life. Man can imitate God in this respect only to the degree that he can create longevity. But it would be hard to argue that longevity is not a pale imitation of immortality.

The relationship between nature and art, God and man in the passage quoted above is a clear example of Hobbes's division of science into analytic and synthetic branches. In his telling, science could proceed in two directions. One could attempt to determine the causes of known phenomena by analyzing them or breaking them down into their constituent parts, or one could begin with the parts or effects and build them into phenomena. The former method Hobbes called analytic or resolutive the latter synthetic or compositive. Because of the nature of sense perception, though, one can accomplish more with the compositive method than the resolutive.

The problem with the resolutive method is that "in knowledge by sense, the whole object is more known, than any part thereof; as when we see a man, the conception or whole idea of that man is first known, than the particular ideas of his being *figurative, animate*, and *rational*."[65] These latter are what Hobbes calls "parts," and he specifies that he does not mean by that term a man's head or shoulders. We grasp the whole idea of man immediately. This idea is composed of various characteristics which we silently or unconsciously add together, such as body, animate and rational.[66]

Resolution of wholes, such as man, into parts, or effects, is done through reason. Because, though, we receive our knowledge of these wholes through sense perception, which is inherently faulty, this resolution is difficult, and may well be incomplete: "[Y]et in natural philosophy, where all questions are concerning the causes of the phantasms of sensible things, it is not so easy to discern between the things themselves, from which those phantasms proceed, and the appearances of those things to the sense."[67] Hobbes gives the example of a man believing that the sun is the width of a foot, and mistaking something appearing round from afar, which turns out to be square (these examples would seem to be drawn from Heraclitus and Descartes, although Hobbes does not mention them by name).[68]

---

[65] Hobbes (1839, 66–7).
[66] Hobbes (1839, 4).
[67] Hobbes (1839, 75).
[68] See Heraclitus (1996, 11), fragment 3, "[The sun's] breadth is <that> of a human foot." See also Descartes (1995, 113): "Sometimes towers which had looked round from a distance appeared square close up."

Another potential flaw in the resolutive method is that any phenomenon is susceptible to multiple explanations. As he puts it in *De Homine*,

> Since the causes of natural things are not in our power, but in the divine will, and since the greatest part of them, namely the ether, is invisible; we that do not see them, cannot deduce their qualities from their causes. Of course, we can, be deducing as far as possible the consequences of those qualities that we do see, demonstrate that such and such *could* have been their causes.[69]

Despite the difficulty of determining what the parts of any whole are, Hobbes claims that the ultimate cause of all universal things is self-evidently motion: "[T]he causes of universal things ... are manifest of themselves (as they say commonly) known to nature; so that they need no method at all; for they have all but one universal cause, which is motion."[70] This materialist starting point already suggests that Hobbes is foreclosing the possibility of a realm of incorporeal spirits. In making this assertion, though, Hobbes is able to simultaneously indicate that giving a complete account of the causes or parts of any particular thing we encounter in the world, in particular man, may be impossible, but also that we do have access to a universally valid and self-evident starting point from which to initiate compositive, or synthetic reasoning. This starting point is geometry.[71]

On the basis of this distinction between compositive and resolutive methods, and their relative capacities, we can understand the often repeated notion that for Hobbes, we only know what we make.

> Both of these methods of proof are usually called demonstrations; the former kind [beginning with causes] is, however, preferable to the latter [reasoning from effects]; and rightly so; for it is better to know how we can best use present causes than to know the irrevocable past, whatsoever its nature. Therefore, science is allowed to men through the former kind of *a priori* demonstration only of those things whose generation depends on the will of men themselves.[72]

We do not, however, have a complete account of man or of nature. Despite knowing that motion is the ultimate cause of everything, we cannot know the irrevocable past that caused man. When, therefore, we

---

[69] Hobbes (1998a, 42). This fact was part of the basis of Hobbes's disagreement with Boyle about the usefulness of the air-pump, and the experimental approach in general. See Shapin and Schaffer (1989).
[70] Hobbes (1839, 69–70).
[71] Hobbes (1839, 71).
[72] Hobbes (1998a, 41).

imitate man in constructing the state, we are making an imperfect and incomplete copy.

Hobbes's method in creating the state is not only synthetic. It is also hortatory. Unlike the resolutive method which seeks knowledge of causes, the compositive method seeks "what may conduce most to the *generation* of some propounded *effect* from many *accidents*; or in what manner particular causes ought to be compounded for the production of some certain effect."[73] The effect Hobbes wanted was a peaceful state. He did not hope to accomplish his goal by creating a state as a perfectly faithful image of man. If the Leviathan was an imitation of man as we find him, it would be as unstable as all previous regimes have been. Instead, Hobbes aimed to teach

> a true and certain rule of our actions, by which we might know whether that we undertake be just or unjust. For it is to no purpose to be bidden in every thing to do right, before there be a certain rule and measure of right established, which no man hitherto hath established. Seeing, therefore, from the not knowing of civil duties, that is, from the want of moral science, proceed civil wars, and the greatest calamities of mankind, we may very well attribute to such science the production of the contrary commodities.[74]

The way in which Hobbes teaches this lesson is only in part through his doctrine of natural law and the relation between protection and obedience. The logical system he built on his description of man is in fact highly rhetorical and was not in fact the resolutive endeavor it appeared to be. Rather, the description of man is resolutive in appearance, but in fact synthetic. That is, in deconstructing man, and reducing him to a function of appetite and aversion, and especially the aversion to death, Hobbes wanted to build a new image of man, and inculcate that idea into the minds of his readers.

Hobbes claimed that what he offered in *Leviathan* was science, but also that self-knowledge was enough to confirm even to the non-scientific reader the truth of his account. In a rather long-winded three sentences in *De Corpore*, Hobbes echoes the introduction of *Leviathan* in claiming that the truth of his political science can be verified both through the synthetic and analytic methods:

> *Civil* and *moral philosophy* do not so adhere to each one another, but that they may be severed. For the causes of the motions of the mind are known, not only by

---

[73] Hobbes (1839, 68).
[74] Hobbes (1839, 9–10).

ratiocination, but also by the experience of every man that takes the pains to observe the motions within himself. And, therefore, not only they that have attained the knowledge of the passions and perturbations of the mind, by the *synthetical method*, and from the very first principles of philosophy, may by proceeding in the same way, come to the causes and necessity of constituting commonwealths, and to get the knowledge of what is natural right, and what are civil duties ... for this reason, that the principles of the politics consists in the knowledge of the motions of the mind, and the knowledge of these motions from the knowledge of sense and imagination; but even they that have not learned the first part of philosophy, namely, *geometry* and *physics*, may, notwithstanding, attain the principles of civil philosophy, by the *analytical method*.[75]

In other words, Hobbes presents as synthetic what is meant to be understood by the majority of readers, who are not scientists, analytically. Or, Hobbes's artificial construction in *Leviathan* is meant to appear as a description of an immediately obvious whole. We can see this more clearly by following what Hobbes says next in *De Corpore*:

For if a question be propounded, as, *whether such an action be just or unjust*; if that *unjust* be resolved into *fact against law*, and that notion *law* into *command* of him or them that have *coercive power*; and that *power* be derived from the *wills* of men that constitute such power, to the end that they may live in peace, they may at last come to this, that the appetites of men and the passions of their minds are such, that, unless they be restrained by some power, they will always be making war upon one another; which may be known to be so by any man's experience, that will but examine his own mind.[76]

This formulation makes sense only if we make certain unwarranted assumptions. For example, that peace is the highest good for a community and is the purpose for which the state came into being; that the thinker in question is willing to consult his own mind; that he be more concerned with the peace and stability of his regime than whatever good may accrue to him from the unjust action; and most importantly, that longevity is his highest priority and therefore that coercive power will be an effective check on his actions and the actions of others. Analytic thinking will only arrive at these conclusions if the one examining his thoughts has already been convinced of Hobbes's synthetic model. It is these assumptions that form the basis of Hobbes's logical system and that he most wanted to inculcate.

---

[75] Hobbes (1839, 73–4).
[76] Hobbes (1839, 74).

A PERFECT SYSTEM: THE INESCAPABLE FEAR OF DEATH AND THE STATE OF NATURE

If anyone in the past had had real knowledge of the causes of peace and war, they would have taught them to others, and, Hobbes says in *De Corpore*, "*it seems unlikely that* [mankind] *would ever have to fight again.*"[77] We should pay careful attention to Hobbes's evidence for this suggestion:

> For what shall we say? Could the ancient masters of Greece, Egypt, Rome and others, persuade the unskilful multitude of their innumerable opinions concerning the nature of their gods, which they themselves knew not whether they were true or false, and which were indeed manifestly false and absurd; and could they not persuade the same multitude to civil duty if they themselves had understood it?[78]

We see here again that Hobbes quite intentionally does not consider the possibility that other regimes and cultures might have had other priorities than peace. It should be enough to recall that for Pericles dying in battle for Athens is the greatest good for an Athenian, for us to realize that Hobbes was fully aware of such alternatives.

The strong implication in Hobbes's statements about ancient and absurd pagan religions is that if entire communities can be brought to believe in the preposterous things the ancient Egyptians had said about their gods, they can certainly be persuaded to accept Hobbes's political proposals – even if this system is not entirely true and even if they did not fully understand it. Hobbes implies here that it will be wholly possible to persuade those of his time and beyond of the truth of his system, even if it is based on an inaccurate account of human nature and the nature of politics. This system can, moreover, be propagated and handed down regardless of whether those who are doing the handing down understand the system or not. In *Behemoth*, Hobbes excerpts several passages from Diodorus Siculus about the philosopher priests in various societies, the Druids, the Magi and Egyptian and Ethiopian priests who exerted great political power despite the improbability of their teachings. This, he says, was in order to show "what the reputation of those sciences can effect among the people."[79] Human beings, Hobbes is saying, will believe in crazy things that are logically inconsistent. The basis of this persuasion is not rationality but the power of the teachers.

---

[77] Hobbes (1839, 5).
[78] Hobbes (1839, 8).
[79] Hobbes (1990, 95).

A Perfect System 81

I do not mean to imply that Hobbes thought what he proposed was as far-fetched as he says paganism or scholasticism were, but that he thought he had a degree of leeway if parts of his system diverged from his own view of human nature. We know that Hobbes suspected Aristotle of not believing his own teaching on metaphysics and of teaching it only because it fit with Greek religion, and so would keep him out of trouble. In *Leviathan*, Hobbes asserts about Aristotle's theory of essences that "it may be he knew [it] to be false Philosophy; but writ it as a thing consonant to, and corroborative of their Religion; and fearing the fate of Socrates."[80] Hobbes had a different goal in mind, but a similar strategy. He thought his system was much closer to the truth than scholasticism, though still, as we shall see, not a perfect fit. It is also clear that he did not think an arid and strictly syllogistic account of his politics would be convincing to the vast majority. Hobbes took advantage of the leeway he had in this regard to promote what he saw as the politically salutary fear of death. In his account, this fear appears as something that should be instilled as if it were an unacknowledged civic virtue. This is done partly by presenting his recommendations as if they were scientific conclusions.

In *De Cive* Hobbes claims to have discovered "*two absolutely certain postulates of human nature,*" one of which was cupidity, and the other, "*the postulate of natural reason, by which each man strives to avoid violent death as the supreme evil in nature.*"[81] This fear of death is "a real necessity of nature as powerful as that by which a stone falls downward."[82] He claims further that "there is in every man a kind of supreme stage of fearfulness, by which he sees the harm threatening him as the worst possible, and by natural necessity does his best to avoid it."[83] In the *Elements of Law*, a "natural necessity of nature" drives men to "avoid that which is hurtful," and "above all that terrible enemy of nature, death, from whom we expect both the loss of all power, and also the greatest of bodily pains in the losing."[84] The worst part of this state is, in *Leviathan*, the "continuall feare, and danger of violent death."[85]

---

[80] Hobbes (2012, 1082).
[81] Hobbes (2004, 6).
[82] Hobbes (2004, 27). Lott (1982) traces the causal relationship between the fear of death and obligation as Hobbes sets it out in *Leviathan* (2012), and Hobbes (1839). For him, as for many scholars, our reaction to the fear of death, as Hobbes presents it, is a strictly physical reaction over which we have no control.
[83] Hobbes (2004, 39), translation slightly changed.
[84] Hobbes (1999, 79).
[85] Hobbes (2012, 192).

In *De Cive*, Hobbes claims to have demonstrated everything in the work with certainty except that monarchy is in all cases the best regime. This amounts to a claim to have offered demonstrable proof of what he calls an absolutely certain postulate of human nature: that man flees violent death as an absolute evil.

The demonstration Hobbes puts forward to establish the necessity of fleeing death is based on his depiction of the state of nature. This image, it turns out, is particularly well suited to suppress and abstract from man's desire for immortality. The desire to live beyond one's time simply makes no sense in the natural state, and this is why Hobbes uses this imagery to present the bare facts of life and death. By appearing to reduce man to his most fundamental drives in the state of nature, and then building his system from this point, Hobbes also gives his system an air of scientific logic.

The great obstacle that must be overcome in the state of nature is the segment of mankind that is not willing to practice the equality of nature. The member of this group, as Hobbes puts it, "supposing himself superior to others, wants to be allowed everything, and demands more honour for himself than others have; that is the sign of an aggressive character."[86] These men engage in conflict not because of economic scarcity, another major cause of strife in the natural state, but because of vainglory, and for "[i]ntellectual dissension." "There is nothing more offensive than this," Hobbes writes, "nothing that triggers a stronger impulse to hurt someone" than "showing hatred and contempt for each other, by laughter or words or a gesture or other sign."[87] In *The Elements of Law* this group is, in fact, "the greatest part of men," who "upon no assurance of odds, do nevertheless, through vanity or comparison, or appetite, provoke the rest, that otherwise would be contented with equality."[88] In *Leviathan* as well, Hobbes speaks of the danger posed by those who, take pleasure "in contemplating their own power in the acts of conquest, which they pursue farther than their security requires."[89] Mankind in his pre-political predicament can be divided into two groups: those who are reasonable, and will accept the principle of equality for the sake of peace, and those who are contentious and will "use Violence ... for trifles, as a word, a smile, a different opinion, and any other signe of undervalue, either direct in

---

[86] Hobbes (2004, 26).
[87] Hobbes (2004, 27).
[88] Hobbes (1999, 78).
[89] Hobbes (2012, 190).

their Persons, or by reflexion in their Kindred, their Friends, their Nation, their Profession, or their Name."[90] The conflict between these two groups results in the war of all against all which makes the natural state intolerable.

In order to escape this condition, reason suggests certain laws of nature, the first of which is "*to seek Peace.*"[91] The rest of the laws of nature follow from this first injunction, and they are held together by contracts that all members of society make with each other. These contracts, in turn, since a man's word is not strong enough to hold him to his obligations, must be reinforced by something more reliable. In *The Elements of Law*, Hobbes makes the central role of the fear of death for his system explicit: "And if no covenant should be good, that proceedeth from the fear of death, no conditions of peace between enemies, nor any laws could be of force; which are all consented to from that fear."[92] "The Passion to be reckoned upon," for Hobbes, "is Fear," and in particular, the fear of "[t]he Power of those men they shall therein Offend."[93] In other words, a stable commonwealth is held together by the fear of men with swords. Stability stems from the appointment of a sovereign with absolute power of life and death over citizens, and who will, in Hobbes's terms, "over-awe" them through terror.[94] The institution of the sovereign solves the problem of conflict. The odds of being executed for a capital offence in a perfect Hobbesian system must be 100 percent. The Leviathan is founded on the premise that if the sovereign creates enough fear, he can compel obedience. If Hobbes is right about his certain postulate about human nature, the problem of achieving stable politics has at long last been solved by the institution of such a sovereign.

The fear of death, though, is not absolute in the state of nature. We can understand that if one is going to die of starvation, risking his life to get food is the only reasonable option. Self-defense also requires overcoming the fear of violent death in order to survive. This makes sense in Hobbes's system. The case of those who risk their lives for the sake of glory or to avenge perceived slights, though, is not so straightforward. From Hobbes's descriptions of the state of nature, and the general equality that pertains there, the vainglorious may have little better than

---

[90] Hobbes (2012, 192).
[91] Hobbes (2012, 200).
[92] Hobbes (1999, 86).
[93] Hobbes (2012, 216).
[94] Hobbes (2012, 190).

a 50 percent chance of surviving their attempts to force others to give them the honor they think is their due. This is a poor risk for a creature that is compelled to avoid death, and especially violent death "by a real necessity of nature as powerful as that by which a stone falls downward."[95] Hobbes clearly expects that these encounters will at least occasionally end in a fight to the death. Readers, the reasonable ones, cannot help but think of those who live this way as being quite insane. It might be the case that making the odds still worse will prevent such people from engaging in this dangerous behavior, but it is also possible that for this type of person, longevity simply is not the priority it is for the more modest sort.

We will, in fact, uncover one of the most important facets of Hobbes's educational rhetoric by delving further into his presentation of the irrationality of pride in the state of nature. By placing glory seekers in the state of nature, Hobbes is able to portray them as so completely irrational that their motivations need not be examined too closely. Hobbes does not go into very much detail about why human pride is so powerful. He sets it out as a fact that is confirmed by everyone's experience, but he also actively shapes his presentation so as to create a division between the sane who can keep their pride in check, and the crazed who cannot.

What glory seekers seek, though, seems quite paltry given the risks. In the state of nature, these "endeavour to destroy, or subdue one an other" for "delectation only," and take pleasure in "contemplating their own power in the acts of conquest."[96] It is simply a form of pleasure seeking that for inscrutable reasons of upbringing or natural character men pursue despite its irrationality. What is strikingly absent from this presentation, though, is the alternative that Hobbes was intimately familiar with: the vision of immortality presented by Pericles. In the funeral oration, Pericles urged the Athenians to risk their lives for the sake of something much more valuable than their lives. Dying for Athens, we recall, was a good deal. Joining oneself erotically with Athens was a means of attaining something permanent and transcendent that made sense of life and death. By confining his description of glory seekers almost entirely to the natural state, Hobbes is able to side-step this very powerful objection. He also abstracts almost completely from considerations of family, faction or class, admitting in *De Cive* that he considers men in the natural state, "as if they had just emerged from the earth like mushrooms."[97]

[95] Hobbes (2004, 27).
[96] Hobbes (2012, 190).
[97] Hobbes (2004, 102).

In the state of nature, there is no family or tribe, no Athens, no permanent structure to which one can attach oneself and join. Isolated with "no account of Time; no Arts; no Letters; no Society," and therefore no way for one's memory to persist after death, the man who kills for the pleasures of glory could not be acting more irrationally.

By describing glory seekers primarily in the state of nature, Hobbes is able to deny, without argument, that the desire for glory aims at anything more than mundane and ephemeral advantages. He is also able to claim that no society can be "based" (in Latin, *iniri*, which carries a connotation of "beginning" or "initiated") on glory. This is because the universal desire for glory causes a universal desire for domination, which all cannot have equally. Political society is thus founded on fear. Hobbes will claim later that this fear results in mutual agreement to form society. But he will also claim that agreement entered into under duress is legitimate before the existence of law. What is conspicuously absent from this equation is the fact that what men really fear is the one whose love of glory and other attributes are so powerful, and his fear of death so slight, that he is able to subdue the rest.

The description of man before political society points to, without naming, the existence of men whose pride, and desire for glory is itself the foundation of society. When Machiavelli, for example, thought about the origins of political society, he thought of great founders such as Romulus, Cyrus, Theseus and Moses. With the complicated exception of the last, Hobbes rarely or never mentions these. As Hobbes must have been aware, though, these founders and subsequent rulers were nearly always the focal points of early civilizations. The most permanent archeological evidence of any civilization invariably consists of funerary works, and other monuments dedicated to the ruler. This artifice testifies to the fact that these rulers wanted more than the advantages of this world. They wanted to overcome death, and to be remembered. Very often they wanted to be deified.

It is also true that even a society founded on fear need not be sustained by it. Periclean Athens was not held together by the fear of death. The real criticism of all previous societies, with the possible exceptions of Rome and Egypt, is that they were short-lived. On the other hand, from the point of view of those living in many of them, these societies were everlasting, and conferred a kind of immortality on their citizens. Hobbes, through his atomized description of individuals, never directly confronts the challenge that the funeral oration of Pericles represents. He implicitly denies the possibility that the individual can be subsumed by his country. Leviathan, it seems, comes closest to achieving immortality the more it denies it to its citizens.

Hobbes's state of nature is not a scientific demonstration, but a rhetorical device in part designed to increase fear of death. Just as the Leviathan serves as an important image of sovereignty, so the state of nature provides a vivid image that focuses the mind on mankind's vulnerability and the bleakness of human existence.[98] Immediately before his first presentation of the "estate of nature," Hobbes outlines this type of strategy, which should be familiar from what we have seen of Aristotle's *Rhetoric*, in *The Elements of Law*, where he speaks of

> [a]nother use of speech ... by which we increase or diminish one another's passions ... And as in raising an opinion from passion, any premises are good enough to infer the desired conclusion; so in raising passion from opinion, it is no matter whether the opinion be true or false, or the narration historical or fabulous. For not truth, but image maketh passion; and a tragedy affecteth no less than a murder if well acted.[99]

Hobbes understood the power of images, and used them to great effect. He understood that truth on its own was not very persuasive, and therefore reckoned on passion. *Leviathan* stirred the passions of its readers, and made itself felt more through notoriety than sound arguments. Casting out superstition and making politics more rational was a major goal of Hobbes's philosophy. But it is easy to overstate the degree to which he was engaged in what, in hindsight, would be the narrative of Enlightenment replacing error with truth and reason. Hobbes had grave doubts about the potential rationality of mankind, and his goal was not simply to deliver the truth to his readers. His goal was peace, and he was willing to bend the truth to attain that goal. Hobbes was more of a sculptor than a geometer.

---

[98] For a discussion of Hobbes's use of the leviathan as an image and visual strategy, see Bredekamp (2007, 29–60).

[99] Hobbes (1999, 76).

4

The Hollow Religion of *Leviathan*

We have seen in Chapters 2 and 3 that Hobbes used a complex form of rhetoric in order to have a specific practical effect on his readers. His goal in his scientific work, *De Corpore*, as with the scientific language of his political works, was achieving this effect, and not propounding the truth as he saw it. In *De Corpore*, Hobbes's goal was to attack the scholastic learning of the universities, but more importantly, he wanted to shake the metaphysical grounding of that teaching. This metaphysical foundation, and the dangerous opinions about immortality it engendered, was, for Hobbes, one of the ultimate sources of the religious warfare of his time.

The most pernicious development of such thinking, Hobbes claims, was the mixing of Aristotle's philosophy with Christianity. Of course, it was easier for Hobbes to lay the blame for what he saw as Christianity's errors at the feet of Aristotle than at the feet of Jesus. Hobbes's explicit claim was that he wanted to free Christianity from the accretions of Greek philosophy it had gathered, and at the same time to reform the ecclesiastical institutions that had subsequently become corrupt. Just as reforming the universities was only to be the outward expression of a much deeper cultural transformation, so the reordering of the church would only be possible on the basis of a seismic shift in the religious opinions of European society. It is thus not surprising that Hobbes's religious writings, and especially what he set down in the third part of *Leviathan*, provoked the most hostile response from his contemporaries. It is also in this part of *Leviathan* and the reaction to it that we see Hobbes's rhetorical strategy at work most clearly.

As I will show in this chapter, Hobbes had several goals in writing part three of *Leviathan*, all of which were aided by the general outcry the work produced. His aims included an attack on Christianity and revealed religion generally. But this attack was not enough to explain everything in the theology and ecclesiology of *Leviathan*. The perennial difficulty in interpreting this part of the work comes from the paradox that Hobbes both is and is not serious about this theology. To this is added the further paradox that what Hobbes proposes here is a rigid civic religion in which thought is free and which, therefore, no one has to believe.

In this chapter, I argue that Hobbes did not want or expect the specific points of his doctrine to be accepted, but thought its underlying principles, which he does not set out explicitly, would be. The ultimate goal of Hobbes's theology in *Leviathan* is the creation of a society relying on a loose religious structure, which is accepted and supported by the sovereign. Individuals in this system will adhere to the principles of this religion (but not to Hobbes's specific theology) in the belief that doing so is a free choice. The most important consequence of adhering to this religion will be a powerful and pervasive commitment to self-preservation. This commitment, which will imperceptibly become the core value of politics and religion, results less from the explicit teaching of the Bible, as traditionally understood, than from an interpretation of the Bible that insidiously renders Christianity hollow and uncertain.

WHY HOBBES WROTE PART THREE OF LEVIATHAN

The greatest difference between Hobbes's earlier political works and *Leviathan* is the extended discussion of religion in the second half of the work. The purpose of this section of *Leviathan* was not obvious and has remained a source of controversy from the book's publication until today. The seemingly perpetual ambiguity of these pages and the perplexity they have caused are, I will suggest, a clue to their purpose.

A common explanation of Hobbes's motive is that he wanted to alter the episcopal structure of the church in his day. As Garsten puts it, "The central problem of Hobbes's political thought was how to undermine the clergy's claim to have an authority separate from that of the political sovereign."[1] This is a reasonable claim, especially given Hobbes's later statements in defense of *Leviathan* that imply that this was the main complaint of his critics. In the dedication to the king of his

---

[1] Garsten (2010, 521). Malcolm (2012, 195) also speaks of Hobbes's "great campaign against the abuse and undermining of temporal power by spiritual or pseudo-spiritual forces."

1662 *Seven Philosophical Problems*, Hobbes offers an apology for *Leviathan*, claiming that

> [t]here is nothing in it against episcopacy; I cannot therefore imagine what reason any episcopal man can have to speak of me, as I hear some of them do, as of an atheist, or man of no religion, unless it be for making the authority of the Church wholly upon the regal power; which I hope your Majesty will think is neither atheism nor heresy."[2]

These apologetics, though, seem to distract from the fact that Hobbes's most serious, and most influential, critics attacked him primarily for what they took to be his undermining of the core aspects of the Christian religion, not because they were afraid he might undermine their position vis-à-vis the king. Hobbes did want to challenge the power of the church, but any change was to be the result of a deeper shift in religious thought that he wanted to effect, not the cause of such an alteration. I am much closer to Johnston, then, who argues that Hobbes was engaged in a project of cultural transformation.

However, if Johnston is correct when he claims that "[t]he second half of *Leviathan* is designed to shape the thoughts and opinions of its readers in ways that will make the argumentation of the first half persuasive and compelling," we are forced to conclude that Hobbes was an utter failure.[3] The fact that the third part of that work was much more offensive than the first half cries out for explanation.

The implicit assumption of Johnston and most other commentators is that whether Hobbes was trying to abolish religion or appease his readers, he wanted to be persuasive in a straightforward way. He wanted his readers to be convinced. The fact that no one was convinced tends to be brushed aside as an inconvenient fact that reveals nothing of Hobbes's actual intentions.[4] It is, though, as I will show in this and the next chapter, very difficult to argue that Hobbes could not have predicted that his work

---

[2] Hobbes (1845b, 5).
[3] Johnston (1986, 120).
[4] Johnston himself acknowledges that "[t]he provocative character of his interpretation was evidently intentional, and the furor it raised was probably not entirely unwelcome." Hobbes engaged in this strategy, Johnston claims, in order to "jolt his readers out of their old ways of thinking, to provoke them into reconstructing their own interpretations" and to transform them "into more rational and predictable beings." But Johnston does not push this suggestion any farther or suggest how exactly Hobbes thought such provocation would make his readers more rational and predictable. His assumption seems to be that readers would be shocked initially, but would finally accept Hobbes's arguments (Johnston 1986, 137).

would be controversial, and in fact that Hobbes did not expect to be taken seriously in a straightforward way. Even before delving into the details, we must ask ourselves if someone famous for being one of the most astute observers of human nature to ever have lived, who had already written controversial works and suffered the consequences, could possibly have been so naive and out of touch with contemporaries as to be blindsided by the reaction to his interpretation of scripture.

In general, contextualists argue that Hobbes was not alone in having strange religious beliefs. They point to those, such as Milton, who were also mortalists and materialists and were contemporaries of Hobbes. No one, though, could seriously suspect Milton or Tyndale of being nonbelievers. Hobbes, on the other hand, stood out for being reviled by Christians of every stripe, and for what his critics supposed was his goal: the subversion of Christianity in its entirety. For all their oddness, very few seventeenth-century interpreters of scripture could be accused of having this goal.

In part three of *Leviathan*, Hobbes lays out an internally consistent interpretation of the Bible. He sets out what is necessary for salvation and how to avoid damnation. He explains several difficult points of theology and offers a comprehensive biblical history. In this section of *Leviathan*, we learn how God does and does not speak to us. Hobbes does not, though, offer a very clear reason for doing so.

In the preface to the reader of *De Cive*, he had said that his aim in the section on religion in that work was to "show that the right of Sovereigns over citizens, which [he] had previously proved by reason, is not in conflict with the holy Scripture."[5] In the dedicatory epistle of *Leviathan*, he offers an explanation that is at once more vague and more polemical for his treatment of the Bible: "That which perhaps may most offend, are certain Texts of Holy Scripture, alleged by me to other purpose than ordinarily they use to be by others."[6] What this other purpose is, he does not say. Nor does he clarify matters when he begins part three, where he says that his aim is to explain "the Nature and Rights of a CHRISTIAN COMMON-WEALTH."[7] Rather than pre-emptively defending his political theory against the charge that it conflicts with the Bible, as he does in *De Cive*, Hobbes seems in *Leviathan* to be building an entirely new structure from the ground up on the basis

---

[5] Hobbes (2004, 12).
[6] Hobbes (2012, 4, 6).
[7] Hobbes (2012, 576).

of scripture[8] – a new structure that coincidentally coincides with what he had sketched in part two. We may assume, as many have, that the purpose of his theology is the same in both *De Cive* and *Leviathan*, but I will contend in this chapter that Hobbes has quite a different goal in mind.

It would be reasonable to assume that Hobbes's goal was the reconciliation of his theology with his materialism, and this is certainly part of what he is doing. Neither this reconciliation, though, nor an attempt to accommodate Christianity to his politics, another popular theory, can fully explain all the theological positions he stakes out.[9] In particular, neither of these lines of argument can account for the elaborate theory of hell introduced in *Leviathan*, which will be the subject of Chapter 5.

Of course, another possible motivation for the lengthy third part of *Leviathan* is Hobbes's sincere belief in the Christianity he elaborates there. Noel Malcolm, for example, has written that "[w]here Hobbes's unorthodox theology is concerned, it is hard to escape the conclusion that he wrote as he did for one compelling reason above all: he believed that what he wrote was true."[10] One must wonder, though, if Malcolm is correct, why Hobbes stood out so distinctly among his contemporaries for what they saw as a blatant lack of sincerity. It is well known that in the seventeenth century, the term "atheist" was hurled at theological opponents when "heretic" would have been closer to the truth. But Hobbes really did seem to his contemporaries to be a wholehearted non-believer, in a way that Milton, again, with his own quite unorthodox opinions, did not.

Malcolm, too, though, recognizes that part three of *Leviathan* is not simply a work of scholarship. It is combative, offensive and defensive. It is, in other words, tactical.[11] Of course, this does not preclude someone being sincere in arguing for a position, but it does suggest that Hobbes was being far more rhetorical than Malcolm seems at points to claim, and that the third part of *Leviathan* was not only a statement of faith. If, as

---

[8] This is likely the root of Pocock's theory that the second half of Hobbes's (2012) *Leviathan* is essentially a parallel work. Pocock (1973, 148–210).
[9] These are the two most common explanations offered for Part Three of Hobbes's (2012) *Leviathan*. Among those who see Hobbes's goal as a reconciliation of his theology with his materialism is Martinich (1992). Among those who see Hobbes primarily engaged in an effort to make his politics more acceptable to Christian readers are Polin (1981), Leo Strauss (1965), specifically in *Natural Right and History*, with the caveat that Strauss' position on Hobbes changed over time and is not easy to pin down (see Stauffer 2007 on this issue).
[10] Malcolm (2012, 195).
[11] On this, see Malcolm (2012, 195).

Malcolm claims, Hobbes wrote what he did because he thought it was true, but in such a way that he would be persuasive to others, rather than as a scholarly exercise, Malcolm would have to accept that Hobbes failed completely in his endeavor.

If, on the other hand, we begin with the premise that Hobbes, in fact, wanted to provoke the reaction he did provoke, much of the perplexity about his motives and methods vanishes. As mentioned above, it is in the sections on religion in *Leviathan* that Hobbes's provocative rhetorical strategy is clearest. As a prelude to the thematic treatment of several topics in Hobbes's theology, then, it will be particularly useful to see how a reader like Clarendon responded to part three of *Leviathan*.

CLARENDON'S PARADIGMATIC ATTACK ON THE THEOLOGY OF LEVIATHAN

Edward Hyde (1609–1674), who would become the First Earl of Clarendon, met Hobbes when he was a young man and liked him. They were both in the exiled court of Charles I in France. They were also, however, intellectual rivals. Clarendon suspected Hobbes of being less than fully committed to the Royalist cause. Hobbes knew this, and, when he showed Clarendon part of *Leviathan* before the completion of the work, he warned him that he would not like what he was about to read there.[12] Indeed, Clarendon did not like what he read and seems to have been instrumental in stripping Hobbes of royal protection, thus precipitating Hobbes's return to England.[13] Clarendon himself, though, later fell out of favor with Charles II, and, while exiled in France, wrote his monumental *History of the Rebellion*. The project he turned to immediately afterward was a work entitled *A Brief View and Survey of the Dangerous and pernicious Errors to Church and State, in Mr. Hobbes's Book, Entitled Leviathan*. This book was complete by 1670 but not published until 1676.

Clarendon was a highly intelligent reader of *Leviathan*, and he was a high-profile figure. John Locke owned a copy of *A Brief View*.[14] Clarendon was, in fact, precisely the kind of reader Hobbes had hoped for, since he fulfilled the rhetorical strategy I outlined in Chapter 2, the kind of reader who delighted in outsmarting Hobbes and deducing his

---

[12] Hyde, Earl of Clarendon (1676, 7).
[13] The best account of this episode is Collins (2007).
[14] Parkin (2007, 322).

true motives. Clarendon himself says that his goal was "to manifest, and expose the poison that lies hid and concealed."[15] My contention is that in *A Brief View*, Clarendon is connecting the dots that Hobbes had left for another to find. In so doing, Clarendon, and critics like him, said openly and loudly what Hobbes could not say – for example, that "*Moses* was no true Prophet."[16]

A truth discovered is better than one received and Clarendon could not help but trumpet the truths he discovered in Hobbes's book. In this he was not alone. For all his animus, though, Clarendon had to admit that there were some points in *Leviathan* that "learned men" also maintained, and some with which he himself agrees.[17] This was also typical of many contemporary attacks and made it difficult to dismiss Hobbes's theology outright. These critics, especially theologians, were drawn irresistibly to demonstrate their superior knowledge of scripture, biblical and church history.

Hobbes's goal was to raise doubts about the possibility of immortality as understood by Christianity, and with his attacks, Clarendon furthered that goal and made *Leviathan* more widely read than it otherwise might have been. Parkin notes that for "many early readers, *Leviathan* was a difficult and paradoxical work whose implications were very hard to read," and that for the first few years after its publication, it "had attracted surprisingly little public comment."[18] Parkin goes on to say that "Clarendon's importance, and the relevance of his critique to the politics of the period ensured that the book was read."[19] Clarendon, for example, who calls[20] Hobbes "a professed adversary to Eternity," spells out the implications of Hobbes's reasoning about religion that were not immediately apparent.

The theology of *Leviathan*, according to Clarendon, gave permission to its adherents to engage in whatever forms of vice they liked, while perhaps still believing that they were Christians. Since, in the seventeenth century, atheism was usually thought to stem from the indulgence of the passions, this put Hobbes in the camp of atheism. As Tenison, Archbishop of Canterbury, says in a 1695 sermon, atheists risk their souls, "for the

---

[15] Hyde, Earl of Clarendon (1676, 9–10).
[16] Hyde, Earl of Clarendon (1676, 196).
[17] Hyde, Earl of Clarendon (1676, 220). See also 233 for his praise of chapter 39, and 302 for his agreement with Hobbes about the ills of the schoolmen.
[18] Parkin (2007, 121, 136).
[19] Parkin (2007, 322).
[20] Hyde, Earl of Clarendon (1676, 285).

sake of a few vile Lusts, and inordinate Passions, the fruit of which is present shame, and inconvenience: They lose their hopes of being like Angels for ever, that they may enjoy a few *Brutal Pleasures* for a few days on earth."[21]

Clarendon, though, does sense something deeper and even more dangerous than atheism at work in part three:

> It seems to be the greatest charity he can expect, to be believed to be a man that believes nothing of the immortality of the Soul, of the Eternal Life, Hell, Salvation, the World to come, and Redemption, which all other Christians do believe, and believe all to be evident out of Scripture. Since it is a less fault not to believe them, how destructive soever, then to imagine that he takes all that pains, and uses all that raillery upon the Scripture, to shew how liable the Word of God it self is to be ill handled, and perversely interpreted by a great and bold Wit.[22]

Hobbes was not, according to Clarendon, simply an atheist trying to tailor the Bible to fit his political theory. Nor were his interpretive flourishes dictated by his materialism. He wanted to show just how far one could go in offering an apparently consistent reading of the Bible and thereby foster the religious uncertainty that Clarendon complains of. It would have been more acceptable if Hobbes had simply attacked the Bible outright. The insidious course Hobbes takes instead is far more dangerous. For Clarendon, "[t]his desperate Art hath enabled his most devoted Proselytes to apply Texts of Scripture to all their profane, impious, and unclean purposes," and this, "unavoidably must carry them to Hell, let the situation of it be where it will."[23] Those who learned their biblical hermeneutics from Hobbes, Clarendon says, could use scripture to justify just about anything.

Since, for Clarendon, Hobbes was pushing the interpretation of scripture beyond all reasonable bounds, he was reluctant to engage with Hobbes in matters of textual exegesis. In Clarendon's attack, then, we find a demonstration of the difficulties even Hobbes's most astute adversaries faced in attempting to refute his positions without being drawn into his mode of arguing. Clarendon opens his attack on part three by stating that he will not stoop to Hobbes's level in arguing directly with the interpretations of scripture there:

> I shall not ... wait upon him in the particular Surveys of his glosses upon, and interpretations of the several Texts of Scripture, with which he is bold ... lest the sobriety and gravity of Scripture be too much exposed to the critical Licence of

---

[21] Tenison (1695, 9).
[22] Hyde, Earl of Clarendon (1676, 230–1).
[23] Hyde, Earl of Clarendon (1676, 231).

Grammarians, or the greater licentiousness of petulant and profane Persons, who chuse the Scripture for both the matter, and the language for the argument of their common and loosest discourses; which exorbitancy is much propagated since the publication of Mr. *Hobbes* his writings.[24]

Rather than attack Hobbes's specific interpretations, Clarendon urges that *Leviathan* "may be fitter for a general disapprobation and discountenance by the Sovereign power, or Ecclesiastical autority" because it

[e]xposes Religion to the irreverant examination of dissolute persons, and prostitutes the sacred mysteries of our Faith, the Incarnation of our blessed Lord and Saviour, the Trinity, the Sacraments, the precious pledges of our Salvation, to a Philosophical and Mathematical Inquisition; and under the notion of translating proper and significant words and terms, in the understanding whereof all Learned men have agreed, into vulgar and common Language, which no terms of any Art ever admitted.[25]

Hobbes indeed, Clarendon notes, claims to accept the notion that the difficult truths of Christianity must be accepted, as one swallows bitter pills whole rather than chewing through them and, as Hobbes says, "sifting out a Philosophical truth by Logic as such mysteries as are not comprehensible," but Hobbes contradicts this principle over and over again in these chapters by digging too deep into the meaning and implications of scripture.[26] In order to demonstrate Hobbes's inconsistency, Clarendon is forced, either against his will, or having forgotten his vow not to do so, to restate Hobbes's arguments, which, he worries, are "little less than Blasphemy to repete."[27] But repeat them, he does, along with all their unstated implications. Despite his stated intention, Clarendon is forced to accuse Hobbes of using "very ill Logic" in his interpretations and to engage in debates about translation and other specific hermeneutic matters.[28]

One important example of Clarendon engaging with a specific piece of text is his attack on Hobbes's interpretation of 2 Kings 17–18, which describes Namaan's asking permission to bow to a foreign god at the bidding of his master. Hobbes's point here is that, according to the Bible, if one's ruler demands that we deny Christ or worship gods in which we do not believe, we must obey. Since "Profession with the tongue is but an

---

[24] Hyde, Earl of Clarendon (1676, 199–200).
[25] Hyde, Earl of Clarendon (1676, 200).
[26] Hyde, Earl of Clarendon (1676, 202). Hobbes makes statements about accepting scripture being like swallowing pills whole in Hobbes (2012, 578), (1998b, 238).
[27] Hyde, Earl of Clarendon (1676, 204).
[28] Hyde, Earl of Clarendon (1676, 247).

externall thing" and as long as we remain faithful to Christ in our hearts, we have "the same liberty which the Prophet Elisha allowed Namaan the Syrian."²⁹ Hobbes goes on to quote the passage in question almost exactly as it appears in the King James translation.³⁰ Clarendon, though, protests that if we follow the translation of "Dr. *Lightfoot*, a man eminently learned in the Hebrew" we find that Namaan "craved pardon for Idolatry past, and not begged leave to be Idolatrous for the time to come."³¹ He claims further that even if Hobbes were following the correct translation, Namaan clearly had special permission from Elisha, which is not something the ordinary citizen can claim. Clarendon stays with this topic for quite some time, marshaling numerous verses against Hobbes's theory, including what seems to be a decisive statement from Jesus that "[w]ho so denieth me before men, I will deny him before my Father which is in Heaven."³² In contrast to Namaan, Clarendon raises "the example of those three in *Daniel*, who chose to be thrown into the hot fiery furnace, rather than fall down before the Image which *Nebuchadnezzar* had set up."³³

The real problem with Hobbes's line of argumentation here, Clarendon realizes, is its implications not only for those with dissenting views in the present but also for Christian martyrs of the past. Hobbes in fact seems to alter his position on martyrs from *De Cive* to *Leviathan*. In the former, Hobbes maintained that when one must decide between obeying the prince or obeying God, one should not resist the prince, but rather, "Go to Christ through Martyrdom."³⁴ He then threw down the following gauntlet: "If anyone thinks this is a harsh thing to say, it is very certain that he does not believe with his whole heart that JESUS IS THE CHRIST, *the Son of the living God* (for he would long to be dissolved [*dissolui*] and to be with Christ)."³⁵ Perhaps realizing that there were altogether too many

---

²⁹ Hobbes (2012, 784).
³⁰ The only difference being that in 2 Kings 5:18 where Hobbes has "*when I bow my selfe in the house of Rimmon*," the KJV has "when I bow *down* myself" (my italics).
³¹ Hyde, Earl of Clarendon (1676, 250). In fact, it seems that Hobbes and the KJV have this correct. There is no indication, in the Oxford Annotated Bible at least, that Namaan was speaking only about past idolatry.
³² Hyde, Earl of Clarendon (1676, 253), Matthew 10:33.
³³ Hyde, Earl of Clarendon (1676, 294).
³⁴ Hobbes (2004, 245).
³⁵ Hobbes (2004, 245). The allusion here is to Philippians 1.23, where Paul says that he has "desire to depart, and to be with Christ," (KJV). "Dissolvi" here, which is the word in the Vulgate, has a connotation of "being destroyed," which is also present in the Greek: "τὸ ἀναλῦσαι καὶ σὺν Χριστῷ εἶωαι."

who were willing to take up this challenge, Hobbes takes quite a different tack in *Leviathan*.

The framing of the question itself in *Leviathan* suggests what Hobbes wants his readers to think of martyrs: "But what shall we say of all those Martyrs we read of in the History of the Church, that they have needlessly cast away their lives?"[36] The Latin here is even more pointed, referring to "*Historiis aliisque Legendis* [Histories and other Legends]."[37] As Malcolm points out, this may be an allusion to *The Golden Legend*, but also "could have a dismissive sense."[38] Further noting that the etymological root of "martyr" is the Greek μάρτυς, which means "witness," he claims that this term can only apply to "those that conversed with him on earth, and saw him after he was risen: For a Witnesse must have seen what he testifieth, or else his testimony is not good."[39] This definition limits true martyrs to a very few disciples who actually spoke with Jesus and saw him in the flesh. Dying is no part of martyrdom, Hobbes maintains, for it is not "the Death of the Witnesse, but the Testimony it self that makes the Martyr."[40] Worse still, martyrs who die for their beliefs will not be with Christ at all, because, "being not called thereto, tis not required at his hands; nor ought he to complain if he loseth the reward he expecteth."[41] The ominous suggestion here is that one may in fact be damned for dying needlessly while thinking oneself a martyr.[42] In the theology of *Leviathan*, this is so because taking this course is tantamount to disobeying the sovereign, which is in fact a sin.

Although Hobbes seems to allow that martyrdom is a possibility in *De Cive* while denying it in *Leviathan*, his goal in both works, in fact, is the same. In both iterations, the reader is forced to wonder whether he is absolutely certain that disobeying the sovereign and being executed for it will result in his admission to heaven. By raising doubts about this, Hobbes wants to make obedience to the law appear to be the safer and more reasonable choice. Notice that while he strongly suggests that one may go to hell while believing oneself a martyr, Hobbes does not raise the

---

[36] Hobbes (2012, 786).
[37] Hobbes (2012, 787).
[38] See Malcolm's note, Hobbes (2012, 787).
[39] Hobbes (2012, 786).
[40] Hobbes (2012, 788).
[41] Hobbes (2012, 788).
[42] To make this more pointed, Hobbes's teaching on martyrs in *Leviathan* (2012) implies that St. George, the patron saint of England, would be damned, since he died for disobeying his sovereign and did not speak directly with Jesus.

possibility that not dying a martyr may result in the same outcome. For Hobbes, one is more likely to arrive in heaven by keeping quiet and avoiding any trouble with the authorities on religious grounds, than one is by dying for one's faith.[43]

This is precisely what Clarendon objects to. "Salvation," Clarendon says of Hobbes's system, "would be gotten at too cheap a rate," if one were allowed to deny with the tongue what one believed in the heart.[44] Clarendon, in responding to Hobbes, has to spell out the fact that as a practical matter, "[o]ur Saviour had provided very ill for the propagation of his Faith, if he had left a latitude for men to deny him in their words, so they confessed him in their hearts. How many Converts would that secret, and reserv'd belief and confession have produc'd?"[45] For Calvin, the death of martyrs was strong evidence of the truth of Christianity: "It is therefore no small proof of the authority of scripture, that it was sealed with the blood of so many witnesses, especially when it is considered that in bearing testimony to the faith, they met death not with fanatical enthusiasm ... but with a firm and constant, yet sober godly zeal."[46] Calvin and Clarendon here may be saying something very similar, but Clarendon is forced into stating the matter in highly pragmatic terms in order to counter Hobbes's suggestion that martyrs had cast away their lives for no reason. Clarendon goes on to spell out what Hobbes only hints at: martyrs suffer from "want of Wit and understanding," and "the expedient [Hobbes] hath found might have saved many hundred thousand lives of the Christians."[47] Paradoxically, Clarendon's reader is forced to wonder if Hobbes might be correct. Is the teaching of the local priest sure enough to bet one's life on it?

This uncertainty is reinforced by the doubts Hobbes stirs up about the authorship, and therefore authority, of the Bible. Clarendon suspects that Hobbes's real goal in raising such questions was "to lessen the reverence that was accustom'd to be paid to the Scriptures themselves, and the authority thereof, before he could hope to have his

---

[43] Without entering into a longer excursus, I would suggest that this is a large part of Locke's message in *The Reasonableness of Christianity*. There, it turns out, Christianity is a reasonable religion, and reasonable people do not get into trouble with the police.
[44] Hyde, Earl of Clarendon (1676, 251).
[45] Hyde, Earl of Clarendon (1676, 252).
[46] Calvin (2008, 42).
[47] Hyde, Earl of Clarendon (1676, 256, 252).

interpretation of them hearken'd unto and received."[48] This supposed strategy, of course, makes little sense: once a reader has lost faith in the authority of the Bible, why would a new textual interpretation be any more persuasive than the discredited one? On the surface, Clarendon's charge seems reasonable, but in trying to outmaneuver Hobbes, he in fact plays into his hands by going a step too far. For those who had been perplexed about Hobbes's theories on the authorship of the Bible and his interpretations of various biblical terms, Clarendon lays bare their significance:

And after the whole foundation of Christian Religion is laid upon the Word of God, and so often mention throughout the Scripture of several particular words spoken by God, and with such declaratory circumstances, that he is said to have spoken face to face, and as a man speaks to his friend, as he did to *Moses*, Mr. *Hobbes* takes great pains to make it believed that he never spake at all, and then we can have none of his words.[49]

Clarendon makes it clearer than Hobbes does that the point of part three of *Leviathan* is to raise grave doubts about the origins of the Bible and the possibility of prophesy and miracles. In an age plagued by religious controversy, where differing sects argued about almost everything, Hobbes, Clarendon repeatedly stresses, attempts to create controversies where none had ever existed before, which is quite a feat.[50] In piecing all of this together, Clarendon recognizes that Hobbes fosters a kind of "comfort that is in the uncertainty" about what happens to us after death, and that "if a King compel a man to it by the terror of death, or other great corporal punishment, it is not Idolatry."[51] He suspects that "his design is rather to perplex and disturb . . . then to enlighten and inform them."[52] Clarendon's attack, although it might have convinced readers not to take seriously the explicit theology of *Leviathan*, which no one of consequence took seriously anyways, is unlikely to have lessened the perplexity or uncertainty that Hobbes really did hope to create. By exposing what he thought to be Hobbes's true intentions, Clarendon unwittingly helped to propagate Hobbes's real goal: undermining hopes for immortality and making the fear of death seem more reasonable.

[48] Hyde, Earl of Clarendon (1676, 197).
[49] Hyde, Earl of Clarendon (1676, 203).
[50] Hyde, Earl of Clarendon (1676, 285, 286).
[51] Hyde, Earl of Clarendon (1676, 223, 315).
[52] Hyde, Earl of Clarendon (1676, 245).

THE HERMENEUTIC CIRCLE

Hobbes did not think his theology would ever be implemented in any straightforward way. We have seen that Clarendon thought that Hobbes was not entirely serious about what he was saying in part three of *Leviathan* and suspected that part of his goal might in fact have been to show just how far a brilliant interpreter could go in revising the traditional understanding of the Bible. In this he was on the right track. But neither he nor any other early critic I am aware of noticed the fundamentally circular argument that underlies Hobbes's entire teaching on theology. By following this circular argument, this section will untangle a paradox that has struck many readers; as Martel puts it, *Leviathan* appears to be a

> work of supreme hypocrisy ... here is a writer who complains that deceptive textual exegesis has mesmerized people into following a series of false prophets, leading to the English civil war. Yet Hobbes himself seems to claim that in *Leviathan* he and he alone offers a correct reading of Scripture ... he sounds like one of the many charlatans he is so quick to denounce.[53]

The key to unraveling this paradox lies in not taking Hobbes too literally.[54]

Hobbes sketches in *Leviathan* a civil religion in which thought is free. Hobbes did, in fact, want such a religion to be established, but he did not expect that it would look like the one he described. He did not expect that anyone would adopt this theology wholesale any more than he expected a future sovereign to use the book as a literal blueprint for a new regime. He did, though, want both his theology and his political theory to have a real impact on the world. On the other hand, he does record his hope at the end of part two that his book may one day fall into the hands of a sovereign "who will consider it himselfe, (for it is short, and I think clear,) without the help of any interested, or envious Interpreter; and by the exercise of entire Soveraignty, in protecting the Publique teaching of it,

---

[53] Martel (2007, 24). Martel in general comes closest to my own view. I agree with his astute observation that Hobbes, "seems to be appropriating the sovereign 'last word' even while appearing to defer to that sovereign authority" (2007, 45). From this observation, which applies especially to Hobbes's interpretation of scripture in *Leviathan* (2012), Martel argues that Hobbes is engaged in a deconstruction of authority itself and the empowering of all readers. I argue, by contrast, that Hobbes undercuts his own authority in this circular fashion in order to foster uncertainty.

[54] Garsten (2010, 521) shows that one of Hobbes's strategies for undermining belief in transubstantiation was claiming that Christians had interpreted the words of Jesus too literally. It is reasonable to apply to Hobbes's texts the same hermeneutic methods Hobbes uses on other texts. One should be wary, then, of reading Hobbes too literally.

convert this Truth of Speculation, into the Utility of Practice."[55] He thus hopes that *Leviathan* will succeed and not be "as useless as the Commonwealth of *Plato*."[56] He seems to mean here that no one successfully transformed a regime on the basis of Plato's *Republic*, but that it might be possible for someone to do so on the basis of *Leviathan*.

The greatest obstacle to the achievement of this goal, Hobbes worries, is that his hope will be useless because of "how different this Doctrine is, from the Practise of the greatest part of the world, especially of these Western parts, that have received their Morall learning from *Rome*, and *Athens*; and how much depth of Morall Philosophy is required, in them that have the Administration of the Sovereign Power."[57] On reflection, this latter statement forces us to wonder how useless Plato's philosophy really was. Although no one emulated the *Republic*, Hobbes sees the moral philosophy that originated in Athens as the greatest challenge to his own project. Plato's influence was, in fact, profound. There were no republics based on Plato's *Republic*, but Plato's thought insinuated itself into all of Western thought. This is in no small part because Greek philosophy permeated Christianity, as Hobbes sets out to prove in part four of *Leviathan*. It may be that Plato's thought was influential in ways that Plato could not have predicted. Hobbes, with the benefit of hindsight and Plato's example, may have hoped to achieve more control over his own influence. John Dowell, in his 1683 work thought Hobbes's argument that Greek philosophy had such a negative impact on Christianity was preposterous since no early Christian bishop was a philosopher.[58] But Dowell fails to see just how subtle are the lines of influence Hobbes traces.

At the end of chapter 33 of *Leviathan*, Hobbes gives authority to the sovereign to interpret scripture, saying that "[f]or, whosoever hath a lawfull power over any Writing, to make it Law, hath the power also to approve or disapprove the interpretation of the same."[59] The meaning of this statement appears straightforward: If the sovereign has the authority to make the teaching of the Bible legally binding, he also has the power to decide which interpretation will be authoritative. This seems to flow

---

[55] Hobbes (2012, 574).
[56] Hobbes (2012, 574).
[57] Hobbes (2012, 574).
[58] Dowell (1683, 6ff.). For Hobbes's assertion that "most of the pastors of the primitive church were ... chosen out of the number of these philosophers" see Hobbes (1840c, 388–9). In Hobbes (2012, 758), moreover, Hobbes also says that after Alexander conquered the Israelites, Greek religion began to corrupt Judaism.
[59] Hobbes (2012, 608).

naturally from the sovereign's absolute power, and his duty, as set out in chapter 18 of *Leviathan*, to decide "*what Doctrines are fit to be taught.*"[60]

But on what basis does the sovereign know that he has the authority to interpret the Bible as he sees fit? On the basis of the interpretation Hobbes offers in *Leviathan*. In other words, the sovereign, who can be an individual or a large number of individuals in an assembly, must already be convinced of Hobbes's interpretation before he can assume the authority to make his own interpretation authoritative. It is important to emphasize here that Hobbes's explicit teaching is that it will be possible for a sovereign assembly to come to agreement about an authoritative interpretation of scripture. This means in effect that it will be Hobbes's reading of scripture that will be authoritative, or that whatever interpretation the sovereign offers will have to fit within the framework of Hobbes's interpretation. It is, in fact, Hobbes who has power over the text in this case, and thus Hobbes who rules the sovereign indirectly.[61]

Hobbes insists that the sovereign must be the authoritative interpreter of scripture, but his own interpretation is in many places quite specific. It seems the sovereign will be quite constrained as far as his interpretation is concerned. For example, Hobbes's theory of the trinity is very unusual. One could argue that Hobbes himself claims that his positions are provisional.[62] However, his theory that the sovereign must be the sole authoritative interpreter of scripture is based squarely on his theory of the trinity and biblical history. How could the sovereign know he (or they) had this authority to interpret without accepting Hobbes's account of how that authority fell into his hands? The sovereign thus seems bound to accept Hobbes's theory that between the ascension and return of Jesus, the sovereign of every state must be the authoritative interpreter of scripture. If the sovereign wanted to offer a different interpretation of the trinity, he would only have the authority to do so on the basis of a prior acceptance of Hobbes's interpretation of the Bible, along with his interpretation of the trinity. This line of thought, though, takes Hobbes too literally.

---

[60] Hobbes (2012, 272).

[61] It is not, therefore, that Hobbes wants Charles to become a godlike creator-sovereign, as Miller (2011) maintains. Hobbes himself is this sovereign. I do not, therefore, accept Miller's argument that Charles was the primary addressee of *Leviathan*. I am in closer agreement with Miller when he states that "[p]hilosophers must imitate the creator" (Miller, 2011, 79).

[62] "I can acknowledge," he says, "no other Books of the Old Testament, to be Holy Scripture, but those which have been commanded to be acknowledged for such, by the Authority of the Church of *England*," Hobbes (2012, 586, see also 700, and especially 708).

The real power Hobbes exerts over the text lies in how he changes the way his readers see it.[63] After exposure to Hobbes, and later Spinoza and Locke, it became impossible for most readers to see the Bible in the same way their ancestors once had. Once we grasp this, it becomes much easier to see the way in which Hobbes both is and is not serious about his theology.

The theology Hobbes sets out, then, in *Leviathan*, is simultaneously authoritative and provisional. To heap paradox on paradox, private belief in Hobbes's system is free, but only on the basis of his interpretation of both the Bible and the mind. In other words, the toleration Hobbes seems to want for private belief can only be accepted on the basis of a prior acceptance of a more fundamental premise about what can be known for certain about religion, and the relative importance of this life and the next.[64]

This confusing situation can only be untangled once we see that the ultimate goal of the theological sections of *Leviathan* is to raise reasonable doubts about any absolutely authoritative reading of the Bible. Once these doubts set in, individual citizens will be less willing to risk their lives for their private beliefs, because they will not be absolutely certain that they are correct. Once it becomes clear that no one can really be certain of the absolute truth of any interpretation of the Bible, and that there is no way to verify what another believes and that there will always be differences of opinion in religious matters, citizens will hold to their own beliefs without feeling the need to impose them on others or to expose them to rigorous examination by others. At the same time, the state, composed of similarly minded individuals, will not see any advantage in terms of promoting peace and stability, in legislating every aspect of worship, let alone belief. Such an outcome will not arise from a discovery of the previously unseen sprit of toleration in Christianity.

---

[63] Eliot (1975, 38) speaks of this phenomenon thus:

> The existing monuments form an ideal order among themselves, which is modified by the introduction of the new (the really new) work of art among them. The existing order is complete before the new arrives; for order to persist after the supervention of novelty, the *whole* existing order must be, if ever so slightly, altered; and so the relations, proportions, values of each work of art towards the whole are readjusted.

[64] In addition to laying the intellectual and cultural groundwork for toleration in *Leviathan* (2012), Hobbes also, as Tuck argues convincingly, tried to intervene in the political debate about toleration in England, writing several works on heresy later in life. See Tuck (1990).

It is only on the basis of profound uncertainty that any theory of toleration can be built.[65]

Hobbes, as I will show in the next section, does in fact want a civil religion, but not of the sort he explicitly outlines in *Leviathan*. He does not describe the inevitability of differing private beliefs in order to make a concession to this plurality, but in order to encourage it.

A CIVIL RELIGION IN WHICH THOUGHT IS FREE

In this section, I argue that for Hobbes, the classical ideal of a civil religion, the boundaries of which are contiguous with the political borders, had important advantages over the religiously fragmented times in which he lived. Precisely because of the nature of this fragmentation, though, Hobbes did not think one sect would ever be able to dominate the others once and for all. His solution to this problem was to foster religious uncertainty and anxiety, which would make religious toleration possible.

Hobbes states in chapter 38 of *Leviathan* that his theology is unusual and provisional:

> But because this doctrine (though proved out of places of Scripture not few, nor obscure) will appear to most men a novelty; I doe but propound it; maintaining nothing in this, or any other paradox of Religion; but attending the end of that dispute of the sword, concerning the Authority (not yet amongst my Countreymen decided), by which all sorts of doctrine are to bee approved, or rejected; and whose commands, both in speech, and writing (whatsoever be the opinions of private men) must by all men, that mean to be protected by their Laws, be obeyed.[66]

This passage does not appear in the Latin *Leviathan*, perhaps because of its focus on contemporary English events. The fact that there is a Latin edition, though, is evidence that Hobbes's teaching cannot be taken to be

---

[65] Consider, for example, how surefooted and straightforward the argument against freedom of belief is for Cardinal Bellarmine (2012, 86):

> [f]reedom of belief is destructive for those to whom it is allowed, for it is nothing but the freedom to err, and to err in the matter where error is most dangerous. For the true faith is only one (Ephesians 4, 'one Lord, one faith, etc.'); therefore the freedom to move away from that one faith is the freedom to rush into the abyss of errors. Just as it is not beneficial to allow sheep the freedom to wander through the mountains, and it is not beneficial to free the ship from its steering oar and allow it to be carried freely by the wind, so also it is not beneficial to allow the peoples freedom of belief after they have joined the one true faith.

[66] Hobbes (2012, 708).

directed at England only.[67] His strategy, moreover, as stated here, would seem to be counter-productive. In the midst of the religious confusion of the Civil War period, he is proposing an entirely new theology and ecclesiology, and even eschatology, as a solution. In other words, at a time when innumerable sects disagreed about almost everything, Hobbes thought that introducing a novel and paradoxical new teaching would quickly put an end to all religious disagreement. He also expected to convince those whose concern seems primarily otherworldly by asserting that his main goal is solving a secular problem. Hobbes further undermines his argument here by stating explicitly that he is advancing a mere hypothesis about the nature of heaven and hell and the means by which one is saved: matters about which one must be absolutely certain.

It would be hard not to see something preposterous in Hobbes's strategy here. He is undoubtedly serious about wanting to end warfare, or at the very least, civil war caused by religious strife. At the same time, he also undoubtedly sees the advantage of religious uniformity backed up by an absolute central government. The founders of ancient republics such as Rome, for example, "have in all places taken care; First, to imprint in their minds a beliefe, that those precepts which they gave concerning Religion, might not be thought to proceed from their own device, but from the dictates of some God or other spirit" and this, Hobbes says, was "in order to their end, (which was the peace of the Commonwealth,) that the common people in their misfortunes, laying the fault on neglect, or errour in their Ceremonies, or on their own disobedience to the lawes, were the lesse apt to mutiny against their Governors."[68] And although Hobbes seems to have thought this strategy was impossible to adopt literally, he could have opted to argue on behalf of the most powerful religious sect in England, in the hope that it would win supremacy and drown out the others. This strategy would have fit better with the Hobbes of realist imagination. Instead, he suggests that the sovereign should adopt a theology he knew would be offensive to everyone.

There is also the question of why Hobbes thought these particular doctrinal positions would be more conducive to peace than more traditional ones. The passage quoted above follows Hobbes's argument that the kingdom of heaven will be a real commonwealth on earth. This, as many critics pointed out, was a far less exalted vision than traditional

---

[67] Hobbes, in fact, removed several, but not all, references to the Civil War from the Latin version.
[68] Hobbes (2012, 176–8).

interpretations of heaven. We are forced to wonder why Hobbes thought a civil religion with this particular vision of heaven would be especially effective at establishing peace, since that is the basis on which he recommends his theology. Since religious and civil law will ideally be the same in Hobbes's system, civil obedience is the surest means to salvation. Why not, then, make heaven as enticing as possible, rather than an eternal version of this life? Hobbes's real goal could not, in any straightforward way, have been the one he explicitly spells out in the above quotation.

In fact, Hobbes could see, as any observer of English history would have, that neither Henry VIII, nor Elizabeth, nor Mary, let alone James I or Charles I, had been able to overcome the problem of religious faction. Neither Catholicism, nor any brand of Protestantism was ever going to be the exclusive creed of England. The arguments among intellectuals about the correct understanding of Christianity were, Hobbes, knew, interminable. "For," he says, "according to the usual curiosity of natural philosophers, they could not abstain from disputing the very first principles of Christianity."[69] As he says further in another context, "To please neither part is easy; but to please both, unless you could better agree amongst yourselves than you do, is impossible. Your differences have troubled the kingdom, as if you were the houses revived of York and Lancaster."[70] Hobbes decided to overcome these problems in a novel way; he pleased neither part. He would create a type of religious conformity not by winning widespread agreement with his specific doctrinal points but by gaining acceptance of his premises through insinuation. In the following section, we will see that the most important of Hobbes's innovations was in the realm of personal belief.

In outward appearance, though, what Hobbes proposes in *Leviathan* is similar in several ways to both the civil religions of classical antiquity and the covenant-based arrangement described in the Torah.[71] In chapter 39 of *Leviathan*, Hobbes argues, on etymological and other grounds, that a church, in the true sense of the word, is "[*a*] *company of men professing Christian Religion, united in the person of one Sovereign; at whose command they ought to assemble, and without whose authority* [injussu]

---

[69] Hobbes (1840c, 390).

[70] Hobbes (1840b, 434).

[71] The similarity of Hobbes's system to ancient civil religion and his "Judaization" of Christianity has been noted by Beiner (2011) and Mitchell (1996, 64); see also Robert P. Kraynak, who highlights Hobbes's "Jewish Christianity" in "The Idea of the Messiah in the Political Thought of Thomas Hobbes" (1992), and Daniel J. Elazer (1992) in the same issue. Also, Eldon J. Eisenach (1981, 62).

they ought not to assemble."[72] He thus makes the church contiguous with the state and denies that there can be a universal church, or one whose authority extends beyond any particular state. The message of Christianity is universal, but there can be as many Christian churches as there are states, just as the ancient Greek *poleis* could each worship their own iteration of Zeus or Athena. This notion was not alien to Catholicism, of course, with its local saints. Much of the argument in chapter 42 of *Leviathan* is directed against the possibility that a citizen is bound by the authority of foreign religious authorities, in particular the pope, against the wishes of his own civil sovereign. The only authority priests or ministers have in a state, Hobbes argues, derives from the authority of the sovereign.

Religious rules, moreover, are nothing but recommendations until they are made law by the sovereign.[73] And it is the sovereign who authorizes an interpreter whose reading of scripture will be authoritative. This could not come about, Hobbes claims, by echoing Plato's *Republic*, "till Kings were Pastors, or Pastors Kings."[74] The Latin *Leviathan* here, instead of "Pastores," which he uses elsewhere for "pastor,"[75] is "Doctores," which means "teacher" and carries a broader connotation. Moses is the model for this type of sovereign authority to make God's commandments laws, although Hobbes adds the unusually republican claim that Moses had this authority not directly from God, but from the consent of the Israelites.[76]

Hobbes further lauds the practice, which he claims was common in the ancient world, of regularly reading out the laws of the commonwealth in church assemblies. This practice is an attempt to reduce any possible distinction in the minds of citizens between civil and religious law.

THE HOLLOWNESS OF PRIVATE BELIEF

If one considers the fostering of religious uncertainty to be Hobbes's main goal, his bizarre interpretations of scripture start to make more sense. Just as Hobbes created an internally consistent political system based on assumptions about human nature he knew to be overly simple, so he

---

[72] Hobbes (2012, 732).
[73] Hobbes (2012, 812).
[74] Hobbes (2012, 812).
[75] Hobbes (2012, 797).
[76] Hobbes (2012, 812–16, 740).

creates a theory of theology and ecclesiology that would, on its face, convince no one. Just as his goal in part two of *Leviathan* is not what he claims it to be, so what he hopes to accomplish in part three is not in any direct sense what it seems to be. The space Hobbes seems to allow for a plurality of personal beliefs is a case in point.

Laws regarding religion, in *Leviathan*, must necessarily be confined to outward words and actions. This is because "internall Faith is in its own nature invisible, and consequently exempted from all humane jurisdiction; whereas the words, and actions that proceed from it, as breaches of our Civill obedience, are injustice both before God and Man."[77] This is a further similarity with ancient religions, which focused more on correctly performed ritual than inner conviction. An important difference, though, is that there is no independent priesthood in Hobbes's system. The sovereign retains all power over religious matters and can therefore alter these at will if he deems it necessary.

The kind and degree of religious toleration Hobbes would allow has been a source of scholarly debate. Hobbes does in some passages seem to allow for a degree of toleration, but seen in the context of his thought as a whole, it becomes clear that what he meant by toleration is not necessarily what later thinkers meant by the term. Of particular importance is the statement Hobbes makes in the forty-seventh chapter of *Leviathan* about Independency, which he suggests "is perhaps best."[78] This statement seems to be in sharp contrast to Hobbes's repeated insistence on the need for religious uniformity. Malcolm makes the useful suggestion that

> [i]n just one essential way, Hobbes's general theoretical position could look favourably on the Independents: their leading thinkers had, on the whole, given up claims to jurisdiction by divine right over the people, and most of them were content to put all such jurisdictional power, including the power to regulate the Church, in the hands of the civil sovereign. In this respect, Hobbes was indeed their natural ally.[79]

In other words, as long as there was a fundamental agreement that one's religious beliefs should not interfere with the government, one could believe what one wished. This is a kind of toleration based on a more basic agreement.

In the seventeenth century, the theory that citizens could maintain whatever private beliefs they wished so long as they conformed outwardly

---

[77] Hobbes (2012, 822).
[78] Hobbes (2012, 1116).
[79] Malcolm (2012, 63).

to the state religion was controversial. Clarendon thought that by this logic, the Jews would never have been able to deny the gods of the Egyptians or follow Moses out of Egypt.[80] He and others also worried that this practice would put an end to the evangelical mission of Christianity. The point Hobbes really wanted to make here, though, is that it is in fact impossible to monitor or verify the private beliefs of others.[81] He also stresses that private beliefs are "not voluntary, nor the effect of the laws, but of the unrevealed will."[82] It would make no sense, Hobbes seems to imply, to persecute individuals for beliefs over which they have no control. The will is the result of appetite, and appetite is decisively shaped, Hobbes argues, by external factors and our physical constitution. A rational religion, then, would not, as medieval inquisitors did, presume to be able to know what an individual really believed, nor would it persecute individuals for their beliefs, even if they could be known, because they are involuntary.

What, then, are we to make of the claim, Hobbes makes much earlier in the work, that the sovereign is able to "[c]onforme the wills" of all his citizens?[83] The sovereign also plays an educative role in teaching subjects their duties and the grounds of his authority. "*Erroneous conscience*" is one of the things Hobbes claims weakens a commonwealth. When one's conscience is in conflict with the law, it is simply a matter of confusion on the subject's part.[84] If the sovereign, then, can, and indeed must to some extent, shape the wills of his subjects, and religious belief is a function of the will, why could he not inculcate uniformity of religious belief, thereby obviating the need to excuse a plurality of those beliefs? If Hobbes is serious about the capacity of the sovereign to create such a unity, we are forced to wonder again why Hobbes does not go all the way in establishing a civil religion that requires both outward and inward conformity?

The most obvious reason is that Hobbes did not in fact think that the sovereign would be able to inculcate the kind of religious uniformity that

---

[80] Hyde, Earl of Clarendon (1676, 196).
[81] Chabot (1995, 404, 408) argues that, according to Hobbes, "inner life is off-limits to the sovereign, if only because he would lack the techniques that would enable him to reach within and condition people into submission," and that Hobbes sought to "instill the skeptical habits of mind that enable us to manage the tension between law and conscience that this achievement brings with it."
[82] Hobbes (2012, 738).
[83] Hobbes (2012, 260).
[84] Hobbes (2012, 502).

was required in a place like Sparta.⁸⁵ The sovereign is said to be able to conform the will of citizens "by terror."⁸⁶ If the sovereign successfully convinces his subjects that his laws are in fact God's laws, and disobedience will result in both execution and damnation, he has a great deal of terror at hand with which to conform their wills. If, however, the sovereign could not successfully convince them of the holy status of his laws, he would have only the threat of physical harm to persuade them. Hobbes readily admits that when there is a conflict between the commands of God and those of the sovereign, it would be totally irrational to follow the sovereign and risk hellfire. If Hobbes expected, as he claims to, that citizens would believe the sovereign was arbiter of their fates here and in the hereafter, and was thus able to "reduce all their Wills, by plurality of voices, unto one Will," which Hobbes claims is a real unity, why does he repeatedly stress the fact that there must be a free space for private beliefs which are beyond the reach of the sovereign?⁸⁷

The reason, or part of the reason, for many of Hobbes's more unusual doctrinal points, as I will show especially with regard to hell, is that he is trying to say things that resonate with various religious sects of his time. Almost everyone could find something in *Leviathan* that sounded somewhat appealing. Hobbes did not want to be dismissed out of hand, which he might have been had his theology been entirely alien on its face. The appeal to some kind of freedom of belief, for example, sounds like a concession to the interiority of Christianity, which might have appealed to certain Protestants. The problem that Hobbes's theory of the will posed for this freedom only appeared upon reflection.

Hobbes is clearly aware that most Christians feel the need for outward expression of their inner faith. Otherwise he would not have tried to deny that this was necessary. Hobbes's method of arriving at his conclusions about private belief, though, forces his readers to reevaluate the nature of their inner lives. *Leviathan*, according to the introduction, is the result of introspection, and the reader is asked to read himself in order to verify the truth of Hobbes's claims. In the first chapters of *Leviathan*, though, the inner life is described in terms it would be difficult for an ordinary reader to verify from introspection: the human mind is an anxiety-driven chaos of incoming and decaying sense perceptions, colliding in random, or

---

⁸⁵ See Ryan (1983, 197–218).
⁸⁶ Hobbes (2012, 260).
⁸⁷ Hobbes (2012, 260).

nearly random, order to produce man's thoughts, memory and imagination.

Not only are our inner thoughts involuntary, they are also unstable and constantly changing. It is, therefore, too much to ask that human beings attempt to regulate these thoughts. In explicit contradiction to Matthew 5:28, Hobbes says both in *Leviathan* and *Behemoth* that there is nothing wrong with imagining "being possessed of another man's goods, servants, or wife," or dreaming of another's death.[88] Controlling such desires is, according to Hobbes, a nearly impossible goal and too great a burden, especially for young men. Expecting human beings to be able to repress their sinful desires before they even arise only ensures that they will despair of their inability to comply and do whatever their priests command in order to atone. There is no way to know precisely the reason for our appetites or what they will be in the future. Holding such a hard line when it comes to private thought would therefore be futile.

Because we can never fully discover the reasons for our own passions, we remain fundamentally mysterious to ourselves. That human beings have difficulty understanding themselves is a fundamental part of Christianity, and one of the main themes of Augustine's *Confessions*. But while Augustine states, "I find my own self hard to grasp," and asks, "What then am I, my God? What is my nature?" He also claims, through addressing God directly, to be able to transcend the limits of his mind: "Here I am climbing up through my mind towards you who are constant above me. I will pass beyond even the power of my mind which is called memory, desiring to reach you by the way through which you can be reached, and to be bonded to you by the way in which it is possible to be bonded."[89] For Hobbes, it is not possible to be bonded to God, to ascend beyond the human mind or to address God. This will remain impossible even after the resurrection. Hobbes's mechanistic description of the passions seems to leave little room for a soul that can be moved by God.

A spiritual journey or ascent is also out of reach for Hobbes. This concept, which pervades Christianity from the early notion of the Christian as a *viator* to John Bunyan's *The Pilgrim's Progress*, one of the most widely read works of English literature, rests on the development of inner religious feeling. Hobbes would call this enthusiasm or inspiration, that is, delusions or visions stemming from unbridled imagination and the

---

[88] Hobbes (2012, 452), see also Hobbes (1990, 26).
[89] Augustine (1998, 193–4).

belief that God is a spiritual entity that can have direct contact with human beings.

For Hobbes, natural reason is man's God-given tool for understanding true religion, and only those whose rational faculty is sufficiently developed can properly understand the Bible. Since reason is "not to be folded up in the Napkin of an Implicit Faith," all interpretation of scripture must be rational.[90] Hobbes does suggest that there is a distinction between those words of God that are above reason and those that are not. Still, he holds that there is nothing in revelation contrary to reason. On closer inspection, Hobbes merely asserts that there is a very fine line between what is and is not above reason without explaining how to differentiate between the two. Hobbes rarely claims that anything in scripture is beyond his own capacity to understand (the notable exception being the concept of purgatory, which he nonetheless denies on logical grounds).[91] In fact, Hobbes says that if we cannot understand something in the Bible, "the fault is either in our unskilfull Interpretation, or erroneous Ratiocination."[92] Similarly, when a prophet or holy man offers contradictory teachings or teachings that do not accord with natural reason, his reputation must be diminished and his teachings rejected.[93] There is also no suggestion in the first two parts of *Leviathan* that human beings must accept certain propositions on faith; everything we need seems to be set out in the law of nature, which is entirely accessible to reason.

One of the bitter pills that the pious assume to be true without further examination is the divine status of the Bible. Hobbes, though, takes his time in chewing on this proposition. In chapter 33 of *Leviathan*, Hobbes raises questions about the authenticity of the Bible. There is no independent authority to prove the authorship of the works of scripture, and, as Hobbes says, this "is the only proof of matter of fact."[94] Although we cannot establish who wrote these works, we can, from circumstantial evidence, discern when they were written. It turns out that many books of the Bible, at the very least those from *Genesis* to *2 Chronicles*, were written, "long after" the time they describe.[95] Moses, for example, could not have written the so-called books of Moses since Deuteronomy mentions that no one knows

---

[90] Hobbes (2012, 576).
[91] Hobbes (2012, 998ff.).
[92] Hobbes (2012, 576).
[93] Hobbes (2012, 182ff.).
[94] Hobbes (2012, 588).
[95] Hobbes (2012, 590).

where the tomb of Moses is.⁹⁶ Similarly, in *Genesis* the author speaks of a time past when the Canaanites were in Israel, although they were always in the land when Moses lived (this is an implicit rejection of the possibility that God could have revealed future events to Moses).

Finally, Hobbes accepts the account in the apocryphal book of 2 Esdras, which claims (according to Hobbes's interpretation), that all of the books of the Old Testament, having been burnt and lost, were rewritten by Esdras (Esdras is the Greek rendering of Ezra) after the Jews returned from Babylon.⁹⁷ From Hobbes's interpretation of this account, it would seem that the current text of the Bible is incomplete, and quite possibly corrupt. If Hobbes is correct, not only is individual interpretation uncertain, but God meant this to be the case. There are four books of Ezra. The first two are the canonical Ezra and Nehemiah. The third and fourth books are often called 1 Esdras and 2 Esdras, which is why Hobbes initially says that only "the third and fourth" of Esdras were apocryphal while he quotes a passage from "the second book," meaning, 2 Esdras. There was a renewed interest in 2 Esdras beginning in the Renaissance among both Protestants (especially dissenting Protestant groups) and Catholics, for reasons ranging from the book's focus on eschatology and the status of the soul to its many predictions.⁹⁸

Hobbes, though, after quoting the passages that seem to imply that all of the works of the Old Testament had been burned, quotes another passage from 2 Esdras (14:45–6), which comes twenty-three verses later and seems unrelated to the point he is making. In the passage, God tells Esdras: "*The first* [twenty four books] *that thou has written, publish openly, that the worthy and unworthy may read it; but keep the seventy last, that thou mayst deliver them onely to such as be wise among the people.*"⁹⁹ The standard interpretation of Hobbes's time, which began with Pico della Mirandola, is that these seventy books were in fact the books of the Kabbalah.¹⁰⁰ Hobbes, though, does not explain what this passage means or why he includes it. Readers who were not as versed as

---

⁹⁶ Hobbes (2012, 590).
⁹⁷ Hobbes (2012, 598). Although Hobbes at first offers this explanation as a suggestion ("if the Books of *Apocrypha* ... may in this point be credited"), he later simply accepts this point as fact: "*Esdras*, who by the direction of Gods Spirit retrieved them when they were lost." Hobbes also accepts this theory in chapter 42, Hobbes (2012, 818). Esdras is the Greek rendering of Ezra.
⁹⁸ See the introduction to Alastair Hamilton's study (1999).
⁹⁹ Hobbes (2012, 598). See also *The Apocrypha of the Old Testament; Revised Standard Version* (New York, 1957), 48.
¹⁰⁰ Hamilton (1999, 96).

Hobbes in contemporary biblical criticism would, then, be left with the thought that there were seventy books of the Bible that Esdras held back, and to which they had no access. This could imply that one who relied on his or her own interpretation of the Bible was doing so on the basis of an incomplete text. This passage also makes it clear that God believes only certain wise men were capable of understanding scripture fully; the word "apocryphal" after all, can mean either spurious or hidden. In fact many books of the New Testament were considered apocryphal because of their esoteric doctrine.[101]

As noted, Hobbes makes a plausible claim that Moses did not write the books of Moses and that the subsequent books were not written by those the texts claim were their authors. If we accept these claims and Hobbes's interpretation of 2 Esdras, then presumably the original books of Moses would not have contained the evidence Hobbes uses to prove that Moses did not write them. This means that Esdras, whose own works were excluded from the canon, was not as faithful a transcriber as he claims to be and that our text of the Old Testament is in fact corrupt. At the very least, this approach would force readers to be aware that there are serious questions surrounding the authenticity of the Old Testament, to which Protestants gave such weight, and about their own capacity to understand these texts.

The New Testament similarly turns out to be suspect according to Hobbes. It was collated by a group of ambitious church fathers who, erroneously, "endeavoured to passe their Doctrine, not for Counsell, and Information, as Preachers; but for Laws, as absolute Governours."[102] Hobbes claims that despite the character of those who established the canon, he is "perswaded they did not therefore falsifie the Scriptures, though the copies of the Books of the New Testament, were in the hands only of the Ecclesiasticks"[103] Even raising the possibility that the texts could have been corrupted forces readers to wonder whether Hobbes had perhaps been too easily persuaded in this case, especially given his view of human beings as generally self-interested and his numerous statements to the effect that ambitious people often lie about spiritual matters and that a large number of Church policies are "manifestly to the advantage of the Pope."[104] On this view, Christian readers are likely to be

---

[101] Hamilton (1999, 3).
[102] Hobbes (2012, 600).
[103] Hobbes (2012, 600).
[104] Hobbes (2012, 186). See also chapter 47 of *Leviathan*.

left with an irresolvable anxiety about their ability to hear the word of God through scripture.

Edwin Curley argues that Hobbes's statements about the New Testament are an example of what he calls "suggestion by disavowal."[105] This is, for Curley, Hobbes's irony at play. According to Curley, Hobbes had to resort to this sort of irony because he was very likely an atheist who wanted to conceal his atheism from most readers, while conveying it to some. I agree with Curley that Hobbes uses irony. I also agree with his suggestion that when Hobbes says that ambitious and corrupt priests were unlikely to corrupt the text of the Bible to further their own ambitions, he was planting precisely the opposite thought in readers' minds. Curley, though, does not give Hobbes or Hobbes's readers enough credit. Almost no one of consequence has ever been fooled by Hobbes's irony. What Curley and others unearth as Hobbes's esoteric teaching is in fact his exoteric teaching. Hobbes wanted to sow doubts in the minds of as many of his readers as he could, not only in the minds of an ingenious minority.

Since there is now, at the very least, a shadow of doubt about whether we can take everything in the Bible at face value, it becomes more difficult to accept the proposition that Jesus is the Christ solely from our own reading of scripture. This poses a problem for Hobbes's assertion that we must have faith that Jesus is the Christ in order to enter heaven because "[t]he most ordinary immediate cause of our beleef, concerning any point of Christian Faith, is, that wee beleeve the bible to be the Word of God."[106] If we cannot trust our own reading of scripture, though, we must trust the sovereign's interpretation and must obey whatever laws he makes, whether derived from the Bible or not. It was proper for the Jews to obey Esdras and to accept his account of the origin of the law, for example, because he "was the High Priest, and the High Priest was their Civill Soveraigne" and, Hobbes concludes, "it is manifest, that the Scriptures were never made Laws, but by the Soveraign Civill Power."[107]

By treating the Bible as he would any other text, Hobbes implicitly challenges its sacredness; it is to be read "without Enthusiasme, or supernaturall Inspiration."[108] Rather than being moved by the word of God,

---

[105] Curley (1992).
[106] Hobbes (2012, 934).
[107] Hobbes (2012, 818).
[108] Hobbes (2012, 584). James Farr notes that "once we work through the metaphors, 'inspiration,' materially speaking, is air blown into a man, or, we might say, inspiration for Hobbes is just hot air."

readers are to examine the Bible for logical consistency and the reasonableness of its claims to truth and grant assent to the proposition that Jesus is Christ. Hobbes, it should be clear, has done everything in his power to undermine the traditional sources of personal belief.

CONCLUSION

Hobbes does not allow a space for private belief because he is a champion of freedom of thought or liberty of conscience. It would be more accurate to describe what Hobbes allows as a private space for uncertainty and anxiety. Hobbes attempts to undermine the confidence individuals have in their own reading of the Bible and to render them uncertain of the origins and truth of their own most firmly held beliefs. This is done not simply by refuting the claims of the Bible by means of reason, but by harnessing those elements of Christianity that disposed human beings to peace – obedience, awe, humility – and removing or transforming those elements that did not – faith, love and communion with God. The net result of this procedure is not that citizens would become atheists, but that they would not be entirely sure of their own beliefs and would be subject to an irremediable restlessness.

The nerve of this restlessness is the fundamental circularity of Hobbes's argument. Hobbes denies that the sovereign has the capacity or the responsibility to demand uniformity of belief among his citizens. At the same time, the sovereign is supposed to have the absolute power to compel total obedience from them. The latter point is decisive. Individuals can believe what they like about God and the afterlife, so long as that belief does not interfere with the sovereign's ability to exact obedience through the fear of physical violence. The laws the sovereign lays down are religious laws, but since citizens need not believe this and can even have private teachers instruct them in other doctrines so long as they do not act on them,[109] the power of the sovereign in fact rests not on the religious status of the law, or the religious beliefs of citizens, but on physical force. For this to work, a fundamental lack of certainty among citizens about the prospects for immortality is necessary.

It is only possible to accept the idea that individuals will differ in their beliefs and that a plurality of sects can exist within a state on the basis of a prior assumption that it is impossible to verify the truth of any religious conviction. This means that the acceptance of a diversity of religious

---

[109] Hobbes (2012, 822).

Conclusion

beliefs rests on a more fundamental belief and agreement about what can be known about religious matters; this is diversity on a foundation of uniformity. The circularity here arises because the toleration of different religious opinions is only possible if citizens already believe that they cannot have certain knowledge of what will happen to them after death, and that therefore they should not risk their lives for the sake of their beliefs. In this context, longevity becomes a higher priority.

Hobbes, then, does envision a civil religion in his state, but not of the sort that he explicitly describes. I noted above the similarities between the system Hobbes describes and ancient civil religions; legalistic, with an emphasis on external actions and words. On the other hand, trying to determine exactly what sort of church Hobbes had in mind, and what his precise thoughts on toleration were, might be a red herring. Much of the scholarly debate about these issues is fueled by the fact that Hobbes made many different statements, often difficult to reconcile, about these matters. If he had had very specific proposals in mind for the kind of toleration he wanted, and the church hierarchy he envisioned, he would likely have spelled these out more clearly. He is very clear about the degree and kinds of power a sovereign should have. He is not, though, unequivocal about how the government will be set up, or even whether the sovereign must be a single individual. His aim was to clarify the nature of sovereignty and to let others work out the details. In religious matters too, Hobbes is less concerned with the details than with the underlying framework.

The real goal for Hobbes was not the literal adoption of his specific proposals, but the inculcation of his principles. His proposals are a means to that end, rather than the end itself. The most important changes Hobbes wanted to enact were on the plane of ideas. The most important idea Hobbes wanted his audience to absorb was that hopes for immortality were uncertain, and that a long and comfortable life is therefore the most rational, even the most moral, goal that man can have. If this thought could be ingrained across society as a foundational idea, if all, or most, people could be brought to agree that peace is the highest good we can know for certain, Hobbes would have succeeded in instituting a core element of ancient civil religion: the fundamental *nomos* that is simultaneously law and custom, and which Pindar claimed was king of all.[110] Hobbes wanted to ingrain his idea about the primacy of self-preservation as deeply as the Spartans ingrained the opposite thought.

---

[110] Pindar (1997, 385, 387), cf. Plutarch (1991, 169 [151]).

The sovereign is entitled to determine what counts as scripture, and he is the authoritative interpreter of it. Ideally, his decisions in this regard will be guided by a prior, probably unacknowledged, acceptance of Hobbes's principles. Whatever the sovereign decides, he will in all likelihood remain within the framework of the wider society. Insofar as Hobbes established that framework, Hobbes is the real sovereign.

5

Hell and Anxiety in Hobbes's *Leviathan*

Perhaps the best example of Hobbes's indirect legislation in religious matters as described in the previous chapter is his treatment of hell. Hobbes's interpretation of hell sparked some of the most incendiary responses from the first readers of *Leviathan*. Modern scholars, though, generally overlook Hobbes's vision of hell, and this choice is at once surprising and understandable.[1] It is understandable because the belief in hell among Westerners has declined at a faster pace than has belief in God or heaven.[2] This oversight is surprising, however, because the fear of violent death is the foundation of Hobbes's political thought and Hobbes clearly states that the fear of hell is greater than the fear of violent death and that citizens are often more afraid to sin than they are of breaking civil laws.[3]

---

[1] Although some scholars who focus on Hobbes's religious thought mention his unusual interpretation of hell without much comment, for example, A.P. Martinich (1992); J.G.A. Pocock (1971), the whole issue is conspicuously absent from other works, such as F.C. Hood (1964) and Warrender (1957).

[2] A 2008 poll of 35,000 respondents by the Pew Forum found that belief in hell has continued to decline (based on comparisons with a 2001 Gallup poll). According to a theologian interviewed for the report, "Skepticism about hell is growing even in evangelical churches and seminaries" (Charles Honey, "Belief in Hell Dips, but Some Say They've Already Been There," *Pew Forum*, http://pewforum.org/news/display.php?NewsID=16260 (accessed August 2008)). D.P. Walker (1964) notes that the gradual lessening of the fear of hell, and attacks on the orthodox view of hell, began in the mid-seventeenth century. More recently, Philippe Ariès (1991, 573, 576–7) notes that "sociological studies show that belief in an afterlife is declining at a much faster rate than faith in God among people of Christian cultures" and, in particular, that belief in the traditional concept of hell has all but disappeared.

[3] "But if the command be such, as cannot be obeyed, without being damned to Eternall Death, then it were madness to obey it, and the Counsell of our Saviour takes place (*Mat.* 10.28) *Fear not those that kill the body but cannot kill the soul*" (Hobbes 2012, 928–30).

This does not appear to be a serious problem in Hobbes's thought since he says that salvation depends on obedience to civil law, which is the same as divine law, and an inner faith that is beyond the sovereign's reach. Since capital punishment in this world leads to damnation in the next, avoiding violent death appears to be the only pertinent consideration. This, though, only makes Hobbes's discussion of hell more puzzling. On the basis of his political theory, there would seem to be no reason for him to stake out a position on what hell will be like. Indeed, he never raises this topic in *De Cive* or *The Elements of Law*.[4] Still less clear is why Hobbes's description is so bizarre, and it is bizarre even by the standards of seventeenth-century England. Hobbes must have known that the image of the damned fornicating after the Second Coming would have rubbed Puritan sensibilities the wrong way. In fact, the strangeness of this image is likely part of the reason, so few scholars discuss it.

Those who study Hobbes and religion can be divided roughly into those who think that he is a believer of some sort, and whose theology is either a more or less orthodox type of Calvinism[5] or, despite his sincerity, highly idiosyncratic,[6] and those who believe that the theological sections of his works are a sop to his contemporaries or an impish subversion of Christianity.[7] A general theme in most of these authors is that Hobbes's treatment of religion is an attempted synthesis of Biblical Christianity and materialism or a natural religion that flows from modern science, and that whatever he is doing to religion, his goal is promoting political stability and peace.[8]

That Hobbes is trying to alter Christianity somehow for the sake of peace is quite familiar in Hobbes scholarship, and I accept this position and agree in general with those who claim that Hobbes is attempting to undermine Christianity. The process or mechanism by which he does this, however, and what it means to undermine Christianity, can be specified to a greater degree than has been done so far. This chapter, through an examination of Hobbes's description of hell, is an attempt to provide at

---

See also Hobbes (2012, 502, 510, 532, 698); Hobbes (2004, 80, 135, 234–6); Hobbes (1999, 162), and Hobbes (1990, 50).

[4] It is possible that Hobbes had not worked out his theory of hell before writing *Leviathan*. The frontispiece of *De Cive* is dominated by a traditional Last Judgment, including what appears to be a standard set of demons and devils torturing the damned and casting them into hellfire. On Hobbes's use of imagery, see Bredekamp (2007).

[5] For example, Hood (1964).

[6] See Mitchell (1996).

[7] Curley (1996, 256–71); Strauss (1963, 1965, 1959).

[8] Milner (1988, 400–25); Springborg (1975, 289–303).

least some of that specificity. The assumption, which is still quite common, that Hobbes wants to usher in a secular political system or create a nation of atheists is proleptic, and in light of work done by Mitchell, Tuck and others is untenable. However, it is equally untenable to maintain that Hobbes hopes individuals will continue to believe in the same way they had previously.

I argue that Hobbes's interpretation of hell is meant to redirect individuals' anxiety about whether they are destined for heaven or hell into anxiety about whether there is a heaven or hell, and if so, how they could know anything certain about either. Hobbes did not expect that citizens of his state would accept all the specific points of his theology or that they would become secularists or atheists; he hoped, rather, that they would be left with an indeterminate belief they would be averse to examining. There is an affinity between this view and the religious attitudes of many in the West. The impossibility of certain knowledge about the correct path to salvation is also the precondition to thinking about religion as a personal choice. Rather than a sharp break with the past, then, Hobbes's treatment of hell is best seen as an attempt to refract an older form of anxiety in a new direction that retains something of its Christian character. This becomes clear when one examines Hobbes's description of hell in light of his epistemology and his selective use of modern rationalism in his interpretation of both hell and the concept of faith.

I begin with a discussion of Hobbes's account of hell and a comparison with other views that were current in seventeenth-century England. I next discuss Hobbes's epistemology and materialism and their importance to the political and religious sections of *Leviathan*. I conclude with an explanation of how the previous sections contribute to Hobbes's rhetorical strategy.

HOBBES'S REINTERPRETATION OF HELL: A FARRAGO OF HERESIES

The soul, Hobbes claims, is nothing but the "breath of Life" or anima of the "*Body alive*" and not the incorporeal substance many believe it to be.[9] When a person dies, the soul, or breath of life, leaves the body, and only a "dead carkasse" remains.[10] At the Second Coming, each person will be restored to life, or reanimated, and after the final judgment the elect will be

[9] Hobbes (2012, 974).
[10] Hobbes (2012, 947).

given immortal and spiritual, although corporeal bodies while the damned are given mortal, "grosse and corruptible" ones.[11]

The kingdom of God will be on earth, according to Hobbes, and not in the sky or anywhere close to God.[12] There will be no marriage or procreation among the blessed, since this would lead to rapid overpopulation, especially if they will inhabit the New Jerusalem which will descend from heaven, and which, according to the verses Hobbes draws our attention to and accepts without comment, will be 2,250,000 square miles in area, or somewhat smaller than Australia, and made entirely of gold and gems.[13]

Hobbes claims initially to be uncertain about the location of hell, suggesting from certain passages in Job and Isaiah that it might be underground or underwater among the ancient race of giants, or from Revelation that it will be a lake of fire, or from Exodus that it is simply a place of complete darkness away from the elect.[14] He goes on to note that the word "hell" derives from the Hebrew word *Gehenna*, the name of a garbage dump outside Jerusalem that was periodically set on fire in order to clear the stench. Hobbes, though, later rejects all of these interpretations because "now there is none that so interprets Scripture."[15]

Hell, Hobbes eventually claims, will be on earth and the damned will live after the resurrection in a state of "grief, and discontent of mind, from the sight of that Eternall felicity in others" until they are cast into the everlasting fire and die a second death.[16] Since, Hobbes reasons, Paul cannot have had the damned in mind when he says that the body will be "*raised in incorruption ... glory*" and "*power*," he cannot have meant that they would have eternal life or be subject to eternal torment. The second death is painful, but at least it is quick.[17] Since the damned will not burn and suffer eternally, though, the everlasting fire mentioned several times in the Bible would seem to be superfluous. Hobbes alludes to his solution to this problem in chapter 38 when he says, "men may be cast successively [into the fires of hell] one after another for ever."[18]

---

[11] Hobbes (2012, 992).
[12] Hobbes (2012, 726).
[13] Hobbes (2012, 724–6).
[14] Hobbes (2012, 712).
[15] Hobbes (2012, 714).
[16] Hobbes (2012, 716). Hobbes makes the same claim in the appendix to the Latin edition, having "B" say, "Thus the reprobate will rise again, it seems, to a second death"; Hobbes (2012, 1160).
[17] Hobbes (2012, 718).
[18] Hobbes (2012, 718).

It is not until chapter 44, however, that Hobbes spells out the full and gruesome implications of his interpretation, as if he had to prepare the reader gradually to hear them. Unlike the Elect, the damned will marry, procreate and raise children before they are killed at some unspecified time.[19] There is no hope of salvation for the children of the damned, who will also be annihilated, but not before having children of their own. This procession of corruptible bodies will provide an endless supply of fuel for the fire, and there will thus be no contradiction between the biblical passages about a second everlasting death and the everlasting fires and torments of hell.

The specific tortures of hell described in the Bible, such as "*the worm of conscience*," "*gnashing of teeth*" and "*Brimstone*," are metaphors for the mental pain and anxiety the reprobate will suffer from the sight of the endless happiness of the Elect.[20] Similarly, the notion that Satan along with other devils and demons will torture the damned is a mistake that stems from the importation of pagan demonology and untranslated words.[21] The word "Satan" signifies any "Earthly Enemy of the Church."[22] These enemies, who Hobbes likens to "evill and cruell Governours," will torment the damned after the resurrection.[23] Before being annihilated, then, the damned will live much as those who live in the present world do under bad, and perhaps Hobbes wants to suggest, non-Hobbesian, government.

What exactly Hobbes means by hellfire, though, is complicated by the fact that he explicitly claims that it is meant metaphorically, but then speaks about it as if it were real. This is an intentional ambiguity, and as I will argue below, part of Hobbes's rhetorical strategy. In chapter 38 he states that "it is manifest, that Hell Fire which is [in Revelation 21:8] expressed by Metaphor, from the reall Fire, of Sodome, signifieth not any certain kind or place of Torment; but is to be taken indefinitely, for Destruction."[24] He says further that "it follows, me thinks, very necessarily, that that which is thus said concerning Hell Fire, is spoken metaphorically" and that biblical passages referring to "*Fire*" and "*the fire is not quenched*" are meant "metaphorically."[25] Being cast into hellfire,

---

[19] Hobbes (2012, 992).
[20] Hobbes (2012, 712, 716).
[21] Hobbes (2012, 716 and chapter 45).
[22] Hobbes (2012, 716).
[23] Hobbes (2012, 716).
[24] Hobbes (2012, 712).
[25] Hobbes (2012, 716).

then, simply means being destroyed rather than burning eternally. The argument here seems to be that the wicked will be resurrected, live horrible lives and then die once and for all, their punishment being their horrible lives rather than the second death. As Hobbes claims in chapter 44, "To the Reprobate there remaineth after the Resurrection, a *Second*, and *Eternall* Death: between which Resurrection, and their Second, and Eternall death, is but a time of Punishment and Torment."[26]

But despite repeatedly asserting that hellfire is meant metaphorically, Hobbes also claims in the same context that "of all Metaphors there is some reall ground" and that this applies both to the "*Place of Hell*, and the nature of *Hellish Torments*, and *Tormentors*."[27] Indeed, in arguing that there is no corporeal soul and that the reprobate will be resurrected with corporeal bodies, he claims that "where it is said that any man shall be cast Body and Soul into Hell fire, it is no more than Body and Life; that is to say, they shall be cast alive into the perpetuall fire of Gehenna."[28] Hobbes implies here that hell will consist of real fire and be in a real place, as he does when he says that "The Fire, or Torments prepared for the wicked in *Gehenna, Tophet*, or in what place soever, may continue for ever."[29] Earlier, as part of his argument for the corporeality of angels and spirits Hobbes had claimed that,

they are permanent, may bee gathered from the words of our Saviour himselfe (*Mat.* 25. 41.) where he saith, it shall be said to the wicked in the last day, *Go ye cursed into everlasting fire prepared for the Devil and his Angels*: which place is manifest for the permanence of Evill Angels (unlesse wee might think the name of Devill and his Angels may be understood of the Churches Adversaries and their Ministers) because Everlasting fire is no punishment to impatible substances.[30]

His theory that the resurrected burn once only holds, but he clearly here treats hell as an actual fire in which permanent bodies, such as Satan, can burn forever. Though these passages could be interpreted in light of Hobbes's earlier statements about the metaphorical nature of hell, the suggestion that the damned will die a second death in some specific place certainly clouds the issue.[31]

---

[26] Hobbes (2012, 994).
[27] Hobbes (2012, 716).
[28] Hobbes (2012, 974).
[29] Hobbes (2012, 992).
[30] Hobbes (2012, 628).
[31] In the appendix to the more conciliatory Latin edition of *Leviathan*, Hobbes complicates this issue further by having his character "B" claim first that "[h]eaven and Earth will be renewed, and although the world will be consumed with fire, it will nevertheless not be

Hobbes blurs the line between the metaphoric and literal interpretation of hell most effectively in the following passage:

> And although in Metaphorical Speech, a Calamitous life Everlasting may be called an Everlasting Death; yet it cannot wel be understood of a *Second Death*. The fire prepared for the wicked, is an Everlasting Fire: that is to say, the estate wherein no man can be without torture, both of body and mind, after Resurrection, shall endure for ever, and in that sense the Fire shall be unquenchable, and the torments Everlasting: but it cannot thence be inferred, that hee who shall be cast into that fire, or be tormented with those torments, shall endure, and resist them so, as to be eternally burnt, and tortured; and yet never be destroyed, nor die.[32]

Though this passage can be interpreted to mean that hellfire is metaphorical, it has often been interpreted to mean that there will be a real fire into which the damned will be thrown.[33] Indeed, if hellfire is meant metaphorically, Hobbes leaves open the question as to how the damned actually will die a second death – old age? Illness? Or perhaps execution by the bad governors of hell? Whether metaphorical or literal, though, the overall effect of this ambiguous and confusing presentation is to make hell appear less terrifying, and perhaps less believable or unknowable.

The prospect of dying quickly is less frightening and more humane than that of suffering for the rest of eternity.[34] This was part of what Hobbes wanted to achieve; those who believed that this was an accurate description would have less to fear from following civil law against the teachings of their priests. Similarly, heaven appears less appealing, and much more like a sanitized version of life here on earth than a theocentric view in which the resurrected are in the presence of God.

On the other hand, although this kind of hell does appear somewhat less frightening, there is no lack of gruesome and apparently unnecessary details. Why, for example, does Hobbes dwell on the lack of marriage among the blessed and the endless generation of hopelessly damned children among the reprobate? Why does he present us with the vision of an endless stream of human beings being burned to death? Why does he raise several unorthodox possibilities about hell's location before rejecting

---

annihilated, but real entities will persist," and later, in response to "A's" claim that many of the descriptions of hell appear to be metaphorical that "[h]owever that may be, no determination of the place of the damned has yet been given by the assembled Church – at least, not by ours" (Hobbes 2012, 1146, 1154).

[32] Hobbes (2012, 718).
[33] See, for example, Martinich (1992, 259–60).
[34] As early as 1643 Hobbes denied Thomas White's assertion that annihilation would be worse than eternal torment. See Johnston (1989, 652).

them? And why would Hobbes, who is so concerned with civil obedience, conflate sin with transgressing civil law, and then proceed to deny eternal torment to sinners? In short, why does Hobbes take such liberties with his interpretation of the afterlife, liberties he knew would be controversial, when this interpretation did not in any obvious way further his political goals?

Hobbes admits that his interpretation is unusual, and given the great variety of views espoused in seventeenth-century England, this was no mean feat. Before answering the question of why Hobbes presents hell the way he does, some understanding of the historical context is necessary, particularly since so many scholars point to the similarities between Hobbes's views and those of his contemporaries to demonstrate that his theology was not as strange as it appears today and that he may have been something of an orthodox thinker.

I will, then, briefly discuss other views of hell that share similarities with Hobbes's in order to highlight what is unique in Hobbes's reinterpretation. One recent strategy has been to compare Hobbes's mortalism to that of Milton, and I will discuss this comparison. Hobbes has also been likened to a Calvinist, yet his views on hell and the soul have little in common with those of Calvin. One early critic characterized the theological teaching of *Leviathan* as "a farrago of Christian Atheism," and this is an accurate description of Hobbes's approach.[35] The second half of *Leviathan* has always been difficult to interpret because it is made up of a tangled mix of ideas, many of which, when taken in isolation, resonated with one group or another. Most sects and theologians could find something to agree with among these ideas, but they were always partial agreements. Hobbes's theology, then, had something for everyone, but as a whole was shared by no one. This is particularly the case with Hobbes's portrayal of hell and the soul.

Indeed, one of the most discussed aspects of Hobbes's eschatology is his denial of the immortality of the soul. Some scholars note that this view, though unorthodox, was not entirely unheard of and that Milton and others shared it.[36] If, however, Milton and Hobbes agreed that the soul was mortal, they agreed on little else, as even the most cursory glance at their respective views of hell reveals. Milton wavered between presenting hell as a state of mind and another realm, while Hobbes is adamant that hell will be on earth. Further, no one could confuse Hobbes's Satan, the

---

[35] Parkin (2007, 102).
[36] Martinich (1992, 266); Strong (1993, 138, 152).

bad governor, with Milton's description in *Paradise Lost*. Other points of disagreement include their respective views on predestination and free will. Mintz notes that Milton, in fact, has much more in common with bishop Bramhall's views than those of Hobbes.[37]

Hobbes only raises the issue of the soul's mortality in the context of his discussion of hell, since it is an essential point of his interpretation that individuals can be completely annihilated by the second death and that neither the bodies nor the souls of the reprobate are immortal, something Milton did not believe. It is indeed surprising that scholars who study Hobbes's mortalist views have not noticed this connection with his vision of hell.[38]

That Strong and Martinich emphasize the small point of agreement between Hobbes and Milton (and others) and do not mention the massive and obvious differences in their views of hell is due to their efforts to demonstrate that Hobbes was more orthodox than many think. The source of the view that Hobbes and Milton had a similar conception of the soul is Norman Burns's *Christian Mortalism from Tyndale to Milton*, in which he points out that Milton only openly stated his mortalist position in his *Christian Doctrine*, which was not published during Milton's lifetime (he died in 1674, long after *Leviathan*'s publication) and which lay undiscovered for nearly 200 years.[39] The most likely reason Milton, who was by no means an orthodox thinker, did not openly state this view is the fact that nearly all Reformation Christians considered it blatantly heretical.[40] That Hobbes had the audacity to state this view openly is one of the chief reasons he was so reviled during his lifetime.

Martinich also claims that Hobbes is a type of orthodox Calvinist. Yet Hobbes's view that the soul was only the breath of life was the focus of Calvin's earliest polemical writings. Indeed, Calvin says that those with views such as those of Hobbes "ought to be severely repressed."[41] As Burns points out, "In Calvin's view, at death the souls of the reprobate go directly to their punishment while the souls of the elect go directly to their reward, each state being but a foretaste of what will follow the Last Day."[42] Also, although both Calvin and Hobbes describe hell as

---

[37] Mintz (1962, 118–19).
[38] Hobbes (1999, 97–100) also defends his view of the soul and its connection with hell at length in his answer to Bishop Bramhall (Hobbes, 1840a).
[39] Burns (1972, 148).
[40] Burns (1972, 10–11).
[41] Burns (1972, 23).
[42] Burns (1972, 22–4).

a tortured state of mind, Hobbes claims that this state will end in a second death, perhaps in a non-metaphorical fire, while Calvin believes in the immortality of all souls.

Luther similarly believes that the soul is incorporeal and that heaven and hell are in another realm than the earth. As he says in his commentary on Ecclesiastes,

> thou mayst understād hell to be that place where the soules be kept, being a certayne graue (as it were) of ye soule, without this corporall worlde, as the earth is the sepulcher of ye body ... The dead therefore are out of all place. Euen as after the resurrection, we shall be cleare from place and tyme.[43]

Most orthodox Christians, in fact, both Catholic and Protestant, held that hell, as a parallel to heaven, was eternal. There was both strong scriptural support for this view, and various councils, including that of Constantinople in 543 and the Lutheran Diet of Augsburg of 1530 state that denying the eternity of hell's torments was anathema.[44] Hobbes is thus far from orthodox in this respect as these councils clearly refer to the eternal torture of each damned individual rather than the eternal torture of the species, as Hobbes would have it. Hobbes's claim that the immortality of hell's punishment "is an Immortality of the Kind, but not of the Persons of men" is entirely novel.[45]

This is a complex innovation that allows Hobbes to both agree with orthodox thinkers that there will be a resurrection and Day of Judgment (a crucial point, as denying this was punishable by death),[46] while at the same time claiming immortality for the elect and annihilation for the damned. This stance amounts to a partial agreement with orthodoxy and partial agreement with one of the most serious heresies of the age, that of the Socinians. This sect held that the wicked were never resurrected but were simply annihilated when they died (whereas the elect were resurrected with celestial bodies).[47] Hobbes's unusual combination of claims, that the elect would be immortal and the damned mortal, also brought him into proximity with another unorthodox view: that all would eventually be saved. Adherents of the theory of universal salvation held that sinners would suffer torment for a certain period of time, generally

---

[43] Quoted in Burns (1972, 31).
[44] Walker (1964, 19–22).
[45] Hobbes (2012, 994).
[46] Burns (1972, 15).
[47] Walker (1964, 73–92).

several thousand years depending on the individual's sins, before their eventual salvation.[48]

Hobbes was also unusual in denying what for most in the seventeenth century was the gravest of hell's torments: the mental agony of being deprived of God's presence. A typical statement comes from Robert Bolton, the Bishop of London's 1639 essay, "Of the Foure Last Things": "[A] sensible and serious contemplation of that inestimable and unrecoverable losse, doth incomparably more afflict an understanding soule, indeed, than all those punishments, tortures, and extremest sufferings of sense."[49] The damned do suffer mental anguish in Hobbes's hell, as we have seen, but Hobbes does not place great emphasis on this type of suffering, describing it as "grief, and discontent of mind," a predicament not entirely alien to the living, whose lives are a perpetual and restless desire for power.[50] The mental pain of the reprobate, for Hobbes, stems from jealousy of the lives of the blessed.

Hobbes could not emphasize the distance from God as a source of pain for the damned as his contemporaries did since he would understand this distance in a literal sense, and both the damned and the blessed, inhabiting this planet, will be equally distant from Him. Indeed, it is hubris, Hobbes claims, for man to want to ascend any higher than God's footstool, which is the earth.[51] In the eyes of Hobbes's contemporaries, this interpretation made hell less of a deterrent, and, as we shall see, was simply perplexing.

While many of Hobbes's claims about hell and the soul were unorthodox, they were not necessarily unheard of. But it was the unusual combination of so many unusual ideas, and especially his unprecedented claim that there would be an endless stream of children being born who would be doomed to oblivion from birth, that so confounded Hobbes's readers.

There were, then, a great variety of theories about what happens to one after death in the seventeenth century, and although Hobbes's view has something in common with many of them, he manages, with great ingenuity, to stake out an original position. Through his partial agreement with so many sects, Hobbes draws his readers in and forces them to take his ideas more seriously than they otherwise might have. Hobbes's theology then, could not simply be dismissed, nor could the connection between his theology and his scientific thought.

---

[48] Walker (1964, 67–8).
[49] Bolton (1639), quoted in Patrides (1964, 220).
[50] Hobbes (2012, 716).
[51] Hobbes (2012, 726).

EPISTEMOLOGY, THEOLOGY AND MATERIALISM

Many of those who discuss Hobbes's theology and his epistemology in *Leviathan* hive these off from the work's overarching political goals. Nor do most scholars read Hobbes's epistemology in light of his theology or vice versa. This has made it more difficult to see clearly some of the most important implications of Hobbes's strategy regarding the relationship of religion and freedom of conscience to politics. All of the details in this work, including its theological and epistemological sections, must be seen in light of its political goals and its rhetorical character.[52] As Hobbes says, "they that insist upon single Texts, without considering the main Designe, can derive no thing from them cleerly."[53] Hobbes was free to write separate works of science and theology, and he did so.[54]

We should be wary, then, of Hobbes's claim that the first chapters on sense perception are unnecessary to the work as a whole.[55] In a similar vein, the theological section of the book cannot be seen simply as a long tedious joke designed to ridicule Christianity. Nor, however, is it simply a list of scriptural passages that support the overtly political part of the work (the strategy Hobbes pursues in *De Cive*). Indeed, the labyrinthine theology of Hobbes's *Leviathan* is an integral part of the work's political project, and it is reasonable to suppose that there is nothing extraneous in it.

All knowledge, according to Hobbes, derives from sense perception, on which both natural prudence and reasoning depend.[56] There are no innate ideas. Hobbes does not think that man naturally has an idea of God in his mind or any innate knowledge of a transcendent standard of good or evil. Nor can contemplation alone provide any such knowledge. The mechanistic nature of our sense perception not only makes it impossible for the human mind to grasp metaphysical truths, it also places serious limits on what we can know for certain about the external, physical world since "the object is one thing, the image or fancy is another."[57] We can reason well enough when

---

[52] An exhaustive study of the unity of Hobbes's thought would have to incorporate his historical thought in addition to his theology as well as his natural and political science. For a discussion of the unity of Hobbes's historical and scientific thought, see Robert Kraynak (1990).
[53] Hobbes (2012, 954).
[54] Scholars as diverse as Strauss (1959); Skinner (1997); and Johnston (1986), among others have noted the rhetorical character of *Leviathan*.
[55] Hobbes (2012, 22).
[56] Hobbes (2012, 22, chapter 5).
[57] Hobbes (2012, 24). Tuck (1993, 286ff.) though makes the point that this approach to sense perception on the part of Hobbes and his contemporaries represented an advance

it comes to mental concepts like lines and figures, and we can make our way in the world by way of memory and experience, but our senses are not reliable as a source of scientific knowledge.[58] Hobbes devoted a great deal of time to works on optics and mechanics, but the account of perception in *Leviathan* is truncated and omits several details that are elaborated in *De Corpore* and elsewhere. In *Leviathan*, we learn just enough about our perception to realize that we do not necessarily have an adequate grasp of the external world.

This view of the mind echoes Paul's statement that we see "through a glass, darkly."[59] But unlike Paul, Hobbes does not think that we can have the sort of inner knowledge or experience that many Christians equate with faith. Again, since all concepts derive from the motion of external bodies pressing against our sense organs, any notion of accepting God into one's heart or having any sort of direct communion or communication with God, what Hobbes calls enthusiasm or private spirit is ruled out.[60] As Mitchell notes, "True, the Leviathan is Christ-like, but through him there is no possibility of possessing the interiority of faith."[61] Those who claim to be prophets who have heard God speak are likely deluded by their vivid imaginations or extravagant dreams and should be regarded with extreme suspicion if they teach civil disobedience or anything other than that Jesus is the Christ.[62] In fact, it was "From this ignorance of how to distinguish Dreams, and other strong Fancies, from Vision and Sense" that "the greatest part of the Religion of the Gentiles" arose.[63]

The ear, and not the heart, Hobbes says, is the primary organ by which we can acquire faith. In particular, although faith is a gift of God, it is nothing other than believing pastors and parents who teach that scripture is the word of God.[64] Because we have not heard God speak to us directly and did not see Jesus resurrected as did the apostles (the only true martyrs

---

over earlier forms of skepticism. Although we could not grasp metaphysical truths through our sense, our senses did in fact provide real knowledge of the world.
[58] Shapin and Schaffer show this was one of the sources of Hobbes's disagreement with empiricists and the experimental scientists of the Royal Society such as Robert Boyle.
[59] 1 Corinthians 13:12, AV.
[60] Hobbes (2012, 584, 936).
[61] Mitchell (1996, 71).
[62] Hobbes (2012, 578–60, 674, 932).
[63] Hobbes (2012, 34).
[64] Hobbes (2012, ch.43, 406), Hobbes (2004, ch.18, 238). Pocock (1971, 163), then, is wrong when he claims that for Hobbes, faith is a "faculty of the mind," "distinct from either reason or experience," which we can use to understand revealed history. Cf. also Hobbes (1998a, 72).

according to *Leviathan*), Christians "doe not know, but onely beleeve the Scripture to be the Word of God."⁶⁵ And this belief depends on accurate transmission of the events described in the Bible across several centuries, or, as he puts it, "a beliefe grounded upon other mens saying, that they know it supernaturally, or that they know those, that knew them, that knew others, that knew it supernaturally."⁶⁶ There is no way of knowing whether this transmission has been accurate and we can never have knowledge but only belief about what any author says.⁶⁷ The primary account of the events in which Christians must have faith is the Bible, and Hobbes demonstrates through philology and logical reasoning that both the Old and New Testaments are corrupt and unreliable.

In sum, the human mind cannot derive certain knowledge about metaphysics or religion in general, or the nature and path to heaven or hell in particular, from contemplating innate ideas, having an inner experience of faith or reading the Bible. Reasoning is simply addition and subtraction, and reasoning about one's fate after death on the basis of any of the above is inherently erroneous.

This conjunction of epistemology and theology is significant because it sets out new criteria for acquiring knowledge not only about the natural world but also about religious matters. One effect of this new set of conditions is the separation of outward worship, which can be policed by the civil authorities, and internal belief, which can neither be policed nor, being invisible, compelled by religious authorities.⁶⁸ This was clearly an important step toward abolishing the cruelty of religious inquisitions and persecution of those with heterodox beliefs. Also of great importance for Hobbes is the fact that this division would defuse one of the chief sources of turmoil in seventeenth-century England; namely, the widely preached doctrine that subjects must not obey the king when his commands conflict with the commands of God.⁶⁹ These conflicting sources of authority were a cause of serious distress for many ordinary citizens, and Hobbes's teaching is in part an attempt to reduce this type of anxiety.

While Hobbes seeks to loosen the tension between the civil and religious authorities through the application of his epistemology to theology, this strategy involves heightening another sort of anxiety, namely, anxiety

---

[65] Hobbes (2012, 936).
[66] Hobbes (2012, 226).
[67] Hobbes (2012, 66).
[68] See, for example, Hobbes (2012, 564, 604–6, 780ff.).
[69] Hobbes (1990, 49–50).

about the status of one's beliefs and one's ability to have any certain knowledge about the most important questions, such as the afterlife. The separation of outward action from private belief is certainly in line with much Protestant thought. Take, for example, Luther's statement that "no matter how much they fret and fume, they cannot do more than make people obey them by word and deed; the heart they cannot constrain ... For the proverb is true, 'Thoughts are free.'"[70] The difference between Hobbes and Luther (and others) on this point is that the separation of thoughts and external actions for Hobbes is grounded in a mechanistic account of the mind, rather than the implicit understanding of the heart and soul we find in Luther, and it is this distinction which gives rise to a new type of anxiety.[71]

The political goals of Hobbes's treatment of the Bible and separation of private belief from outward profession (along with his suspicions about the validity of private belief) are clear, but his description of heaven and hell do not appear to serve these goals in any obvious way. The requirements for salvation in Hobbes's system are quite simple: obedience to the country's laws and a will to obey them, as well as faith that Jesus is the Christ.[72] Conversely, disobeying the law is conflated with sin and a breach of faith, and consequently the penalties for serious crimes will be meted out in both this world and the next. The sovereign requires obedience to "all the Civill Laws; in which also are contained all the Laws and Nature, that is, all the Laws of God: for besides the Laws of Nature, and the Laws of the Church, which are part of the Civill Law ... there bee no other Laws Divine," and "[t]here can therefore be no contradiction between the Laws of God, and the Laws of a Christian Common-wealth," or a heathen commonwealth.[73]

We would expect, then, that Hobbes would either remain silent about what the next life will be like, as he does in *De Cive* and *The Elements of Law*, since no such description is necessary to his argument, or that he would emphasize the worst aspects of hell and the best features of heaven, since this strategy would only reinforce the subject's incentives for civil obedience, which, to repeat, is necessary for salvation. Hobbes's argument in chapter 43 of *Leviathan*, that since the most common cause of civil war

---

[70] Luther (1962, 385).
[71] For a good discussion of the materialist basis of Hobbes's account of consciousness in contrast with Descartes's immaterial interpretation, see Frost (2005, 495–517) and Pettit (2008).
[72] Hobbes (2012, 930).
[73] Hobbes (2012, 952); see also Hobbes (2004, 245); and Hobbes (1998a, 72).

is the conflict between the commands of God and those of the sovereign it is necessary to demonstrate that there is no conflict between the two, appears to be sufficient and is made with no mention of heaven or hell (and this is also true of the parallel chapter of *De Cive*).

A common explanation for the unusual character of Hobbes's theology is that it results in large part from his attempt to reconcile his religious views with his materialism.[74] For example, Martinich, one of the few scholars to pay much attention to the issue of hell in Hobbes, notes correctly that the depiction of hell is "quite horrible" and sets this down to Hobbes's desire to "explain how belief in hell is consistent with the scientific view of the world."[75] The only concrete example of a scientific explanation for this vision of hell Martinich offers, though, is that "only a real fire burns real bodies," and that Hobbes was therefore obliged to say that the damned are consumed in the fire and do not suffer eternally.[76] And because the fires are eternal, it is simply a necessary corollary that the damned will procreate and raise children who will be fuel for the fire, since the fire would have no other reason to burn forever.[77]

In the case of Hobbes's description of hell, though, the explanation that its oddness results from an attempt to interpret scripture in a way that is compatible with modern science is simply untenable. To begin with, Martinich falls prey to Hobbes's ambiguity about the metaphorical nature of hellfire. He also outlines the only possible feature of Hobbes's interpretation of hell which admits of some sort of scientific explanation, and although it is plausible that Hobbes thought the damned would not burn eternally because they had gross and corruptible bodies that would be consumed, he never explicitly makes this connection. The closest he comes to this is his assertion that, as quoted above, although the "fire prepared for the wicked" will last forever, "it cannot thence be inferred, that hee who shall be cast into the fire, or be tormented with those torments, shall endure, and resist them so, as to be eternally burnt, and tortured; and yet never be destroyed, nor die."[78] But Hobbes supports this contention not by saying that corporeal bodies cannot withstand fire forever, but by pointing to a supposed lacuna in scripture: "though there be many places [in the Bible] that affirm Everlasting Fire, and Torments... yet I find none

---

[74] See, for example, Farr (1990); Sorell (1986); Mintz (1962); Martinich (1992); Parkin (2007, 115).
[75] Martinich (1992, 260, 258).
[76] Martinich (1992, 259).
[77] Martinich (1992, 259–60).
[78] Hobbes (2012, 718).

that affirm there shall bee an Eternal Life therein of any individual person; but to the contrary, an Everlasting Death."⁷⁹

In fact, in neither chapter 38 nor chapter 44 does Hobbes ever refer to a physical law or any characteristic of the material world as an explanation for his interpretation. Nor does he offer any such justification when defending this interpretation in his response to Bramhall: in both places, Hobbes relies entirely on scripture.⁸⁰ Given the topic under discussion, this is understandable. Hobbes does not raise any questions about the physical possibility of a resurrection of all of the dead, or of a city more than ten times the size of France made of gold and jewels descending from heaven, or spiritual human bodies that can live forever. In accepting these phenomena as unproblematic, Hobbes implicitly accepts the notion of God's omnipotence. Thus, although Hobbes's theology is materialistic, in the sense that it does not rely on incorporeal bodies, it cannot be reduced to, or explained by, its materialism. Rather than attempting to reconcile his theology with the emerging scientific understanding of the world, Hobbes is exploiting the latitude with which the Bible can be interpreted.

In effect, Hobbes leaves citizens free to believe what they want about topics such as hell, but only after insinuating that these beliefs are groundless – an unsettling fact that citizens will not likely want to face directly.⁸¹ Hobbes's theory of the mind cuts individuals off from what they had once regarded as certain knowledge about the world around them and what they could expect after death. Since this knowledge cannot be recovered through study or contemplation, citizens are increasingly likely to avoid thinking about this problem at all.⁸²

HOBBES'S RHETORICAL STRATEGY: HELL

Part of Hobbes's goal is making hell less frightening, and therefore less of a deterrent. He accomplishes this not so much by offering an interpretation he thinks will be accepted, but by offering one he knows will be highly

---

⁷⁹ Hobbes (2012, 718).
⁸⁰ Hobbes (1840a, 97–100).
⁸¹ For a discussion of the theme of homelessness and fear in Hobbes, see Blits (1989, 417–31).
⁸² In some sense, Hobbes is picking up on the Protestant notion of a hidden God, or Deus Absconditus, and combining it with his account of the mind to prove just how incapable man is of acquiring such knowledge. The difference is that the Protestant soul could still have some sort of contact with the hidden God, while for Hobbes God was entirely hidden in every respect.

controversial in an effort to change the way individuals think about the afterlife. In his Verse Autobiography, Hobbes says that he was pleased by the controversy his *Leviathan* caused, claiming that the attacks by innumerable divines, "made it read by many a man, And did confirm the more; 'tis hop'd by me, That it will last to all Eternity."[83] This is not simply Hobbes's attempt to make the best of his infamy after the fact, for he announces in the work's opening paragraph that his readers are likely to be offended by his interpretation of scripture.[84] The notoriety of the work in fact only increased the demand for it and allowed Hobbes to claim that it had "framed the minds of a thousand gentlemen."[85]

The main argument against the view that Hobbes wanted his work to be controversial is that Hobbes's religious statements were, as Strauss says, an attempt at "circumspection" and "accommodation" designed to allow him to "survive or to die in peace."[86] In a similar vein, Cooke argues that Hobbes was trying to cover over the bleakness of his vision, claiming that

Hobbes hid this "nakedness," the exposure of autonomous and also unprotected man to an impersonal, masterless universe, by means of his appropriation of religion. This is how Hobbes deals with the question of what life is for – he hides his conviction of the fundamental absence of an answer to this question behind his appropriation of a transformed Christianity.[87]

In this supposed appropriation though, Hobbes was singularly unsuccessful. He immediately gained various sobriquets in England, including the "Monster of Malmesbury," the "Devil's Secretary" and, perhaps appropriately for the topic under discussion, the "Agent of Hell."[88]

Thus, far from trying to conceal his harsh view of human nature and life's lack of meaning, it was in fact this brutal picture which more than anything has established *Leviathan* as the classic work of philosophy in the English language. None of this escaped Hobbes's contemporaries and the second half of the work did nothing to assuage them, to say the least. As Mintz, in surveying the hostile reaction to Hobbes during the seventeenth century points out,

---

[83] Hobbes (1994a, 261). Gaskin includes a note at this point in the autobiography stating that *Leviathan* was in great demand by 1668, in part because of its notoriety.
[84] Hobbes (2012, 4).
[85] Parkin (2007, 95).
[86] Strauss (1965, 199n).
[87] Cooke (1996, 236).
[88] Parkin (2007, 1).

Hobbes must have known that the line between his brand of theism and seventeenth-century atheism was a thin one and that for many of his contemporaries this line did not exist at all. If safety and a peaceful life were his object he would have had to express his opinions far more circumspectly than Professor Strauss would have us believe.[89]

In fact, the response that Hobbes received was the one he hoped for, and we should therefore see him as a rhetorical success, rather than the rhetorical failure many claim him to be.[90] While so many of his readers and detractors purport to be lifting the veil he places over his true thoughts, they are in fact reading Hobbes the way he wants to be read. If he were in fact trying to avoid controversy, it is hard to see why he devoted increasing space to his increasingly bizarre theology from one work to the next. This is especially the case given that even the single theological chapter of *The Elements of Law* attracted negative attention, not to mention the many hostile responses *De Cive* received for the same reasons.[91]

Hobbes, in fact, wants most of his readers to think themselves capable of seeing through to his real meaning. Indeed, what better way for an analyst of pride, such as Hobbes, to pull his readers in than allowing them to proclaim that they had not been fooled by his subterfuge? Although one did not have to be especially perceptive to notice that Hobbes was somehow unorthodox, his subversion of Christianity is not so obvious or clear that his readers can simply dismiss him as an atheist without attending carefully to his arguments, and this is Hobbes's goal.[92]

As noted above, Hobbes was not obliged to raise the topic of hell at all, and the fact that he did so in the way that he did is further evidence that he was attempting to provoke his readers. Walker notes that there were some figures in the seventeenth century who doubted hell's eternity, but who did not dare to state this opinion openly, and the earliest "surprising example" he finds of someone suggesting obliquely that God was not

---

[89] Mintz (1962, 44).
[90] It is a necessary corollary of Skinner's arguments about Hobbes's use of rhetoric that he failed completely either in trying to hide his true views or in trying to persuade his readers of his orthodoxy.
[91] Collins (2007, 480); Parkin (2007, 25–6, 35ff.).
[92] Strauss is the best-known exponent of the theory that Hobbes is esoteric in the sense of being circumspect, but he too seems to imply that the complete picture is more complex. In one of his later writings on Hobbes, Strauss (1959, 189) claims almost in the same breath that Hobbes "expressed himself with great caution" and that his work was full of "shocking over-simplifications" and "absurdities." A full examination of Strauss's complex treatment of Hobbes's esotericism, though, is beyond the scope of this chapter.

bound to punish sinners forever is a sermon by Tillotson in 1690.⁹³ The danger of openly stating such opinions, Walker claims, led to "a theory of double truth: there is a private, esoteric doctrine, which must be confined to a few intellectuals, because its effects on the mass of people will be morally and socially disastrous, and a public exoteric doctrine, which these same intellectuals must preach, although they do not believe it."⁹⁴ He is thinking here of later thinkers, the most famous of whom are Locke and Newton, who were very guarded with respect to their opinions about the nature of hell. Hobbes was also an adherent of the theory that there were certain truths one should not teach openly, as he indicates when he asks Bramhall to keep his thoughts on free will private because of the "ill use" that might be made of them, but he clearly did not think that the annihilation of the damned was a topic he had to keep to himself.⁹⁵ The frank statements Hobbes makes about such a sensitive topic preclude the possibility that his teaching about the afterlife was esoteric in the usual sense of the word.

Everybody knows that Hobbes's *Leviathan* was attacked in the seventeenth century because of its supposed atheism, but less well noted today is how significant a role his description of hell was in making this such a frequently attacked book. Malcolm states that "this feature of his theory had become a favorite target for his critics."⁹⁶ And as Parkin notes in his work on the reception of Hobbes's work in England, Hobbes's "portrait of Hell as a finite return to earthly existence leaves Tenison, like many of his contemporaries, simply puzzled."⁹⁷ As well, "booksellers ... found Hobbes's highly unusual reinterpretation of Hell objectionable" and tried to have *Leviathan* banned or burned, because it had put "millions of Souls" on the "High-way to eternal Perdition."⁹⁸

The worst part of being damned according to Hobbes is the second death one suffers, which his contemporaries saw as lessening hell's punishment. As Tenison notes in his 1670 work, *The Creed of Mr. Hobbes Examined*, "That which you [Hobbes] make the top of their calamitie, is to be reckoned as a priviledg, because it puts an end to their torment together with their being; the continuance of which cannot make

---

⁹³ Walker (1964, 6).
⁹⁴ Walker (1964, 5).
⁹⁵ Hobbes (1840a, 24).
⁹⁶ Malcolm (2002, 365).
⁹⁷ Parkin (2007, 269).
⁹⁸ Parkin (2007, 114–15); Collins (2007, 483); cf. Mintz (1962, 60).

recompence for that misery with which in the real Hell, it will be oppressed."[99] Bramhall makes a similar charge, stating that there being no "fear of any Torments after death for their ill-doing, they will pass their times here as pleasantly as they can. This is all the Damnation which T. H. fancieth."[100]

Perhaps Hobbes's most dangerous opponent, though, was Edward Hyde, later the Earl of Clarendon. In his book length attack on *Leviathan*, he singled out Hobbes's interpretation of hell for some of his harshest criticism, claiming that "after sixteen hundred years Mr. *Hobbes* should arise a new Evangelist, to make the joies of Heaven more indifferent, and the pains of Hell less formidable, then ever any Christian hath before attemted to do."[101] He goes on to argue that

> the rewards which he hath propounded are of much less value then they are esteemed to be, and the punishment which he threatens, to be less terrible, and of shorter duration then they are understood; and take upon them to suspend the inflicting of any punishment at all upon the greatest sinner until the end of the World, by the mortality of the Soul, equal to that of the Body, and so to undergo no farther trouble till they are again united in the Resurrection; and even then not to be in so ill a condition, as most men apprehend, which is a consolation wicked men stand not in need of, and which no Christian Casuist, before Mr. *Hobbes*, ever presum'd to administer.[102]

Although this critique was not published until Hobbes was eighty-eight years old, Clarendon's opinions predate *Leviathan*'s publication. This is in fact what made Hyde so dangerous. While Hobbes wrote *Leviathan*, both he and Hyde were living among Charles's exiled court in Paris. When Hobbes showed Hyde sections of the work while it was being prepared for printing, he told Hyde that he would not like it. Indeed Hyde did not, claiming in fact that any European government would be within its rights in punishing Hobbes for writing such a work.[103] Since Hyde was one of Charles's closest ministers, it is no surprise that Hobbes was stripped of Royal protection soon after presenting the king with a manuscript copy of *Leviathan*.[104] In short, as Collins notes, "there is ample evidence that

---

[99] Tenison (1670, 217).
[100] Bramhall, (1842–1845, 538–9).
[101] Hyde, Earl of Clarendon (1676, 219).
[102] Hyde, Earl of Clarendon (1676, 222).
[103] Parkin (2007, 95); Collins (2005, 144); Zagorin (2007, 463).
[104] Hyde admitted to having had some hand in excluding Hobbes from court; Zagorin (2007, 464); Collins (2005, 146). I follow Collins' argument addressing the question of why Hobbes would have presented such a manuscript to Charles knowing it would displease him. As Collins notes, this presentation "bears all of the hallmarks of an ad hoc

Hobbes anticipated the controversy that *Leviathan* would spawn."[105] But why would Hobbes want to stir such controversy?

The first question to revisit is why Hobbes would want to make hell less frightening and heaven more mundane if the divine law is the natural law and the natural law obliges man to obey his sovereign, and therefore obedience to the civil law merits entry into heaven as well as commodious life on earth, while breaking the law brings punishment in both this world and the next. The thirty-eighth chapter of *Leviathan*, which describes eternal life and hell, begins in much the same way as chapter 43, which outlines what is necessary for entry into heaven. Both chapters open with the claim that a state cannot stand when someone other than the sovereign can offer rewards and punishments greater than life and death. Each chapter, though, approaches this political problem in a different way, chapter 43 stating that there is no contradiction between civil and divine law and chapter 38 stating that the torments of hell will not be eternal.

If subjects were convinced that they would suffer eternal agony if they disobeyed the sovereign, this would incline them all the more to obedience and there would then be no one who could offer greater rewards or punishments than the sovereign. If hell were less of a deterrent, but nonetheless in the sovereign's hands alone, complete submission to civil law would still be the only reasonable choice. Hobbes makes his highly controversial claims about the nature of hell in the context of his discussion of the political problem of obedience, and the question of why he describes it as he does becomes more acute in light of the fact that this interpretation does not further his political goal in any obvious way.

In fact, this interpretation of hell is evidence that Hobbes did not think that he would be entirely successful in convincing individuals that there is "no contradiction between the Laws of God, and the Laws of a Christian

---

effort by Hobbes to cover his tracks once Charles had unexpectedly returned to France" (Collins, 2005, 144). He goes on to note that "the manuscript lacks a dedication to Charles" and contained several passages critical of Independency which are not present in the printed version. Hobbes in fact had wanted to return to England before Charles's return (if Charles returned at all) but was waylaid by serious illness; see Collins (2005, 145ff.) and also Malcolm (2002), but *pace* Miller (2004).

[105] Collins (2007, 481). Although Collins argues that *Leviathan* was primarily written to signal Hobbes's change of allegiance from the Royal cause to that of the revolutionaries, I would argue that Hobbes was mostly concerned with his ability to continue his philosophic activity rather than any factional allegiance. Clarendon is probably right, if we remove the adjectives, when he claims that "he considers not, nor will be subject to any other Soveraignty, then that of his own capricious brain, and haughty understanding"; Hyde, Earl of Clarendon (1676, 230).

Common-wealth," or that there could be a complete separation between inner belief and one's actions.[106] By claiming that a state will only stand where the sovereign has a monopoly on the most severe punishments and then stating that hell will not be eternal, Hobbes indicates that a certain number of individuals will continue to believe that there is a conflict between civil and religious law, that they can acquire knowledge of God's will independently of the sovereign's interpretation of scripture, and who will therefore continue to be more concerned with punishments after death than with death itself.

This is a corollary of the fact that, according to Hobbes, individuals, who are "in a perpetuall solicitude of the time to come," will always be subject to natural superstitions that are not subject to rational argument.[107] Man in the state of nature initially appears to have no notion of gods or religion, since neither of these are mentioned in chapter 13 of *Leviathan*, and he escapes from the state of nature through rational observation of natural law. In the two chapters surrounding the 13th, though, Hobbes claims both that the seeds of religion will always be present in the human heart and that

> before the time of Civill Society, or in the interruption thereof by Warre, there is nothing can strengthen a Covenant of Peace agreed on, against the temptations of Avarice, Ambition, Lust, or other strong desire, but the feare of that Invisible Power, which they every one Worship as God; and Feare as a Revenger of their Perfidy.[108]

There is, then, a natural fear of invisible powers and an accompanying sense of justice and fear of reprisal from those powers. These fears predate civil society and organized religion, and among a large segment of the population, they have persisted until the present in spite of official religious teachings. Hobbes states in *De Homine* that "[a]ll men are of the opinion that there is an invisible something or invisible things, from which ... all goods are to be hoped and all evils are to be feared," and that almost all human beings have a propensity to believe in one type of divination or another.[109] For this segment of the population neither rational argument nor rigorous biblical scholarship will be able to loosen the grip of these fears and beliefs. Hobbes's strategy, then, is not to convince his readers entirely

---

[106] Hobbes (2012, 952).
[107] Hobbes (2012, 164).
[108] Hobbes (2012, 180, 216).
[109] Hobbes (1998a, 58, 79–80).

on the grounds of reason or scriptural hermeneutics but to persuade them through a subtle manipulation of their fears.

Rather than simply trying to shock his readers, Hobbes attempts to manipulate their anxieties about the afterlife in such a way that they will suspect that it could not be as harsh as their priests claim, but also that they will be afraid to even face the question directly. This is an essential part of Hobbes's attempt to make the fear of violent death, which man can always be sure is a real possibility, the most reliable passion on which to found political society.

Both Mintz and Parkin note that Hobbes forced his opponents to unwittingly change the way they thought about religion; as Mintz argues, he was able to "penetrate their defences by obliging them to adopt the rationalist approach. For the Cambridge Platonists this meant that in refuting Hobbes they ... concentrated on logical arguments for the existence of God and spirit."[110] Similarly, Parkin notes that Hobbes's critics "were obliged to employ his own method of rational argument, thus absorbing his method while they resisted his ideas," and that one of the elegies written after Hobbes's death claimed that those "who his writings still accused in vain / were taught by him of whom they complain."[111] Something similar occurs with Hobbes's discussion of hell, but here his goal is not to turn his readers into materialists but to force them to realize that they cannot know for certain what awaits them after death. Hobbes undermines his readers' confidence that they can have any actual knowledge about the afterlife while at the same time fostering the suspicion that God would not punish them eternally for their sins.

Hobbes plants the suggestion in the minds of his readers that hell is unlikely to be as terrible as many claim it will be. He cannot hope to convince them beyond a shadow of doubt. The suggestion Hobbes makes is that the God who wants to make His yoke light and who puts salvation within such easy grasp is unlikely to be so unmerciful as to torture sinners forever.[112] As Bramhall notes, Hobbes's denial of free will has similar consequences: "[I]f there be no liberty, there shall be no day of doom, no last judgment, no rewards nor punishments after death ... To take away liberty hazards heaven, but undoubtedly it leaves no hell."[113] One does not have to accept all the specifics of Hobbes's theology in order to believe

---

[110] Mintz (1962, 151).
[111] Parkin (2007, 5, 451).
[112] Hobbes (2012, 988–90).
[113] Bramhall (1999, 4).

that this is a reasonable possibility, and suggesting this possibility, rather than convincing readers of the literal truth of his account, is in fact Hobbes's goal.

This becomes clear in light of Hobbes's suggestion, in one of his responses to Bramhall, that he was not serious about his account of hell in *Leviathan* and that he really believes that "after the Resurrection there shall be at all no wicked men; but the Elect (all that are, have been, and hereafter shall be) shall live on earth."[114] This account implies the annihilation of the damned at death or universal salvation and which is consistent with *Leviathan's* denial of eternal torture, but not its description of hell. As well, in *De Homine* Hobbes suggests that "there is no reason why God cannot forgive sinners, at least the repentant, without any punishment having been received by them or by others in their place."[115] Hell, then, becomes less of a deterrent not because anyone accepts Hobbes's account of it, but because no one can be absolutely certain of what it will be like, or whether it really exists. In this way, Hobbes is able to sidestep many of the thorniest religious controversies of his day, such as the debates surrounding predestination and Pelagianism.[116]

The possibility that hell might not be eternal may reduce one's distress about the afterlife, but this possibility in fact conceals and is premised on a source of anxiety that is in some sense even more acute than that which permeates the traditional view. While the non-Hobbesian could believe he or she knew what lay ahead and could make constant progress toward greater knowledge of and closeness to God, no such knowledge or progress are possible for Hobbes. Even the Calvinist who could not know for certain whether he or she was among the elect knew what being among the elect or among the damned meant and could see signs of this fate reflected in life on earth. A student of Hobbes's epistemology could not know anything for certain about the afterlife, especially since, unlike knowledge of salvation which for most Protestant Christians depends on inner faith alone, knowledge of heaven and hell involves concrete details and factual answers to difficult questions, such as whether one will be in God's

---

[114] Hobbes (1840a, 100). Hobbes comes close to saying something similar in the Latin edition of *Leviathan* when he says "from which it follows that the reprobate will not be resurrected at all, except to [undergo] the second death. For the children of God are the only children of the resurrection" (Hobbes 2012, 994). He maintains, though, that the reprobate will in fact be resurrected and that they will die again.
[115] Hobbes (1998a, 74). There is a similar ambiguity in Hobbes (2004, 61–2).
[116] See Gillespie (2006).

presence or not and whether heaven and hell are on earth or not. One can assume or hope that hell will not be eternal but the Hobbesian must admit that, strictly speaking, what awaits us after death is unknowable. Indeed, although Hobbes offers an unorthodox and controversial interpretation of hell, there is no other aspect of his theology about which he is so equivocal.

As noted above, Hobbes begins his discussion of hell by raising the possibility that it could be in various different locations, but then dismisses these possibilities on the grounds that no one else believes this is where hell could be. That no one else interprets the location of hell in this way is an unusual reason for Hobbes to reject these possibilities; he raises no such objection when setting forth the most controversial aspects of his own interpretation of the life of the damned, and indeed he proclaims at various points that his own interpretation is a novelty.[117] These "new Doctrines" are permissible, he claims, in part because he is writing in the midst of civil war and there is no sovereign to offer an official interpretation.[118] But this does not explain why Hobbes lays out his thought process regarding hell's location only to reject it on the basis of what others think, or why he chooses to interpret hell in this particular way.

CONCLUSION

Hobbes's method of exegesis is a demonstration of just how wide a range of interpretations are possible, and in light of this the traditional pictures of hell as well as Hobbes's interpretation appear quite arbitrary, and by offering plausible historical explanations as to the genesis of the various ideas about hell, he fosters a sense of uncertainty in his readers as to the reliability of any scriptural interpretation of the afterlife.[119]

Hobbes's theory that the damned will procreate after the resurrection could only have exacerbated this sense of uncertainty. These passages are among the most controversial statements in the work, and in fact the only major excision Hobbes made between the "Head" and "Bear" editions of *Leviathan* was the sentence stating that "the wicked ... may at the Resurrection live as they did, marry, and give in marriage, and have grosse

---

[117] Hobbes (2012, 4, 708, 1139).
[118] Hobbes (2012, 1139).
[119] For a discussion of contemporary views of the relationship between Gehenna and hell, see Bailey (1986, 187–91).

and corruptible bodies, as all mankind now have; and consequently may engender perpetually, after the Resurrection, as they did before."[120] Although Tuck claims that Hobbes "eliminated" these passages, Malcolm is more accurate when he says that Hobbes's excision was a "toning down" of this "idiosyncratic eschatological theory," since Hobbes retains the subsequent paragraph which discusses the eternal "propagation" of the reprobate.[121] It would be difficult, though, to think that Hobbes took this theory very seriously; he tries to deny he was serious about it when responding to Bramhall and makes quite different statements in *De Homine*, as noted above. Also, Hobbes's keen sense of humor shines through when, in the midst of describing this horrible scene, he says that the passage supporting the marriage of the damned is "a fertile text."[122]

His goal, though, is not simply to make a joke but to point to a problem with no solution. Hobbes claims that his is a legitimate interpretation because "there is no place of Scripture to the contrary."[123] This is not so much scriptural proof, though, as proof that there is great latitude in how Scripture can be interpreted. The Bible, it turns out, cannot offer firm answers about what awaits us after death, and no amount of study can improve this situation. Hobbes claims that he is waiting for the outcome of the Civil War to find out what doctrines his new sovereign will approve, and he makes this claim immediately before describing hell in chapter 38 of *Leviathan*.[124] This means that if the new sovereign teaches that hell will be on another plane of existence and that the damned will be tortured there forever, Hobbes will have to proclaim that he believes this to be the case. If the sovereign is wise, he will see the political advantages of adopting Hobbes's theory, but he may not. Whatever he chooses to do, the official church doctrine will appear quite arbitrary with respect to the unknowable truth. Hell either exists or does not, and if it does, it is either on earth or it is not, but the official teaching of the church, as determined by the sovereign for reasons of his own rather than by superior learning or the strength of tradition, cannot be a guide to which of these is actually the case.

---

[120] Hobbes (2012, 992). On the alterations relating to this issue between the first and second editions of *Leviathan*, see Tuck's introduction to his edition of Hobbes (1996, xlvi) and Malcolm (2002, 349–50, 364–5).

[121] Malcolm (2002, 349); Hobbes (2012, 994) and Tuck's introduction to his edition of *Leviathan* (1996, xlvii).

[122] Hobbes (2012, 992).

[123] Hobbes (2012, 992).

[124] Hobbes (2012, 708).

Hobbes allows that everyone can have his or her own private beliefs about the afterlife as well as other aspects of religion, but this freedom is premised on the fact that the human mind alone cannot know anything for certain about the afterlife, and scripture is similarly unable to offer any reliable answers. The afterlife, and indeed religion as a whole, becomes a matter of opinion rather than knowledge, and as such it becomes a matter of personal choice. Since no amount of independent reasoning or biblical scholarship can lead to any progress in these questions, Hobbes in effect leaves individuals free to make up their minds about that which they cannot possibly know. If one's fate after death is an impenetrable mystery, dwelling on that fact is likely to be a source of great distress. In the face of this irresolvable problem, questions about the afterlife are likely to recede into the background in a more or less unconscious effort to avoid asking them altogether.

6

War, Madness and Death

The Paradox of Honor in Hobbes's Leviathan

> Fortitude is a royal virtue; and though it be necessary in such private men as shall be soldiers, yet, for other men, the less they dare the better it is both for the commonwealth and for themselves.
>
> – Behemoth

> Nor is there any repugnancy between fearing the laws, and not fearing a public enemy.
>
> – Leviathan

We have seen that part of Hobbes's rhetorical strategy, which was in addition a necessary part of his political proposal, was an attack on the metaphysical framework that supported hopes for immortality. Hobbes recognized that a fundamental part of the political problem posed by Christianity was its universalism, and more specifically, the notion that there was a universal standard of justice. The problem of political sovereignty could not be solved as long as individuals held on to this transcendent order. Hobbes therefore had to withdraw the boundaries of justice as well as religion back within the walls of the state. There are, then, as I pointed out in Chapter 4, important similarities between Hobbes's religious teaching and the classical ideal of a civil religion.

It was, though, not only religious hopes Hobbes had to combat. He also had to subdue those who wanted to make a name for themselves through violent means. And though Hobbes recognizes the need for an army that would defend the homeland, he does not want his citizens to exhibit the same sort of self-sacrificing patriotism that characterized those in classical republics. Rather, Hobbes emphasizes the great danger to which individuals are exposed in war.

The worst part of life during wartime, which is the same as the state of nature, Hobbes claims, is the "continual fear, and danger of violent death."[1] And it is this that individuals seek to escape when they establish civil society. Once in civil society, though, Hobbes clearly expects citizens to submit themselves again to the constant fear of violent death in the service of national defense. On this basis, many commentators have concluded that Hobbes is guilty of a glaring contradiction, since, they claim, he can offer no plausible reason a citizen is obligated to fight and risk his life for his country.[2] The individual, it seems, should never be required to do what Hobbes clearly expects him to do. Yet, the desire to preserve one's life at nearly any cost, the apex of rationality in Hobbes's works, must, in the precincts of a national war, be cast aside.

I argue that Hobbes is imposing a simplified and consistently logical vision of man onto what he realizes is the more complex and contradictory truth about human nature. This logical system, which draws on Hobbes's materialism, is essential to his rhetorical educative strategy.[3] And as Hobbes says, "[I]f there be not powerfull Eloquence, which procureth attention and Consent, the effect of Reason will be little."[4] He expects that a desire for honor, and in particular the desire for fame after death, will persist without much need for instruction or encouragement, despite his teaching that one should above all strive to preserve one's life. Hobbes relies on at least some citizens to act in ways he condemns as fundamentally irrational. This paradox in Hobbes's thought, I argue, is an intentional incoherence.

The key to unraveling this intentional incoherence is understanding Hobbes's treatment of honor. Because of its close connection with pride

---

[1] Hobbes (2012, 192).
[2] Johnson Bagby (2009, 89, 100), Walzer (1970, 82); Lloyd (2009, 147).
[3] I read Hobbes's political philosophy, especially in *Leviathan* (2012), as being highly rhetorical, and the scientific aspects of his thought as his most powerful rhetorical strategy. As Kahn (1985, 157) suggests, from one point of view, "the appearance of logical argument in the *Leviathan* is revealed to be the most persuasive and canniest of Hobbes's rhetorical postures." And as Cantalupo (1991, 29) says in discussing Hobbes's tendency in *Leviathan* (2012) to vacillate between rhetoric and science, "*Leviathan* only has pockets of an air-tight philosophical system, and they seem to appear and disappear at the author's will." The work, however, he adds (Cantalupo, 15), was "born perfect." On Hobbes's use of rhetoric see also Garsten (2006), Johnston (1986), Miller (2011), Skinner (1997), Strauss (1963), as well as Shapin and Schaffer (1989) who note that Hobbes's disagreements with Boyle's experiments were partly motivated by political considerations.
[4] Hobbes (2012, 1132).

and glory, the desire for honor is one of the major obstacles to creating a peaceful and stable political community. The other such impediment to promoting a civically responsible fear of death is religion, which I have already discussed.[5] For Hobbes, honor is politically destabilizing and in need of reinterpretation and ultimately excision in its most dangerous forms from the domestic sphere. At the same time though, it is necessary, especially the kind that leads to fame after death, in the inevitable cases of external warfare. In most contexts this type of honor, Hobbes wants to teach his readers, is a form of madness. It relies on a communal bond Hobbes otherwise eschews in favor of preservation-oriented egoism. But in times of war, it is nonetheless, a necessity for the survival of the Hobbesian polity.

THE CENTRAL, BUT PROBLEMATIC ROLE OF THE FEAR OF DEATH

In order to see the intentional incoherence Hobbes sets up with regard to war and honor, it will be necessary to revisit his thoughts on the fear of death from the perspectives of recent scholarship. Until recently, Hobbes scholars have tended to emphasize the role of the fear of violent death as the key factor holding the commonwealth together and maintaining the sovereign in his position of absolute control.[6] This line of interpretation helped to validate a view of Hobbes as a mechanistic thinker for whom human beings act on the basis of fixed and entirely calculable factors.[7] Since individuals are necessarily incapable of escaping their fear of death, according to this narrative, applying enough of this fear is a reliable method of ensuring complete obedience to the sovereign.

Hobbes, though, as we saw in Chapter 3, clearly states that the fear of death is not absolute, and, more importantly, cannot be sufficient to guarantee obedience.[8] The historical circumstances during which

---

[5] I agree with Lloyd (1992, 271), who sates that, "Hobbes took social disorder to be primarily the result of action on transcendent interests," but where Lloyd rightly emphasizes the religious aspect of this issue, I am concerned here with the desire for transcendent honor, or the desire for fame after death.

[6] Ahrensdorf (2000, 582); Berns (1987, 399); Martinich (1992, 267); Oakeshott (1991, 253); Strauss (1963, 16).

[7] Hobbes, as is well-known, is frequently studied in conjunction with some form of game theory. For three of the best-known examples see Kavka (1986), Hampton (1986), Gauthier (1969).

[8] For good synopses of these exceptions to the overriding power of the fear of death see Seery (1996), Kateb (1989), Sreedhar (2010).

Hobbes wrote *Leviathan* provide the most obvious evidence against the efficacy of fearing death; the work was written during a civil war in which a significant percentage of the populations of England, Scotland and Ireland died for the sake of honor, religion and political ends. In addition, Hobbes, in his dialogic history of the Civil War has the elder character "A" claim that a large number of common people cared little for any of these more exalted causes and were willing to risk their lives for either side, "for pay or plunder."[9] Indeed, the first part of *Behemoth* reads like a compendium of motives to fight in the upcoming war, all of which to some degree had to have been stronger than a supposedly overriding concern for personal safety. In *The Elements of Law* and *De Cive* Hobbes states unequivocally that pride (which is connected to honor) will trump the fear of death. For example, he states that "many a man had rather die" than allow another to wreak even non-lethal revenge on him.[10] "Life itself," he asserts, "with the condition of enduring scorn is not esteemed worth the enjoying."[11] In *De Cive*, similarly, he claims that, "most men prefer to lose their peace and even their lives rather than suffer insult."[12] Further, in *Leviathan*, he states that "most men choose rather to hazard their life, than not to be revenged."[13] We also learn in *Leviathan* that honor seekers will continue to risk their lives in duels, and in *De Homine* that when the pains of life become too great, "unless their quick end is foreseen, they may lead men to number death among the goods."[14] In chapter 30 of *Leviathan*, Hobbes also maintains that the fear of death is not enough to dissuade individuals from breaking the law; rights, he says, "cannot be maintained by any Civill Law, or terrour of legall punishment," and a law against rebellion cannot therefore be effective.[15] The desire for self-preservation, then, is not in all cases mankind's highest goal and the fear of death is not simply or naturally the strongest passion, or the *summum malum*, as many scholars suggest.

One recent solution to this apparent inconstancy has been to argue that Hobbes in fact places very little weight on the fear of death, and instead

---

[9] Hobbes (1990, 2).
[10] Hobbes (1999, 52).
[11] Hobbes (1999, 52).
[12] Hobbes (2004, 49).
[13] Hobbes (2012, 234).
[14] Hobbes (2012, 142), Hobbes (1998a, 48).
[15] Hobbes (2012, 522). In this vein I agree with Bejan (2010, 615), that "The problem with punishments is not that they encourage obedience for the 'wrong' reasons, but rather that they cannot be relied upon consistently to provide the kind of constant, overwhelming inducement to obedience (namely fear) requisite to peace."

relies on a hitherto unseen moral sense.[16] Zagorin and Lloyd, the best examples of this approach, both claim that Hobbes seeks to inculcate a sense of moral obligation in citizens and sovereign.[17] This interpretive strategy goes a long way toward resolving some of the difficulties of the earlier position: for example, Hobbes's explicit statement that the threat of corporal punishment can never be so pervasive and effective that it will always hold citizens to their words. This rehabilitation of Hobbes, which is in part an attempt to rescue him from the resilient charge of pessimism regarding the human race, places much more weight on the need for education, which is clearly present in his theory, and represents an important advance in our understanding of his philosophy.

This rehabilitative interpretation, though, overstates the role of moral obligation in Hobbes, just as earlier scholars placed too much weight on the role of the fear of death. Zagorin, for example, claims that following the law of nature, "made for virtuous people and was the right thing to do."[18] He never explains what he means by "the right thing to do," nor provides evidence as to why Hobbes's theory relied on citizens doing the right thing. Nor does Zagorin's understanding of altruism seem entirely coherent. When he claims that "[Hobbes's position] shows pretty clearly that his conception of human nature and human relationships does not in any way exclude the possibility of altruism and human beings seeking the good or happiness of others as part of their own good," he does not seem to realize that doing something for someone else as part of one's own good makes it self-interested, not altruistic.[19] At most, Zagorin proves that Hobbes's system requires a sense of self-interest rightly understood. Lloyd too seems to describe something closer to long-term self-interest than selfless moral duty when she argues that both citizens and subjects are bound to act according to the reciprocity principle, and for the same reasons: it is in the sovereign's interest to treat citizens well and avoid rebellion, and it is in the citizen's long term interest to do that which is conducive to a peaceful and stable commonwealth. Lloyd, though, admits that, if her interpretation is correct, we would have to accept that Hobbes made certain inconsistent statements about the fear of

---

[16] According to Lloyd (2009, 247), we must, "recognize how limited is Hobbes's assumption that men naturally desire to preserve their lives. The only work it does is to explain why we would judge it unreasonable of others to whom we owe no special obligation to fault us for defending our lives . . . it is not needed for anything else in his theory."

[17] Lloyd (2009), Zagorin (2009).

[18] Zagorin (2009, 103).

[19] Zagorin (2009, 86).

death: "[A]lthough Hobbes does not espouse psychological egoism, his language invites that misunderstanding."[20]

In fact, Hobbes is quite explicit about the essential role the fear of death plays in his political theory. As he says in *Elements*: "And if no covenant should be good, that proceedeth from the fear of death, no conditions of peace between enemies, nor any laws could be of force; which are all consented to from that fear."[21] In addition to binding citizens to their covenants, Hobbes is also unequivocal that self-preservation is the primary goal of those forming a commonwealth:

> The finall Cause, End, or Designe of men ... in the introduction of that restraint upon themselves (in which we see them live in Commonwealths,) is the foresight of their own preservation, and of a more contented life thereby; that is to say, of getting themselves out from that miserable condition of Warre.[22]

Hobbes is also quite clear that when it comes to creating a stable polity, "[t]he Passion to be reckoned upon, is Fear," and he means here fear for one's own fate.[23] The problem of self-sacrifice for the sake of the state, then, remains problematic for Hobbes.

WAR, PART ONE: THE EGOIST IN BATTLE

The specific problem the need for soldiers presents to the strictly egoistic system Hobbes presents runs as follows: the citizen, who enters the commonwealth as an individual primarily concerned with his own preservation, can never identify with the community in a way that would make the sacrifice of life in war seem entirely reasonable or desirable. Walzer, discussing Hobbes, outlines this tension well:

> A man who dies for the state defeats his only purpose in forming the state [preservation of his life]: death is the contradiction of politics. A man who risks his life for the state accepts the insecurity which it was the only end of his political obedience to avoid: war is the failure of politics. Hence, there can be no political obligation either to die or to fight. Obligation disappears in the presence of death or of the fear of death.[24]

If the state's primary function is the preservation of the individual's life, demanding that he die in war to preserve the state is a bald contradiction.

---

[20] Lloyd (2009, 243).
[21] Hobbes (1999, 86).
[22] Hobbes (2012, 254).
[23] Hobbes (2012, 216).
[24] Walzer (1970, 82).

As Johnson Bagby argues, "In the end, [Hobbes] could not justify any reason for obligating a soldier to face imminent death for a chance to preserve his country."[25]

There is, though, an argument for going to war founded on egoism built into Hobbes's system. The clearest reason Hobbes gives for soldiers to take up arms in war is that if they do not, the "Soveraign have Right enough to punish [their] refusall with death," and that it is therefore very much in their interest to fight.[26] Soldiers who take "imprest money" also forfeit the right to run away from battle, and this implies that they also abandon their most fundamental right to self-preservation because they have been paid to do so.[27] Because volunteer soldiers have forfeited this right, they may be justly punished with death for cowardice. Running from battle in this case is akin to a capital crime. Although Hobbes makes allowance for conscripts who are cowardly, he maintains that the sovereign retains the right to put them to death. The goal here is to make the fear of certain death at the hands of state's agents outweigh the threat of possible death in battle. As Hobbes explains in an analogous context, "man by nature chooseth the lesser evil, which is danger of death in resisting, rather than the greater, which is certain and present death in not resisting."[28] If the state comes together for the sake of self-preservation, but cannot defend itself, its constitution was in vain. The sovereign facing this difficulty must then leverage the desire for self-preservation to his advantage.

Although one way to do this is to threaten disobedient soldiers with death, the wise sovereign, who is in part the audience of *Leviathan*, could also establish a vast military superiority, or at least a stable balance of power.[29] One goal of Hobbes's sovereign is to unify the largest possible number of citizens, and thereby make the odds of a successful invasion as low as possible: "The Multitude sufficient to confide in for our Security, is not determined by any certain number, but by comparison with the Enemy we feare; and is the sufficient, when the odds of the Enemy is not of so visible and conspicuous moment to determine the event of warre, as to move him to attempt."[30] The implication is that a larger unified multitude

---

[25] Johnson Bagby (2009, 7).
[26] Hobbes (2012, 338).
[27] Hobbes (2012, 338–40). I agree with Warrender who believes that this obligation no longer applies to those in mortal danger (1957, 192). *Pace* Baumgold (1988, 91–2) on the "strenuous obligation" of volunteer soldiers.
[28] Hobbes (2012, 214).
[29] On Hobbes's works as advice to wise sovereigns see Mara (1988).
[30] Hobbes (2012, 256).

will be able to field a larger and better army and deter any opponent from going to war in the first place. Joining an army with overwhelming deterrent power, and thus a very low long-term casualty rate, is far less irrational than joining a vulnerable army that is very likely to engage a more powerful enemy. A wise sovereign will never allow his military to be inferior to potential enemies.[31]

When the sovereign fails to establish such superiority or a stable balance of power, he risks, in Hobbes's system, widespread defection and defeat. Since the pact that subjects make with their sovereign is an exchange of obedience for protection, soldiers are not bound to obey their sovereign if he can no longer protect them. Properly speaking, if the sovereign can no longer protect his subjects, he is no longer the sovereign. And although Hobbes claims that, "*every man is bound by Nature, as much as in him lieth, to protect in Warre, the Authority, by which he is himself protected in time of Peace*" he goes on to say that it would be contradictory "*to destroy him, by whose strength he is preserved.*" This is more a prohibition against actively opposing the sovereign than a command to fight to the death to protect him.[32] Hobbes is quite clear that soldiers are not bound to risk their lives in the face of imminent death, and that it is up to the individual to make this assessment. If a solider or group of soldiers is outnumbered, they are within their rights to surrender and pledge allegiance to their enemy.[33] Soldiers thus act on the same principle as non-soldiers:

For where a number of men are manifestly too weak to defend themselves united, every one may use his own reason in time of danger, to save his own life, either by flight, or by submission to the enemy, as hee shall think best; in the same manner as a very small company of souldiers, surprised by an army, may cast down their armes, and demand quarter, or run away, rather than be put to the sword.[34]

If soldiers' supplies are cut off and they cannot survive otherwise, they may do what they must to remain alive; they are permitted both to surrender and to pledge allegiance to the enemy. A subject is no longer obligated to his former sovereign, "when the means of his life is within the Guards and Garrisons of the Enemy; for it is then, that he hath no longer

---

[31] The other solution to the problem of war, suggested by Strauss, is the "outlawry of war, or the establishment of a world state," although it is unlikely this is the solution Hobbes had in mind (Strauss 1965, 198). See, for example, Schmitt (2007, 52–4, 65).
[32] Hobbes (2012, 1133).
[33] Hobbes (2012, 1134).
[34] Hobbes (2012, 314).

Hobbes's Education in Sanity and Insanity

Protection from him, but is protected by the adverse party for his Contribution."[35] And further,

> a Souldier ... hath not the liberty to submit to a new Power, as long as the old one keeps the field, and giveth him means of subsistence, either in his Armies, or Garrisons; for in this case, he cannot complain of want of Protection, and means to live as a Souldier. But when that also failes, a Souldier also may seek his Protection wheresoever he has most hope to have it; and may lawfully submit himself to his new Master.[36]

Just as the individual retains a right to resist the sovereign because he can never be understood to have given up his right to self-preservation, so soldiers are never bound to die for their country if they can possibly avoid it.

In this section we have seen that Hobbes overcomes Walzer's objection through an argument based on self-interest. We have also seen, however, that on the basis of this argument there is no incentive for going above and beyond a very limited call of duty, but rather an expectation that the fear of death will continue to be the decisive factor determining one's actions. The logical system he proposes leaves no room for courageous action, which, we will see, Hobbes, claims in several places, is necessary for the survival of the commonwealth. This system is in fact an important part of Hobbes's rhetorical strategy to inculcate a more peaceful ethos among citizens.

HOBBES'S EDUCATION IN SANITY AND INSANITY

Hobbes did not expect that the system outlined above would be perfectly replicated in reality, but he did think the world would become a more peaceful place if this way of thinking became more prevalent. Hobbes, therefore, is engaged in an educative strategy that famously involves replacing the works of Aristotle and the scholastics with his own works.[37] Hobbes's teaching on madness, I will argue in this section, serves as a crucial underpinning to this egoistic system, and also reveals the extent to which Hobbes's education involved subtly altering the way

---

[35] Hobbes (2012, 1134).
[36] Hobbes (2012, 1134).
[37] As Tuck (1998, 147) says, the philosophy of Hobbes is, "one of the most profound engagements with the facts of education which is to be found in the main body of western philosophy." For a good recent treatment of Hobbes on education see Bejan (2010). See also Garsten (2006).

individuals thought about and used certain words and concepts.[38] In particular, Hobbes seeks to define as insane those who are willing to risk their lives, along with the political stability of their states, for the sake of honor. In so doing, Hobbes attempts to establish a new standard of normalcy and reasonableness that involves avoiding danger and excessively passionate behavior.[39]

As scholars have noted, Hobbes teaches a new set of virtues which supplant traditional and classical republican virtues,[40] but the chapter in *Leviathan* in which he purports to discuss the intellectual virtues and their defects is primarily a discussion of various types of madness. Virtue is a type of preeminence, but when it becomes too preeminent, according to Hobbes, it is insanity: "to have stronger, and more vehement Passions for any thing, than is ordinarily seen in others, is that which men call MADNESSE."[41] He goes on to explain that the chief causes of madness include, "*great vainglory, which is commonly called pride and self-conceit,*" because "*Pride subjecteth a man to anger, the excess whereof is the madness called rage, and fury.*" A relative term, madness depends on what is considered ordinary, and it is the latter that Hobbes hopes to change. Those who are particularly prone to the excessive pride that leads to madness are those who are not content with equality, but who act rashly, or madly, from a desire for honor and power. It is the demagogues and those who can persuade large numbers of citizens to fight or rebel that Hobbes wants to portray as mad, those Hobbes is thinking of when he says in *Behemoth* that "*there were an exceeding great number men of the better sort [who were eager for war], that had been so educated, as that in their youth having read books written by famous men of the ancient Grecian and Roman commonwealths concerning their polity and great actions.*"[42] In depicting such men, who had been raised on classical literature, as inherently dangerous, Hobbes hopes to temper the ambition

---

[38] Both Mintz (1962) and Parkin (2007, 110ff.) discuss Hobbes's linguistic strategies in this regard. See also Pettit (2008). As Mintz (1962, 151) puts it, Hobbes surreptitiously won over his critics because he was able to "penetrate their defences by obliging them to adopt the rationalist approach." It was partly because of this rhetorical strategy that Hobbes was able to claim that *Leviathan* (2012) had, "framed the minds of a thousand gentlemen to a conscientious obedience to present government, which otherwise would have wavered in that point" (Hobbes 1845b, 336).

[39] In this context see also Cooper (2010) who emphasizes Hobbes's promotion of modesty and humility as an antidote to vainglory.

[40] Berkowitz (2000), Dietz (1990), Johnston (1986), Strauss (1963).

[41] Hobbes (2012, 110).

[42] Hobbes (1990, 3).

of potential Alexanders, those "much taken with reading of Romants," not only by having them worry that they will be perceived as mad, but also causing ordinary citizens to be wary of following such madmen.[43] In *De Cive* moreover, Hobbes warns of those orators like Cataline who, because of their eloquence are able to stir up sedition through "their ability to render their hearers insane," by agitating their passions and thus "minimize the risks [of sedition] beyond reason."[44] Those who follow orators such as Cataline are insane because they are convinced to risk their lives for a cause, and lose their grip on the meaning of "*justice* and *injustice, honour* and *dishonour, good* and *evil*."[45] Labeling someone insane is an effective way to end discussion of the relative value of motives. Thus, by calling those who are filled with pride, anger and lack of discretion mad, Hobbes goes a long way toward changing our perception of men who put their lives at stake for the sake of honor.

For Hobbes, then, being risk-averse is a source of both moral virtue, since it is a requirement of the first law of nature, and sanity. Rather than cultivating the martial virtues as thinkers such as Machiavelli and Sydney urged, Hobbes's system teaches us to avoid ever putting ourselves in harm's way. Goldsmith in this context notes that for Hobbes, "suicides are in fact insane."[46] "Fortitude," "A" says in *Behemoth* "is a royal virtue; and though it be necessary in such private men as shall be soldiers, yet, for other men, the less they dare the better it is both for the commonwealth and themselves."[47] In fact, Hobbes wants not only to promote the fear of death as a civic virtue, but also to foster a fear of ever being placed in dangerous situations, or what we could call the fear of the fear of death.[48] It is through this fear of fear that Hobbes is able to overcome the paradox noted by some scholars that the Hobbesian state is meant to free us from the worst feature of the state of nature, continual fear of death, but must itself rely on fear.[49]

---

[43] Hobbes (2012, 30).
[44] Hobbes (2004, 139–40).
[45] Hobbes (2004, 139–40).
[46] Goldsmith (1966, 123).
[47] Hobbes (1990, 45).
[48] Robin notes that fear is a pervasive political tool today, and that this fear is often not direct, but something akin to what Franklin D. Roosevelt called the fear of fear itself in his "First Inaugural Address" (Robin 2004, 10). Consider also Shklar, who speaks of liberalism as being motivated by "the very fear of fear itself" (Shklar 1989, 29), quoted in Robin (2004, 10).
[49] As Richard Tuck notes in his introduction to *Leviathan*, "(contrary to many people's belief) Hobbes wished to free people from fear" (Hobbes, 1996, xxvi). Although *pace* Ahrensdorf (2000, 584).

This particular paradox is resolved when we realize that Hobbes is talking about two distinct types of fear. As he says in response to an objection to *De Cive*,

> The objectors believe, I think, that fearing is nothing but being actually frightened. But I mean by that word any anticipation of future evil. In my view, not only flight, but also distrust, suspicion, *precaution and provision against fear* are all characteristics of men who are afraid.[50]

Taking precautions against being afraid is a sign of fear; it is possible to, so to speak, be afraid of the fear of death and to insulate oneself against it. For example, a person who avoids skydiving because of a fear of parachute failure is, for Hobbes, experiencing a different kind of fear than the person who, after jumping out of an airplane, realizes that the parachute has in fact failed. Hobbes wanted to promote the less intense of these fears, which is closely connected to his teaching on prudence. When Hobbes discusses the train of thought of the potential criminal running from, "The Crime," to "the Officer, the Prison, the Judge, and the Gallows," he is connecting prudence to the fear of possible and far off consequences, and promoting a general aversion to dangerous behavior.[51] In this way, he was attempting to establish the avoidance of danger as an entirely rational norm. Facing and overcoming our fear of danger might lead to boldness, which Hobbes clearly does not want to encourage. Citizens of the commonwealth will be afraid of experiencing the very intense fear of those who live in an anarchic state of nature, and will therefore prize stability and personal safety above all else.

As noted above, the greatest obstacle to individuals adopting this standard of fearfulness in the secular realm is the desire for honor among glory seekers. Hobbes's system overcomes this problem by making the sovereign the sole source of civil honor (although not of natural honor, which I will discuss in the following section). In chapter 30 of *Leviathan*, which describes how a sovereign should educate his citizens regarding equality before the law, Hobbes says that "The honour of great Persons, is to be valued for their beneficence, and the aydes they give men of inferior rank, *or not at all*. And the violences, oppressions, and injuries they do, are not extenuated, but aggravated by the greatness of their persons."[52] If we compare this statement with

---

[50] Hobbes (2004, 25, my italics). For a good treatment of the persistence of fear in Hobbes's thought see also Blits (1989).
[51] Hobbes (2012, 42).
[52] Hobbes (2012, 536, my italics).

Hobbes's frequent indictments of the classically educated and war-hungry elites of his time, it becomes clear that he was attempting to encourage a more humane standard of honor based on charity. Those who contravened this standard, Hobbes hoped to label reckless and mad.

This is evident in Hobbes's discussion of one of the more dangerous pastimes among civilians in his time: dueling. Hobbes claims that "at this day, in this part of the world, private Duels are, and always will be Honourable, though unlawful, till such time as there shall be Honour ordained for them that refuse, and Ignominy for them that make the challenge." Francis Bacon attempted such a transformation of the definition of honor in 1614 in his piece written against the practice of dueling; he proposed that those who knew the true meaning of fortitude and honor would direct their desire for immortal renown through "great and lofty services to the commonwealth and would view duels as unworthy of a true gentleman."[53] Hobbes is sympathetic to duelers since he recognizes that the dishonor involved in not accepting the challenge could be damaging to a person's future. He therefore recommends mild punishment for those involved, since it is unjust for princes and governors to "countenance anything obliquely, which directly they forbid."[54] Changing the law is clearly not enough. Only a more fundamental change in attitudes and mores could make refusing a duel acceptable and this is part of Hobbes's strategy in describing those who use violence "for trifles, as a word, a smile, a different opinion, and any other sign of undervalue, either direct in their persons or by reflection in their kindred, their friends, their nation, their profession, or their name," as one of the root causes of anarchy. Historically,[55] the practice of dueling in England reached its peak in the early seventeenth century, but gradually became less common and less lethal. Historians tend to agree that this was indeed the result of a changing view of what was considered honorable.[56]

We cannot help but think of those who would risk their lives for a word (calling a man a knave was one of the chief causes of duels in the seventeenth century), or a smile as not only irrational, but as reckless and possessed by the type of rage Hobbes describes as madness.[57]

---

[53] Peltonen (2001).
[54] Hobbes (2012, 476).
[55] Hobbes (2012, 192).
[56] Shoemaker (2002); Andrew (1980).
[57] Historically, the practice of dueling in England reached its peak in the early seventeenth century, but gradually became less common and less lethal. Historians tend to agree that

In Hobbes's system, self-preservation is supposed to be the highest priority, and only madmen deviate from this priority.

It is partly on this basis that we can understand Hobbes's ever-perplexing right to resistance. For Hobbes, even dying out of respect for the law would appear crazy; citizens never give up their right to resist, and, as Walzer notes, "Given Hobbes's theory, the behavior of Socrates [in Plato's *Crito*], is literally inexplicable; Hobbes would have to say that the man was mad."[58]

WAR, PART TWO: THE PERSISTENCE OF HONOR

Despite his prescriptive description of man as primarily concerned with avoiding death, and casting as mad those who do not do so, Hobbes recognizes that, despite his educative efforts, a certain desire for honor that leads one to potentially deadly acts of heroism would remain a part of human nature, and, indeed, a necessity for the state in times of war: the natural punishment for cowardice, Hobbes says, is oppression.[59]

For the most part, Hobbes's use of the term honor involves worldly affairs and what is useful to one while alive, including a sense of individual dignity that must be respected. To honor, Hobbes says, is "[t]o Value a man at a high rate," and honor itself is "[t]he manifestation of the Value we set on one another."[60] In general, unlike glory or vainglory, which is something one attributes to oneself, honor for Hobbes is something that others bestow upon us because of our superior power and out of some hope of gaining aid or avoiding offense.[61] In the tenth chapter of *Leviathan*, the list of things for which one is honored is more focused on immediate goods such as receiving great gifts, having one's advice followed, being obeyed, being trusted and loved.[62] This account of honor is consistent with Hobbes's description of human beings as seekers of power and commodious living and avoiders of pain. Gaining public offices and riches are honorable from this point of view because they fit within this economy of power. Hobbes, though, also uses the term honor to refer to

---

this was the result of a changing view of what was considered honorable (Andrew 1980; Shoemaker 2002).

[58] Walzer (1970, 81).
[59] Hobbes (2012, 572).
[60] Hobbes (2012, 136).
[61] Hobbes (2012, 88). On the distinction between glory and honor see especially Slomp (2000, 38–40).
[62] Hobbes (2012, 136).

future, non-worldly, goods, such as fame that outlives the individual, and the attendant pleasure in imagining these. In *The Elements of Law* Hobbes is more explicit about the distinction between the "imaginations of honour and glory, which ... have respect to the future," and sensual pleasures, "which please only for the present and taketh away the inclination to observe such things as conduce to honour."[63] It is this type of honor in particular that I am concerned with here.

As I have indicated above, neither Hobbes's teaching on insanity nor the egoistic explanation of why soldiers fight is the whole story for Hobbes, nor do these fit particularly well with observable phenomena, as Hobbes must have been aware. Clearly soldiers faced with an enemy's superior military might do not always defect or abandon their countrymen or government. Nor do soldiers remain and fight in dangerous situations simply through fear of the military police, or because they might otherwise forfeit their pay. No amount of money can compensate for one's death if individuals are the psychological egoists some Hobbes scholars have claimed. Hobbes draws attention to this tension in the "Review and Conclusion" of *Leviathan* when he adds what is often called the extra law of nature, which says that subjects are bound to protect their sovereign in war.[64] Volunteer soldiers must be bound by something more than the fear of death, or narrow self-interest, because of the positive act of signing on. As we shall see, this obligation is founded precisely on the love of honor Hobbes finds so dangerous in civil society. Just as Hobbes acknowledges that the fear of death can be overcome, so he knows that the system he describes is not fully in accord with his own understanding of human nature. Hobbes does not want to eradicate the love of honor that drives individuals to seek immortal fame in war. He sought to tame this desire through education, but he did not expect or want to be entirely successful in this endeavor. In fact, he believed the residual desire for honor could be harnessed in the armed forces.

Kateb is one of the most vocal critics of Hobbes's apparent irrationality in this regard, which he describes as "a kind of hysterical doublethink."[65] He claims that Hobbes, although usually rational and desirous of peace at home, was blinded by "an unpurged patriotism or ethnocentrism" when it came to external enemies: "He tries to see through everything except national feeling. He cannot shake free of the sickest of all sick political

[63] Hobbes (1999, 61).
[64] Hobbes (2012, 1133).
[65] Kateb (1989, 382)

thoughts, the abstract we. To want nationhood, whether the numbers are few or in the millions, is to *want* war and death."[66] Hobbes, then, according to Kateb, wants to promote both longevity at home and death in wars abroad. The contradiction Kateb and numerous others have noted does in fact exist in Hobbes's theory, and, given how often this contradiction is observed, and how unlikely that Hobbes would have missed it, it should be understood as an intentional incoherence.

That is, Hobbes quite consciously expects individuals to act on the basis of opposing priorities in different situations: to fear the laws at home but not to fear the public enemy.[67] Despite the rigidly logical account of how and why soldiers will act in wartime sketched in the previous sections, and despite his claim to have "sufficiently, or probably proved all the Theoremes of Morall doctrine," Hobbes was aware of the inadequacy of his educational framework in this crucial respect. In fact, such inadequacy was essential to the survival of the commonwealth. Just as Hobbes taught that rebellion leads to a state of anarchy which is worse than anything, but also recognized that this fact would not prevent irrational citizens from rebelling from a negligent prince, so he relies on the fact that the educational dam he builds to hold back the politically disruptive desire for honor would fail when foreign enemies threatened the state.[68] The incoherence in Hobbes's thought is not that he needs soldiers to fight, but cannot explain why they would do so. Rather, he undermines the self-interested system he presents to explain why they would fight by claiming that no state can be secure on the basis of this kind of narrow self-interest, but requires for its defense acts of courage motivated by a desire for honor.

The laws of the commonwealth and culture, according to Hobbes, can only go so far in manipulating what is considered honorable. As Hobbes says, when discussing natural and conventional honor vis-à-vis divine worship,

because not all Actions are signes by Constitution; but some are Naturally signes of Honour, others of Contumely, these later (which are those that men are ashamed to do in the sight of them they reverence) cannot be made by humane

[66] Kateb (1989, 382). It is true that Hobbes says that garrisons and forts are necessary on a state's frontiers, and that this upholds "the Industry of their Subjects." He also maintains that this posture for war is conducive to something like a balance of power, and that, "there does not follow from it, that misery, which accompanies the Liberty of particular men" (Hobbes 2012, 90).
[67] Hobbes (2012, 1133).
[68] Hobbes (2012, 572).

power a part of Divine worship; nor the former (such as are decent, modest, humble Behaviour) ever be separated from it.[69]

We have seen that Hobbes expects the sovereign to be the sole arbiter of civil honor. But, as he explains, there are also, in addition to institutional or conventional forms of honor, also natural forms: "There be some signes of Honour, (both in Attributes and Actions,) that be Naturally so; as amongst Attributes, *Good, Just, Liberall*, and the like; and amongst Actions, *Prayers, Thanks,* and *Obedience.*"[70] Wearing the king of Persia's robes could be either honorable or dishonorable depending on the king's decrees (as in Hobbes's example). Courage, great actions, and ambition for great honors, will always be honorable for Hobbes, and disobedience will always be a form of dishonor, as will weakness or cowardice.[71]

When Hobbes speaks of excusing "men of feminine courage" from fighting in war, he can only mean that the standard soldiers are to follow is that of manly courage.[72] It is clear that Hobbes regards women as unfit for the dangerous activities of a solider,[73] and since Hobbes defines courage as "the Contempt of Wounds, and violent Death," he must mean that most soldiers will be able to overcome their fear of death.[74] As noted above, Hobbes mentions in several places that many would rather die than suffer insult, and given this, the very punishment for cowardice in the army, in addition to being branded as "womanly," may entail such a degree of dishonor that many would rather die than submit to it. Indeed, as Johnson Bagby, notes, in Hobbes's *The Whole Art of Rhetoric*, he "lists several things of which men are ashamed. To throw down their arms and run away is considered cowardly."[75]

The standard of manliness Hobbes indirectly implies here involves a sense of communal belonging that Hobbes tries to prevent in civilian life, and is part of the ethos of duty which survives to this day in military units. Indeed, the bond among soldiers is a rare exception to Hobbes's individualism, and overall fear of civic association.[76] Hobbes seems to sanction this bond, because, "the strength of an Army, [consists in] the

---

[69] Hobbes (2012, 572).
[70] Hobbes (2012, 562).
[71] Hobbes (2012, 136ff.).
[72] Hobbes (2012, 338).
[73] Mansfield (2006, 174).
[74] Hobbes (2012, 1132).
[75] Johnson Bagby (2009, 60).
[76] Boyd (2001).

union of their strength under one Command."⁷⁷ Mansfield says that, "Hobbes deserves the mantle ... of having created the sensitive male," and that Hobbes was "more wary of men than favorable to women," because he is "mainly against manliness."⁷⁸ This is a good description of Hobbes's vision for civilian life, but as his comments about "men of feminine courage" and the need for soldiers to overcome their fear of death and wounds imply, Hobbes favors manliness in the army, or at least that type of manliness embodied by Sidney Godolphin. It is remarkable that *Leviathan* also opens and ends (in its English edition) with the image of Hobbes's "most noble and honoured friend," who did not fight and die out of fear of punishment, but from courage and love of country and who managed to combine the apparently contradictory traits of fearing punishment at home while being fearless in the face of the enemy.⁷⁹ This type of courage is necessary to the survival of the state. As Hobbes says in *De Homine*, "just as the state is not preserved save by the courage, prudence and temperance of good citizens, so is it not destroyed save by the courage, prudence and temperance of its enemies." ⁸⁰ Clearly, the egoistic explanation of why soldiers fight cannot account for this.

Nor can the egoistic description of soldiers explain Hobbes's statements about the power of an able commander to motivate his troops. When discussing the character of the best military commander in chapter 30 of *Leviathan*, Hobbes states that "[h]e must ... be Industrious, Valiant, Affable, Liberall and Fortunate, that he may gain an opinion both of sufficiency, and of loving his Souldiers. This is Popularity, and breeds in the Souldiers both the desire and courage, to recommend themselves to his favour."⁸¹ The courageous acts of a soldier can only be acts that put him in mortal danger, and therefore require him to overcome his fear of violent death. Johnson Bagby, misses the mark when she claims that "Hobbes wishes to undermine any idea of heroism, because it contradicts so dramatically his insistence that fear of death should be the decisive factor in our political and religious choices."⁸² The desire to impress one's commander through courageous and heroic acts is a desire to be honored by him as well as one's unit, army and country more generally.

---

⁷⁷ Hobbes (2012, 274).
⁷⁸ Mansfield (2006, 173–4).
⁷⁹ Hobbes (2012, 1133).
⁸⁰ Hobbes (1998a, 89).
⁸¹ Hobbes (2012, 550).
⁸² Johnson Bagby (2009, 6).

This phenomenon is not alien to modern warfare. Gray notes that inspirational commanders of the sort Hobbes recommends are, "a perennial phenomenon in war, a cause of wonder and admiration ... they have the capacity to inspire their troops to deeds of recklessness and self-sacrifice."[83] This willingness to die in battle for the sake of one's fellows or commander is not necessarily a rational calculation, and the sentiment that drives a soldier to such action runs counter to Hobbes's claims that man is entirely egoistic. Gray, explains this phenomenon thus: "I may fall, but I do not die, for that which is real in me goes forward and lives on in the comrades for whom I gave up my physical life," and further, "He who has seen men throw away their lives in battle when caught up in communal passion or expose themselves recklessly and carelessly to mortal danger will be cured forever of such easy [psychological egoist] interpretations of human motivation," and further, "Nothing is clearer than that men can act contrary to the alleged basic instinct of self-preservation and against all motives of self-interest and egoism."[84]

When Hobbes, seemingly incongruously, ends the paragraph in which he excuses men of feminine courage by proclaiming that when the commonwealth is in great danger, all those who are able must fight to defend the state, and must fight with courage, he indicates that in certain situations, the collective insanity Kateb brands patriotism will indeed overcome the scruples of the naturally timorous.[85] I am persuaded by Baumgold that Hobbes's "political analysis discriminates between political elites and ordinary subjects, and it was the ambition of the former for power that occupied his attention," and that those he was most concerned about were potential Alexanders.[86] Only some individuals are driven by a desire for honor that has the potential to threaten the state and fewer still have the potential to be the next Caesar.[87] Hobbes hopes to tame the most dangerous excesses of the latter two groups, but relies on a residual capacity both to act courageously, and to inspire such actions on the part of others, who are not naturally so disposed.[88]

---

[83] Gray (1998, 106).
[84] Gray (1998, 46–7, 80).
[85] Hobbes (2012, 340).
[86] Baumgold (1990, 75).
[87] See, for example, Hobbes (1999, 78): "And thus the greatest part of men, upon no assurance of odds, do nevertheless, through vanity or comparison, or appetite, provoke the rest, that otherwise would be contented with equality."
[88] This is not alien to modern warfare. Gray notes that inspirational commanders of the sort Hobbes recommends are, "a perennial phenomenon in war, a cause of wonder and

Hobbes clearly recognizes that individuals are willing to risk their lives and die for the sake of fame after death. He tends to say that this impulse is not entirely rational. In *De Homine*, for example, he says that,

> Even though we think of fame after death as being neither unpleasing nor useless for others, we are nevertheless mistaken in looking at the future like the present, because we shall not experience it, nor can we mere mortals estimate its worth. For we would be making the same mistake as we would were we to be grieved because we had not been famous before we were born.[89]

Hobbes, does, however, also admit that the desire for fame after death is both useful and a worthwhile goal:

> Desire of Praise, disposeth to laudable actions such as please them whose judgement they value ... Desire of Fame after death does the same. And though after death, there be no sense of the praise given us on Earth, as being joyes, that are either swallowed up in the unspeakable joyes of Heaven, or extinguished in the extreme torments of Hell: yet is not such fame vain; because men have a present delight therein, from the foresight of it, and of the benefit that may redound thereby to their posterity.[90]

Although Slomp claims that "Hobbes never thinks that honour can compensate for loss of life," Hobbes here maintains that dying for the sake of such praise is indeed worthwhile, and at the very least not vain, and is something for which some people will naturally strive.[91] The "delight" Hobbes describes here that "pleases them whose judgement they value" might have been described by a later writer as camaraderie; a sentiment that characterizes much modern writing on warfare. Gray, to return briefly to his observations on men in battle, describes the connection between camaraderie and transcendence:

> The sense of power and liberation that comes over men at such moments stems from a source beyond the union of men. I believe it is nothing less than the assurance of immortality that makes self-sacrifice at these moments so relatively easy. Men are true comrades only when each is ready to give up his life for the other, without reflection and without thought of personal loss ... Immortality is not something remote and otherwordly, possibly or probably true and real; on the

---

admiration ... they have the capacity to inspire their troops to deeds of recklessness and self-sacrifice" (Gray, 1998, 106).

[89] Hobbes (1998a, 60).
[90] Hobbes (2012, 152).
[91] Slomp (2000, 41). This passage also implies that both Slomp and Abizadeh, are not telling the whole story when they maintain that for Hobbes, individuals are willing to fight to defend their honor, or avenge signs of contempt, but not to attain honor (Abizadeh, 2011). See also on intellectual vainglory Kraynak (1982).

contrary it becomes a present and self-evident fact ... I may fall, but I do not die, for that which is real in me goes forward and lives on in the comrades for whom I gave up my physical life.[92]

Hobbes's acknowledgment of the reasonableness of performing laudable actions, which must include giving one's life for the sake of posterity, or to please one's commander, "whose judgement they value," is in jarring contrast to his statements about the soldier's right to defection in the face of mortal danger, and to the entire tradition of interpreting him as a psychological egoist. This seeming contradiction is all the more striking because many of Hobbes's strongest statements about the soldier's right to pledge allegiance to a more powerful enemy, disregarding all considerations of tradition, national identity and ignominy, come immediately after his claims that it is entirely possible to combine opposing sets of priorities in the same individual. As one epigraph to this article states, "Nor is there any repugnancy between fearing the Laws, and not fearing a publique Enemy," and Hobbes himself attests that Godolphin did in fact embody this apparent contradiction.[93] Moreover, Hobbes admits that in combining fear of the law at home, and courage in the face of the enemy, he is doing something that many hold to be impossible: "There is therefore no such Inconsistency of Humane Nature, with Civill Duties, as some think."[94] The prudential and sane calculations that keep individuals out of danger within society must be silenced in favor of this kind of honor in war. Civil duty requires that we fear death and corporal punishment from the state, while human nature urges many to risk their lives for the sake of honor.

There is, moreover, evidence that Hobbes differentiates between the kind of violent death a soldier might suffer, but which he saw coming and could prepare for, and the violent death of those who could not do so. To take one less well-known mention of death, Hobbes says in *Thomas White's De Mundo Examined*, "Of the good things experienced by men, however, none can outweigh the greatest of the evil ones, namely sudden

---

[92] Gray (1998, 46–7). Drew Gilpin Faust notes in *This Republic of Suffering* (2008), that "A dying Confederate asked a friend, 'Johnnie if a boy dies for his country the glory is his forever isn't it?'"

[93] Hobbes (2012, 1133). Pace Johnson Bagby who states that "The man whose courage is good if he follows a good cause may still exist, but Hobbes does not mention him" (Johnson Bagby 2009, 127). See also Scott who argues that Hobbes's friendship with Godolphin demonstrates Hobbes's exaggerated dismissal of man's natural sociability (Scott, 2003).

[94] Hobbes (2012, 1133).

[praesentaneae] death."[95] Notice that here the emphasis is on unexpected death rather than death simply, or even violent death. Philippe Ariès, the historian of Western attitudes toward death, notes that dying unexpectedly was for a time regarded as the worst kind of death. Hobbes appears to accept this distinction when he says that the desire for fame after death is not vain. Since the soldier can find joy in contemplating his future fame, his death, though violent, does not, in all cases, qualify as sudden death.[96] This distinction between sudden death and death that we can prepare for may in part explain Hobbes's sparing use of the phrase "violent death" in Leviathan. Despite the heavy reliance on this term by scholars, it only appears three times in Leviathan and only two of these refer to the violent death of individuals. The first use appears in Hobbes's discussion of the state of nature, in which there is "no account of Time; no Arts; no Letters; no Society," and thus no possibility of enjoying any contemplation of fame after death.[97] The other use of the term with regard to individuals is in the "Review and Conclusion" when, as noted above, Hobbes urges the courageous to have contempt for violent death when defending their country.[98] Violent death, then, comes to light as death that will not be remembered and for which one cannot prepare.

This desire, though, can be harnessed for the benefit of the commonwealth. In the state of nature glory seekers are the most dangerous types of person. In civil society, Hobbes makes clear, these characters remain a potential source of trouble. Sedition requires a leader who can inspire others to overlook their own safety, and become, as noted above, "insane."[99] In a clear example of Hobbes revealing the more complex truth beneath his overt logical model of human nature with its compulsory fear of death, he says of such a rabble rouser that,

> He must be a *leader* whom they willingly obey, not because they are obligated by having submitted to his command (for we have argued in this very chapter that men in this situation do not know that they are obligated beyond what seems right and good to themselves), but because they value his courage and military skill, or because they share his passions.[100]

---

[95] Hobbes (1973, 378; 1976, 408).
[96] Ariès (1991, 587).
[97] Hobbes (2012, 192).
[98] Hobbes (2012, 1132). The third use of "violent death" in Leviathan appears in chapter 21, and refers to the violent death of the commonwealth through external enemies (Hobbes 2012, 344).
[99] Hobbes (2004, 140).
[100] Hobbes (2004, 139).

Hobbes, though, is clearly confident that those who have the potential to become Catalines and other individuals who are naturally disposed to courageous actions, can be tamed through education. We find evidence for this in *Behemoth*, where "B" says the following:

> For if men know not their duty, what is there that can force them to obey the laws? An army, you will say. But what shall force the army? ... I am therefore of your opinion, both that men may be brought to a love of obedience by preachers and gentlemen that imbibe good principles in their youth at the Universities, and also that we never shall have a lasting peace, till the Universities themselves be in such a manner, as you have said, reformed.[101]

Hobbes also discusses the possibility of combining courage, which he defines as "Contempt of Wounds, and Violent Death" and "*Timorousnesse*," through "Education and Discipline."[102] Through education, then, the individual can come to see violence in the service of honor within the commonwealth as irrational, and potentially insane, but risking his life in war as a potential source of everlasting fame that is worth dying for.

Hobbes was acutely aware that individuals could be convinced to believe in inconsistent, and even absurd ideas through education. A major part of his philosophical project involved overturning what he took to be the foolish teachings of Aristotle and his followers, "blockheads" such as Suarez and Duns Scotus, which had taken over the universities and propagated nonsensical doctrines for centuries.[103] Hobbes's own philosophy thus comes to appear at first as the attempt to replace scholastic nonsense with a coherent, systematic and rational system. This impression is largely warranted. Hobbes's political philosophy is an attempt to make both individuals and politics more rational, but, at least with respect to the continuing need for a military to fight external wars, he embraces a certain fundamental inconsistency.

CONCLUSION

Hobbes's theory rests on an intentional incoherence between the priorities of the citizen and those of the solider, who, of course, are often the same person. While the private citizen should ideally fear death above all else, the soldier must be able to overcome this fear for the sake of honor. The highest good thus alternates between two opposed poles for

[101] Hobbes (1990, 59).
[102] Hobbes (2012, 1133).
[103] Hobbes (1990, 40–1).

individuals, and often differs in the same individual at different times. The contradiction so many scholars have seen, then, between Hobbes's treatment of civilians and soldiers, rather than being a flaw in his theory, is in fact the result of Hobbes's realization that individuals can and do in fact act on the basis of very different motivators in different situations. What might seem like insane and dangerous behavior in civil society is necessary and praiseworthy in war.

A citizen who fears death and avoids danger is a peaceful citizen. A soldier who fears death and avoids danger is useless. The burden of Hobbes's education was to teach the former disposition, not the latter. Hobbes accomplished this not by arguing that human beings should fear death, but by describing a system of politics which would work perfectly given a fundamental fear of death. The egoistic and quasi-scientific system Hobbes presents is itself the most important part of Hobbes's rhetorical educative strategy. The system seems to break down when compared to reality at points, and especially when it comes to soldiers and war, but, Hobbes seems to have surmised, and as I argued in Chapters 2 and 3, the more readers argued about the mechanics of this system, the more obvious the premises would become. The primacy of the fear of death would not be subject of debate, it would be an assumption. This approach made it easier for Hobbes to recast those who contravened these assumptions as dangerous madmen. Again, these came to be seen as mad not primarily because of any specific arguments Hobbes levels against glory seekers, but through the premises, and even the tone of his description of those who would kill for a smile.

The system Hobbes presents also has the virtue of constituting oblique advice to sovereigns who may be faced with the prospect of going to war with a risk-averse and longevity-obsessed populace. Vast military superiority, perhaps paradoxically, goes hand in hand with the type of citizen Hobbes tries to create. The less risky joining an army is the more likely a risk-averse individual will both join and do what is required.[104]

Establishing such superiority, though, as Hobbes acknowledges, is not enough to win battles or wars. Courageous soldiers will still be necessary,

---

[104] Many observers of international politics have noted that the West has, or is perceived to have, an aversion to casualties in war, which has prompted governments to find ways of minimizing battle deaths in war. Perhaps the most insightful has been Coker (2002, 59) who writes: "The Western way of warfare has become almost entirely instrumental. It is determined almost entirely by what it takes to 'kill' members of the opposing side. By contrast, non-Western strategies ask a very different question: What does it take to persuade soldiers to die for their beliefs?" See also Luttwak (1995, 1999).

Conclusion

as will the sorts of leaders who can inspire their troops to perform acts of bravery, and possibly self-sacrifice. As we have seen, individuals with the potential to be such leaders and such soldiers exist in the state of nature, and remain a permanent phenomenon. Hobbes did not think these individuals needed much cultivation or encouragement, but would appear on their own despite his educational program. The difference, though, is that in civil society, those whose violent acts appear pointless and destructive in the state of nature have the possibility of winning fame after death when their energies are directed in defense of the polity that can serve as a vehicle for this form of immortality. The key for Hobbes was ensuring that this valorous potential remained latent and undisturbed as long as it was not needed. Part of Hobbes's education involves inculcating the sense that there would be no possibility of such immortal fame for violent acts within society.

Hobbes was not optimistic about the possibility of world peace. Given limited space and resources, even if human beings were as Hobbes's system assumes them to be, there would still be war.[105] Given the anarchic state of international affairs, and the lack of a common power to keep nations in check, moreover, Hobbes seems to have thought, as the lawyer says in *A Dialogue Between a Philosopher and a Student of the Common Laws of England*, "You are not to expect such a Peace between two Nations, because there is no Common Power in this World to punish their injustice: mutual fear may keep them quiet for a time, but upon every visible advantage they will invade one another."[106] There will, therefore, always be a place for honor seekers in the world. It seems fair to say, though, that Hobbes did hope for a more peaceful world and that by fostering more stable domestic politics, there would be fewer international wars.[107] In a more peaceful world, Hobbes may have hoped, fewer individuals would be called to make the kind of self-sacrifice Sidney Godolphin made, and more would seek the kind of immortality that comes through great wisdom and learning.[108] This, after all, is the prospect Hobbes must have been savoring, when, in the last line of his *Autobiography*, he writes, "death approaching, prompts me not to fear."[109]

---

[105] Hobbes (2012, 540).
[106] Hobbes (1997, 57).
[107] Hobbes (1997, 57).
[108] Hobbes (1999, 31).
[109] Hobbes (1994b, Curley edition, lxiv).

7

Self-Interest Rightly Understood in *Behemoth*

The Case of General Monck

In Chapters 1–6, I have outlined Hobbes's attempt to undermine the desire for immortality. We have seen that one of his strategies for doing so is juxtaposing a simplified ideal of human nature and a correspondingly simplified ideal regime, with a more subtle presentation of the real complexities of both. In his history of the English Civil War, *Behemoth*, Hobbes is less concerned to stir up controversy than he was in his political works. It is here, though that we see most clearly just how complex Hobbes thought human nature is, and just how overdetermined is the desire for immortality. *Behemoth*, though, is not simply an exposition on Hobbes's view of human nature. He also presents the reader with a new moral ideal, one which would take hold over the course of the following centuries and displace to a great extent the destabilizing notions of honor and salvation we have seen Hobbes oppose in previous chapters. In this chapter, I will give an account of Hobbes's view of human nature as presented in *Behemoth*, as well as the new ideal of self-interest rightly understood, as exemplified by General Monck.[1]

PRELUDE ON THE DIALOGUE FORM

Behemoth is a dialogue between two characters, "A" and "B," about the English Civil War. The opening exchange between these two calls for some comment, which I will offer here as a prelude to the main argument

---

[1] I do not, therefore, agree with those interpretations of *Behemoth* that argue the work was either the presentation of the problem of civil war to which *Leviathan* (Hobbes, 2012) and *De Cive* (Hobbes, 2004) were the solutions (this position is taken by Kraynak, 1982; Mintz, 1962, 46) or those that claim *Behemoth* is an image of Hobbes's political philosophy in action (Holmes, in his introduction to Hobbes, 1990; Lund, 1992).

of the chapter. The exchange reveals that this is a philosophic history behind a vaguely pious facade, and that it is therefore highly rhetorical.[2] This should not be surprising given the general character of Hobbes's writings, but it is worth pointing out that this work of history is very much in line with his political theory generally.[3]

"A" begins by proclaiming that one who looked over England in the years 1640–1660, "as from the Devil's mountain," would have a view of all manner of injustice and iniquity the world could afford.[4] This is clearly an allusion to the temptation of Christ as related in Matthew 4:8–10. In that passage, the devil brought Jesus to a very high mountain from which all the kingdoms of the world were visible. Satan offered all of this to Jesus, who replied that one should worship only the Lord, and not the world. "A," then, appears to be playing the role of Satan who tempts the apparently younger "B."[5] But the temptation is not power over the kingdoms of the world in all their splendor, but knowledge of man's injustice. The world as seen from this prospect has no splendor. The attraction here is very much like the attraction of the history of Thucydides, which, by showing mankind put to an extreme test, reveals the permanent truth about human nature. The temptation here is not accurate knowledge of what happened in the Civil War, but knowledge of human nature.

If "A" plays the role of the philosophic teacher in the guise of Satan, "B" plays the role of student in the guise of both Jesus and Adam. "B," unlike Jesus, is, in fact, attracted by this prospect, because he, like Adam, does not know about good and evil but wants to know the truth about them: "I should be glad to behold that prospect. You that have lived in that time and in that part of your age, wherein men used to see best into good and evil, I pray you to set me (that could not then see so well) upon the same mountain."[6] "B," as an innocent observing the world of good and evil for the first time, will see the turmoil and confusion of seventeenth-century man for what it is, and will thus be open to a new moral

---

[2] I am therefore skeptical of Geoffrey Vaughan (2002, 82), who claims that "[w]hen writing *Behemoth* Hobbes played the historian's part, not the philosopher's."
[3] See, for example, Abosch (2009); Holmes (1990); Kraynak (1982); Vaughan (2002).
[4] Hobbes (1990, 1).
[5] This possible flirtation with Satan in *Behemoth* may have been intended to resonate with the traditional association of the Leviathan with Satan. As Malcolm (2012, 114ff.) quite persuasively argues, though, the primary meaning of Leviathan in Hobbes's *Leviathan* (2012) is "sticking together" and "society."
[6] Hobbes (1990, 1).

teaching; one that prioritizes self-preservation rather than what comes to light as an incoherent and dangerously mercurial desire for transcendence in most of the actors in the Civil War.

THE DESIRE FOR IMMORTALITY AS A CAUSE OF THE CIVIL WAR

Hobbes's explicit theory of human nature in *Leviathan* and *De Cive* seems so plausible to so many modern readers because the desire for power and domination can be observed at the root of so much human activity. Hobbes, in *Behemoth*, also tries to explain the motives of all parties in terms of the desire for power rather than piety, or a concern for the common good. As Vaughan puts it, "B," by the end of the dialogue, "has changed his mind and interprets the actions of people in much the same way as 'A,' seeing corruption and ambition where he had once expected sincerity."[7] Holmes rightly accounts for this move in *Behemoth* by claiming that "a normative bias against dangerous passions and norms helps explain Hobbes's occasional lapses into motivational reductionism. In an ideal world, people would pursue self-preservation alone."[8] The main impression Hobbes wants to impose on the reader is that of a chaotic mass of incoherent desires that must be subjected to order.[9] On the other hand, Hobbes also shows more clearly in *Behemoth* than anywhere else that when speaking of actual individuals and groups, rather than of ideal regimes, it is very difficult, perhaps impossible, to separate the desire for power from the desire for immortality. The two are very often inextricably linked.

The figure of Oliver Cromwell is perhaps the best example of this complex but inextricably linked set of desires. Cromwell was undoubtedly a very pious man who was driven in large part by concern for his soul. He was also a brilliant general who relished victory. By the end of his life, he had essentially set himself up as a hereditary monarch. Historians, though, have always had a difficult time determining what exactly Cromwell's motives were. Somehow a desire for salvation, martial glory and political rule, along with dynastic ambition, coexisted in him. In this complexity,

---

[7] Vaughan (2002, 132).
[8] Holmes (1990, 145).
[9] As Holmes (1990, 120) puts it, "Hobbes skewered all parties in the English Civil War: lawyers, merchants, soldiers, city-dwellers, Commons, Lords, bishops, Presbyterians, king's advisers, and, of course, the people. Stupidity and corruption are ordinary human failings, but seldom have they seemed so effortlessly combined."

Cromwell is emblematic of the variety of forms the desire for immortality could take, as well as the often symbiotic relationship between a desire for transcendence and a desire for power. Hobbes, however, presents him simply as power hungry.

Beneath the chaos of motives, Hobbes is showing that the desire for transcendence is ever-present, and that it can take an enormous variety of forms that are likely confused even in the minds of the actors. Thucydides wanted to show that the same motives would always be at work in human beings and presented the Peloponnesian War as one manifestation of this. Hobbes, in *Behemoth*, does the same. A major difference between the two authors, though, is that Hobbes wants to offer a more concrete plan of political action than did Thucydides.

The particular manifestations of the desire for immortality that Hobbes observed in his own time shaped his presentation of politics and human nature as well as his proposed political solution. There is evidence that in another time and place Hobbes would have preferred a different solution – perhaps a more homogenous society with a strong civil religion. He may, therefore, have agreed with Aristotle that there is a difference between the best regime and the best possible regime here and now.[10] In Hobbes's own time, religion and politics had become so fragmented that no genuine homogeneity of the sort proposed in his explicit political and religious theory was possible. Hobbes had to work with this fragmentation rather than against it. His efforts to blunt the force of religion laid the groundwork for the kind of toleration we find in John Locke.

Before this kind of toleration could come into force, though, Hobbes had to alter the metaphysical framework that guided his contemporaries, as we saw in Chapter 3. He had to argue that there was no absolute standard of right and wrong. Hobbes should, therefore, have agreed with the assessment of his source for *Behemoth*, James Heath's *A Brief Chronicle of the Civil Wars of England, Scotland and Ireland*, who opens his work by claiming that

> [n]o higher or greater cause can be assigned for this war (setting aside the sins of all Times and Nations, to which the Justice of Heaven is seldom long a Debtor) but the fate and catastrophe of Kingdoms and Monarchies, which do at certain periods

---

[10] On the complex relationship between Aristotle and Hobbes, see especially Spragens (1973, 45), who argues that "Hobbes accepted the underlying framework of the Aristotelian paradigm, and this component was perpetuated in his thought as the tacit matrix of his own paradigm. He rejected, however, the focal model of the Aristotelian paradigm and replaced it with quite a different model which he found more satisfactory."

of time taste of that vicissitude and mutability to which other sublunary things are more frequently subjected.[11]

For Heath, the cause of the war was a blind fate that affects all things. In a universe in which there is no good or evil beyond what men call good and evil, this would seem to be the correct view of wars. But for the speakers in *Behemoth*, the war put into clear relief the nature of good and evil. Hobbes does not have the equanimity that Heath seems to. In *Behemoth*, Hobbes wants to refashion how we understand good and evil, and how we make calculations about them.

When faced with a choice between obeying the civil authorities but committing a mortal sin that results in damnation, and not committing the sin but being executed by the state, Hobbes unhesitatingly advocates avoiding hell. This is the only reasonable course of action. Hobbes was a reasonable man and naturally believed in making decisions based on long-term self-interest. Many, though, do not think as clearly as Hobbes does. In forming civil society:

> The Passion to be reckoned upon, is Fear; whereof there be two very generall Objects: one, The Power of Spirits Invisible; the other, The Power of those men they shall therein Offend. Of these two, though the former be the greater Power, yet the feare of the later is commonly the greater Feare.[12]

If men would only think clearly, religion would be the best guarantor of civil peace. From this point of view, the most important part of Hobbes's educational strategy should be the inculcation of firm, uniform, Christian belief in all citizens. Just prior to the passage quoted above, Hobbes also claims that men can be held to their words by a sense of pride and glory in keeping their oaths. Unfortunately, this is only a weak motivator, one that a sovereign cannot rely on. It could do no harm, though, for a sovereign to strengthen this sense of honor to the extent possible.

From these statements, we can discern Hobbes's ideal strategy for a stable, peaceful state; the sovereign would have overwhelming power to threaten and inflict physical punishment on his subjects, and this coercive power would be bolstered by a powerful state religion which had been drummed into every citizen from birth. In addition to physical power and religious power, the sovereign would instill to the extent possible a code of honor, ideally one that would be linked to the state religion. From these few comments, the ideal Hobbesian state would look

---

[11] Heath (1663, 1).
[12] Hobbes (2012, 216).

somewhat like Sparta. This would seem to be the logical conclusion Hobbes would draw from his premises about human nature and the nature of politics and religion.

There are, though, several problems with this reasoning. If we take Hobbes's writings at face value, he did indeed want to inculcate a firm, uniform, Christian belief in his readers.[13] But Hobbes was generally seen as an atheist or an extreme heretic by his contemporaries and by nearly everyone afterward. As we have seen in previous chapters, his goal was not the inculcation of belief in any ordinary sense. Hobbes did not think that the fear of physical violence would simply trump the fear of invisible spirits, and no one was convinced by his claim that breaking the civil law earned one a place in hell. Neither was the promotion of a sense of honor high on the list of Hobbes's priorities. The explicit goal of the Leviathan is the suppression of pride. He may have thought that a desire for glory was not strong enough to hold men to their oaths, but he did think it was a major driver of war. The picture of what Hobbes was trying to accomplish with regard to rational calculation is more complicated than we might at first suppose.

The obvious rejoinder is that Hobbes thought a state could be made peaceful on the basis of overwhelming physical force. Seen in that light, the main point of *Behemoth* would be to accuse Charles I of being insufficiently powerful to keep his kingdom in order. This certainly is one of the main themes in *Behemoth*, but not the most interesting. What must strike most readers is that the book is not a history in the ordinary sense of the term. The actual narrative of the war takes up less than half of the book and is rather perfunctory. The bulk of the dialogue is, in fact, a discussion of the causes of war, and more specifically the motivations of the various groups involved. Again, part of the message is that Charles was not strong enough to prevent the war, but the reason he was not powerful enough is the real key to the work. It is easy enough to say that the sovereign should have overwhelming coercive power, but the means of attaining such force are not obvious. The central right of the sovereign is the power to *"Judge of what Doctrines are fit to be*

---

[13] This belief though would have been subordinated to political concerns, as in ancient civic religions. As Beiner (2011, 61–2) puts it, in *Behemoth* Hobbes was most concerned with "*theocracy* in the proper... sense as a historical regime. Civil religion is acceptable and even desirable from a Hobbesian point of view because it is a mode of theocracy ruled by the sovereign and subordinated to political-nonreligious concerns for civic order. Puritan theocracy – that is, *real* theocracy – is *not* acceptable because it is a subordination of political concerns to religious imperatives."

taught."[14] This power is the 7th in a list of thirteen rights Hobbes says a sovereign must have in chapter 18 of *Leviathan*, but he does not number this correctly, leaving only twelve rights with numbers, thus drawing attention to this decisive one (although this is correct in the Latin *Leviathan*, and so may well have been simply an error on Hobbes's part). This impression is reinforced by two statements we find in *Behemoth* that will serve as the backbone of this chapter.

The first is that "the power of the mighty hath no foundation but in the opinion and belief of the people."[15] The second: "For if men know not their duty, what is there that can force them to obey the laws? An army, you will say. But what shall force the army?"[16] Both of these suggest that the key to a stable and peaceful state is not physical force, but the kinds of beliefs that underpin such force and therefore such stability.

The main goal of Hobbes's work is the subtle manipulation of belief in the service of peace. Hobbes wants to fundamentally alter what we would call culture. To return to the calculation I raised above, Hobbes does not, in fact, want citizens to base their calculations on what they think will get them into heaven and keep them out of hell. Nor does he want them to stake their lives on the possibility of everlasting fame for great deeds. Both of these are undeniably the goals of long-term self-interest. But neither does Hobbes praise those who risk their lives foolishly for the sake of pecuniary gain or other foolhardy short-term goals. What he wants to inculcate is what we can call a kind of medium-range self-interest, namely, longevity.

Behemoth opens with a discussion of the inability of Charles I to properly rule his kingdom because of the corruption of many of his citizens. The chief culprits in this corruption were ministers of Christ who taught that they collectively had the right to govern the whole nation. The second group Hobbes names are Papists, who believed that the nation should be governed by the Pope. Third were the various minor sects: Independents, Anabaptists, Fifth Monarchy men, Quakers, Adamites and others. "And these," "A" says, "were the enemies which arose against his Majesty from the private interpretation of the Scripture, exposed to every man's scanning in his mother-tongue."[17]

---

[14] Hobbes (2012, 272).
[15] Hobbes (1990, 16).
[16] Hobbes (1990, 59).
[17] Hobbes (1990, 3).

Those who instigated the war, according to Hobbes, were those most concerned with an afterlife. Both Catholics and the various Protestant sects are driven by a desire to attain heaven and avoid hell and did not believe that Charles had any authority over spiritual matters. "A" wants to argue that all of these groups are mistaken in this belief: "he that is excommunicate for disobedience to the King's laws, either spiritual or temporal, is excommunicate for sin; and therefore if he die excommunicate and without desire of reconciliation, he dies impenitent."[18] This suggestion fits with Hobbes's official theology, but clearly was not accepted by any of the religious groups he mentions.

Hobbes also blames the war on aristocrats who want to achieve great deeds of their own, for which they will be remembered. They also are in love with an abstract "form" of government, and thus attached to the idea of a transcendent standard of justice, which is connected to democracy. For these, the legal sovereign, Charles I, is not the sole conduit through which one acquires honor and lasting memory, as Hobbes's official theory would have it.

The war was caused primarily by these two forms of corruption on the part of the religious and the glory-seeking democrats. But both forms of corruption can be summed up by their shared desire for immortality that is not dependent on the state. To reiterate the basic premise of this work, the greatest obstacle to a stable and long-lasting polity is the desire for immortality. Hobbes, by laying the blame for the war on these groups in the first pages of *Behemoth*, acknowledges this.

Although Hobbes identifies this desire for transcendence first and foremost, which he could hardly avoid doing, he fairly quickly shifts the narrative to depict the war as a struggle for power and dominance among all of the groups involved.

The first topic the speakers take up after the list of groups involved in the war is heresy. The definition of heresy, we learn, is the responsibility of parliament, and, in fact, the church itself owes its authority to the government. This is clear because historically, "the Popes themselves received the papacy from the Emperor." And, in the example that proves the rule,

The first [pope] that ever was elected Bishop of Rome without the Emperor's consent, excused himself by letters to the Emperor with this: that the people and clergy of Rome forced him to take it upon him, and prayed the Emperor to confirm

---

[18] Hobbes (1990, 8).

it, which the Emperor did; but with reprehension of their proceedings, and the prohibition of the like for the time to come.[19]

The popes, then, acknowledged that their authority came from the sovereign. When the opportunity presented itself, though, they were ready enough to exert power on their own behalf. The example Hobbes cites is that of the Peruvian king, Atabalipa, who was told by a friar that

> Christ being King of all the world, had given the disposing of all the kingdoms therin to the Pope, and that the Pope had given Peru to the Roman Emperor Charles the Fifth, and required Atabalipa to resign it; and for the refusing it, seized upon his person by the Spanish army there present, and murdered him.[20]

"You see by this," "A" concludes, "how much they claim, when they have power to make it good."[21] Over time, moreover, as Hobbes recounts it, the popes gradually introduced measures that reduced the power of the emperors. These included the celibacy of priests, which prevented a king from being also a pope; auricular confession, which underlined the power of priests to damn and save; and transubstantiation, which put the power to create the body of Christ and left ordinary people in awe of their power.[22]

The overwhelming power of religion over men's minds is a theme Hobbes returns to more than once in *Behemoth*. The most dramatic example is that of the Ethiopian priests, who

> spend their time about the worship and honour of their Gods, and are in the greatest authority; when they have a mind to it, send a messenger to the King to bid him die, for that the Gods have given such an order, and that the commandments of the immortals are not by any means to be neglected by those that are, by nature, mortal.[23]

This is a concrete example of kings obeying priests, "not as mastered by force and arms, but as having their reason mastered by superstition."[24] This, Hobbes implies, is the direction in which Europe was tending through the Middle Ages.

"A,' we notice, is not concerned about the truth of the various religious doctrines of his time, but only what effect they have in the power struggle

---

[19] Hobbes (1990, 13).
[20] Hobbes (1990, 11).
[21] Hobbes (1990, 11).
[22] Hobbes (1990, 13–15).
[23] Hobbes (1990, 94).
[24] Hobbes (1990, 94).

with the secular authorities. "For my part," "B" exclaims, the ability of priests to make Christ's body from bread "would have an effect on me, to make me think them gods, and to stand in awe of them as of God himself, if he were visibly present."[25] From this point of view, religious sects and the papacy are just one more group among many vying for temporal power and should be treated as such. The spread of Christianity through the establishment of universities, which "A" likens to Trojan Horses, is presented as purely a matter of increasing the authority of the Pope, with no hint that there could have been any sincere faith among Popes, bishops or anyone else involved.[26] The imperialism of the papacy was a conscious design, and, "A" claims,

> it was an evident argument of that design, that they fell in hand with the work so quickly. For the rector of the University of Paris ... was Peter Lombard, who first brought in them the learning called School-divinity; and was seconded by John Scot of Duns, who lived in, or near the same time; whom any ingenious reader, not knowing it was the design, would judge to have been two of the most egregious blockheads in the world, so obscure and senseless are their writings.[27]

Scholasticism here is presented as a complex ruse designed to fool all of Europe into obeying the Pope. From this Machiavellian perspective, Hobbes makes a Machiavellian suggestion: "Had it not been much better that those seditious ministers, which were not perhaps 1000, had been all killed before they had preached? It had been (I confess) a great massacre; but the killing of 100,000 is a greater."[28] Clear-sighted politicians should not be misled by the supposedly sacred nature of a priest's person, as Baglioni, according to Machiavelli, was with Pope Julius II.[29] This calculation on the part of "A" exhibits a level of *sang froid* we do not normally associate with Hobbes, and one advantage of the dialogue form is that we cannot simply attribute it to him.

The Hobbes of *Leviathan* and *De Cive* would likely point out that the lawful sovereign cannot be accused of injustice by his subjects, and so a purge of seditious ministers would be a real possibility in his system. Hobbes, though, also points out that gross mistreatment of one's subjects will result in rebellion. Unless the flocks of these ministers agreed with the sovereign about the need for such an action, they would certainly regard

---

[25] Hobbes (1990, 15).
[26] Hobbes (1990, 39–40).
[27] Hobbes (1990, 40–1).
[28] Hobbes (1990, 95).
[29] Machiavelli (1996, 62).

the execution of their parish priests as a grave affront. In fact, given the intensity of religious feeling among their adherents, massacring these ministers would likely have catapulted them to the status of martyrs and brought about the war their murder would have been meant to avoid.

By inserting this suggestion, probably the most dramatic of the work, Hobbes wants readers to see religious disputes more in terms of power relations. He wants us to have a more cynical view of what the clergy are really after. Like everyone else, they love to dominate and will do so when given the chance. On the other hand, reflection on the plausibility of this strategy reveals that Hobbes faces a serious problem when it comes to counteracting the negative effects of religious sects and the papacy: Because their power derives from their influence over men's minds, they cannot be defeated by force alone. Hobbes, though, also does not try to defeat them in a straightforward way on their own terms. He does not argue for the truth of one sect over another, but, as we have seen, creates a new theology he does not expect will be taken seriously. If Hobbes is to succeed in his endeavor to create a more peaceful and stable politics, he cannot adopt an overtly amoral position. Instead, as I will argue in the conclusion, his philosophy, for all its bad reputation and supposedly grim view of human nature, must retain at its core something of Christian morality.

Murdering all disloyal ministers would simply have been too shocking to be effective. The greatest part of this shock would have stemmed from the belief, probably impossible to completely eradicate, that priests are somehow sacred and that it is a greater sin to murder them than members of the laity. The reasons for this may be complex and have something to do with the squeamishness associated with killing those who are at least overtly non-violent. But it would be hard to deny that the stigma attached to killing a priest derives from the suspicion that must lurk in the minds of all but the most hardened atheists, if even them, that such an act may offend great hidden powers, and that there will be repercussions in this life or the next.

The suggestion that 1,000 bishops should have been killed, in fact, epitomizes the complex of not very coherent short- and long-term goals that characterizes the participants in the Civil War. Again and again in the first dialogue of *Behemoth*, we find actors motivated by concern for their everlasting souls at one moment, and risking their lives for the sake of money at the next. Almost in the same breath, "A" claims that "there were very few of the common people that cared much for either of the causes, but would have taken any side for pay or plunder," and that the source of their corruption was the ministers who pretended "to have a right from God to govern every one his parish and their assembly the whole nation."[30] "B," moreover, claims that most people weigh "the commodities or incommodities of this present life only, which are in their sight, never putting into the scales the good and evil of the life to come, which they see not."[31] The next time "B" speaks, he claims that questions about the nature of hell and who rules in heaven, among other points of doctrine, were "the cause of all our late mischief," because the variety of answers to these questions has fragmented ordinary people into the various sects whose disputes led directly to the war.[32] Taking the side of parliament or the king for the sake of plunder and following one's minister, or the Pope, because he claims that his authority comes directly from Christ, are not readily compatible motives. Hobbes suggests that both were operating at the same time in a fundamentally irrational way.

Since Tyndale's translation of the Bible into English and the dissemination of it with the aid of the printing press, individuals could read scripture in their mother tongue. This led to a diversity of sects, which, at the beginning of Charles I's reign, "did then appear to the disturbance of the commonwealth."[33] "Every man," "A" says, "became a judge of religion, and an interpreter of the Scriptures to himself."[34] "A" makes it clear that however pious the motivation behind this private interpretation, those who were engaged in it were in no way qualified to do so. As he says, "after the Bible was translated into English, every man, nay, every boy and wench, that could read English, thought they spoke with God Almighty, and understood what he said, when, by a certain number of chapters a day they had read the Scriptures once or twice over."[35] This sincere but incompetent attempt to follow the teachings of Christ was exploited by ambitious clergy who carefully crafted their message to make it as appealing as possible to ordinary people, while still maintaining control over them. "A" tells us that these ministers carefully avoided preaching against "the lucrative vices ... which was a great ease to the generality of citizens," but on the other hand did, "with great earnestness and severity, inveigh often against two sins, carnal lusts and vain swearing."[36] By this

---

[30] Hobbes (1990, 2).
[31] Hobbes (1990, 54).
[32] Hobbes (1990, 55).
[33] Hobbes (1990, 22).
[34] Hobbes (1990, 22).
[35] Hobbes (1990, 21).
[36] Hobbes (1990, 25).

means, the ministers were able to control their listeners by telling them they sinned whenever they delighted in the sight of the opposite sex, which Hobbes says is by nature impossible to prevent.

All of these contrivances of the clergy, either Catholic or Protestant, which Hobbes does his best to present as unadulterated power politics, rest on the fundamental belief of ordinary people that they were bound either for heaven or hell after death. No one would have listened to the Scholastics if this had not been their concern. No one would have cared about which book of prayer was being used, nor been persuaded to care by their ministers, if this was not an ever-present consideration.

Hobbes is well known for his realism and clear-sighted view of the role of power in politics, but it is impossible to understand him properly without always keeping in mind the fact that behind all physical power is the power of ideas. To recall the key quotation of this chapter, "the power of the mighty hath no foundation but in the opinion and belief of the people."[37] And those beliefs come mainly from priests: "So that it is impossible that the multitude should ever learn their duty, but from the pulpit and upon holidays; but then, and from thence, it is, that they learned their disobedience."[38]

One way to solve this problem and ensure conformity in religious education would be to legislate a uniform liturgy across the state. This, though, had blatantly failed in Britain. Charles I had tried to impose the Book of Common Prayer on England and Scotland with famously disastrous results. The reason, "A" says, is connected with the new zeal for individual interpretation of the Bible; when ministers delivered their sermons, "their prayer was or seemed to be *extempore*, which they pretended to be dictated by the spirit of God within them, and many of the people believed or seemed to believe it."[39] "And from hence," "A" goes on, "came a dislike of the *common-prayer-book*."[40] Hobbes suggests both in *Behemoth* and *Leviathan* that a public reading of the laws of England, in the manner of the Jews of the Old Testament, would be an ideal way to demonstrate the unity of civil and religious law. In light of the new religious spirit he describes in *Behemoth*, with its antipathy for formulae and the Book of Common Prayer, we are justified in wondering

---

[37] Hobbes (1990, 16).
[38] Hobbes (1990, 40).
[39] Hobbes (1990, 25).
[40] Hobbes (1990, 25).

if Hobbes really thought the process of instilling religious uniformity could be so straightforward.

Recommending that the laws of England be read in church periodically was really one of the more ham-handed suggestions Hobbes makes, and no one has ever taken it seriously as a solution to the problem of religious fragmentation. In light of the great variety of sects in England, such a solution, even according to Hobbes himself, could not work. As "A" says, "A state can constrain obedience, but convince no error, nor alter the minds of them that believe they have the better reason. Suppression of doctrine does but unite and exasperate, that is, both increase the malice and power of them that have already believed them."[41] As I have argued in previous chapters, Hobbes did not expect anyone to adopt the political system he sets out in a straightforward way, nor did he expect his theology to be taken seriously. It follows, then, that he did not expect future priests to read out laws and points of theology he knew would be unacceptable.

As mentioned above, Hobbes, in the 18th chapter of *Leviathan*, obliquely suggests that the most important power the sovereign has is censorship and the strict control of which doctrines can be publicly taught. Hobbes thus makes a subtle suggestion about the decisive importance of shaping men's thoughts, but then offers a preposterous suggestion for putting this proposal into effect. If we put these two things together, we can see that Hobbes both is and is not serious about his suggestion for promoting uniformity of opinion. He wanted to instill a uniformity of thought without appearing to do so. The nature of that unity would be such that what had been considered heresies could be more openly tolerated, since they would henceforth be undergirded by a deeper agreement about the limits of religiously inspired action. In other words, he wants to have the effect of reading out the laws of the nation to its citizens as if they were religious injunctions without literally doing so. This would seem to be the only method that would work with those who prefer spontaneity and depth of feeling to the rote repetition of a code of laws. Hobbes made suggestions for literal courses of action; he in fact wanted to be implemented surreptitiously; his actual proposals were implausible, but they suggested an indirect course of action that could be very successful.

The other major group "A" accuses of fomenting war in the opening of *Behemoth* is the "great number of men of the better sort" who were overly

[41] Hobbes (1990, 62).

impressed with the "great actions" of the ancient Greeks and Romans, and who "became thereby in love with their forms of government."[42] These, "A" claims, were the most eloquent and persuasive members of the House of Commons. The parallel with the funeral oration in which Pericles urged the Athenians to fall in love with Athens is striking. We notice here, though, the more abstract, almost Platonic, nature of aristocrats falling in love with a "form" of government, rather than a particular nation. The love of liberty and popular government here is equated with a universally valid standard of justice, and tyranny with unqualified injustice. The great actions they sought to undertake on behalf of democracy and justice would, they thought, immortalize them both in England and beyond as liberators. They would, like Brutus, always be remembered as having overthrown a tyrannical monarchy and established a republic.[43]

Hobbes, of course, is not impressed. His goal is downplaying the transcendent aspirations of these men of the better sort and depicting their motives as a confused jumble of long- and short-term goals that were inherently destabilizing. The nobility of Scotland, for example, was driven by mixed motives. "A" claims that he cannot be sure how much religious conscience factored into their desire for war, since he cannot know what is in other men's minds, but he is quite sure that a desire for glory as well as money played a part.[44] These motives can all, Hobbes wants to show, be reduced to a desire for power. Hobbes wants in fact to cast the notion of honor itself as artificial and not something a sensible person would want to die for. Just as he does with religious drivers of the war, Hobbes subtly reduces the quest for honor to a quest for power.

The goal for Hobbes, though, is not the outright elimination of honor, a task that, as I have shown in Chapter 6, he did not think was possible. Honor poses a special problem for the following reasons. We have seen

---

[42] Hobbes (1990, 3). Thomas (2010, 56) notes that "[f]or Tudor commanders, Roman valour was as important an inspiration as medieval chivalry ... This neoclassical stress upon the value of military accomplishment intensified in the mid-seventeenth century, when it acquired quasi-democratic overtones." See also Braddick (2009, 259).

[43] It is important to note here that Hobbes, in speaking of those aristocrats who yearned for freedom, is not, as Skinner (1996) claims, attacking the Roman idea of republican liberty to make way for his own ideas about negative liberty. As Kapust and Turner (2013) convincingly argue, Hobbes is very much drawing on the Roman concept of liberty, in all its complexity. Hobbes's worries about "democratical gentlemen" in his own time were the same in kind as Cicero's worries about Cataline. For both, the worry is about ambitious men who use terms like liberty and democracy as a means to achieve their ends.

[44] Hobbes (1990, 29-30).

that in *Behemoth*, Hobbes makes it clear that the power of a state rests on the beliefs of ordinary people. The sovereign's power rests on men with swords, but as "B" asks, "What shall force the army?"[45] The answer turns out to be education. The universities must teach "love of obedience" as a precondition for a loyal army and a state free of civil war.[46] From this it would follow that those destined for the military should be immersed in an education replete with patriotism and nationalism. In the seventeenth century, this might have taken the form of a cult of personality such as that which accompanied Queen Elizabeth. It could also have included the type of exhortation Henry V gave to his soldiers in Shakespeare's play:

> This story shall the good man teach his son;
> And Crispin Crispian shall ne'er go by,
> From this day to the ending of the world,
> But we in it shall be remember'd-
> We few, we happy few, we band of brothers.[47]

Only this type of devotion and obedience could convince soldiers to put themselves willingly in harm's way. But this manifestly is not what Hobbes has in mind.

Hobbes cannot have meant for the universities to imbue their students with patriotic zeal because of what has come to be known as Hobbes's "de factoism." The rule, as set out most clearly in *Leviathan*, and especially in the "Review and Conclusion," is that citizens owe obedience to those who protect them. Once that protection has ceased, and once there is another who can provide it, the individual is bound to obey the usurper as the legitimate sovereign. Hobbes's university would train future officers not to become confused about their own self-interest by ideas of sacrifice and to disregard tradition. Hobbes both acknowledges the importance of ideas for holding both an army and a state together, but also undermines what was traditionally, and is still today, the content of those ideas.

One specific instance of this is his discussion of escutcheons and heraldry in *Leviathan*. The reason coats of arms and escutcheons are honorable, for Hobbes, is that they confer money and privileges on their holders.[48] Without such riches or privileges, they are not honorable. He acknowledges that the honor of these may also derive from,

---

[45] Hobbes (1990, 59).
[46] Hobbes (1990, 59).
[47] Shakespeare (1997, 1004).
[48] Hobbes (2012, 144).

"some such thing as is equally honoured in other men."[49] What this other thing is, Hobbes does not say. We can surmise that he refers here to the sense of belonging to a centuries-old dynasty. However, the purpose of these passages seems to be the deconstruction, and so deflation, of this sense of tradition. The concept of gentry itself, Hobbes says, is German in origin. It was unknown to the Greeks. The origin of all coats of arms as well as titles stem from the "infinite number of little Lords," who, "continually had wars one with another."[50] Tradition itself did not confer any right separate from that conferred by the king, and so could not be appealed to against the monarch. As "A" puts it in *Behemoth* after tracing the history of the gentry in similar fashion to what we find in the tenth chapter of *Leviathan*, "it cannot be inferred that [the lords] had a right to oppose the King's resolutions by force, nor to enjoy those honours and places longer than they should continue good subjects."[51] In the opening of the dialogue, "A" explains that Charles I held the sovereignty "by right of a descent continued above six hundred years, and from a much longer descent King of Scotland, and from the time of his ancestor Henry II., King of Ireland."[52] "B," apparently uninterested in lines of ancestry, is only concerned with the fact that Charles has "60,000 men, and divers magazines of ammunition in places fortified."[53] This demystifying of heraldry must in part be intended to make it easier to abandon tradition when danger threatened.

Hobbes does not want tradition to be a factor in men's calculations about how to face death. We have seen in Chapter 3 that he wants to diminish the appeal of honor in general. It is true that Hobbes wants the sovereign to be the font of all honor. "A" claims that the sovereign must be liberal with "those that do him service in the wars," but subjects must disregard even this domestically generated form of honor in the face of life-threatening danger.[54] We are left wondering, then, what it is that the universities will teach in order to force the army and everyone else into obedience.

---

[49] Hobbes (2012, 144).
[50] Hobbes (2012, 144).
[51] Hobbes (1990, 77).
[52] Hobbes (1990, 1–2).
[53] Hobbes (1990, 2).
[54] Hobbes (1990, 45).

REFORMING THE UNIVERSITIES

Hobbes never directly addresses the disjunct in his political theory between the need to teach obedience to citizens and soldiers and his efforts to undermine all traditional means of doing so. If we examine the specific passages of *Behemoth* that discuss reforming the universities, though, what he has in mind comes more clearly into focus.

The clergy, "A" tells "B," were enthusiastic about the religious reforms of Henry VIII because they thought that "the pulling down of the Pope was the setting up of them (as to England) in his place."[55] In line with his general strategy, Hobbes makes the plausible, but probably reductionist, claim that the clergy's only concern was power. There is, according to *Behemoth*, not much difference between Episcopalians and Presbyterians on this point, as this bit of dialogue shows:

B. How would the Presbyterians have the Church to be governed?
A. By national and provincial synods.
B. Is not this to make the national assembly an arch-bishop, and the provincial assemblies so many bishops?
A. Yes; but every minister shall have the delight of sharing in the government, and consequently of being able to be revenged on those that do not admire their learning and help to fill their purses, and win to their service those that do.[56]

From the cynical point of view presented in *Behemoth*, the English clergy hoped to keep the monarchy in thrall, because "[i]t seems they did not think it reasonable that a woman, or a child, or a man that could not construe the Hebrew, Greek, or Latin Bible, nor knew perhaps the declensions and conjugations of Greek or Latin nouns and verbs, should take upon him to govern so many learned doctors in matters of divinity."[57] Since the correct understanding of Christianity depends on the proper interpretation of the Bible, and since the proper interpretation of the Bible depends on vast learning that no monarch is likely to have, the clergy was sure to retain a great deal of control in England.

This control depends, as we have seen, on upholding the ruse, perpetrated by Thomas Aquinas and others, that Christianity is really about scholastic theology. Divinity, or church philosophy, "B" claims, is

---

[55] Hobbes (1990, 56).
[56] Hobbes (1990, 89).
[57] Hobbes (1990, 57).

extremely dangerous: "the interpretation of a verse in the Hebrew, Greek or Latin Bible, is oftentimes the cause of civil war and the deposing and assassination of God's anointed."[58] As "A" puts it, "religion has been for a long time, and is now by most people, taken for the same thing with divinity, to the great advantage of the clergy."[59] Hobbes here makes a distinction between divinity, or what today is called theology, which requires a knowledge of several languages as well as the philosophy of Aristotle, and religion, which Hobbes equates with early Christianity and is a matter of inner conviction.[60] In exasperation with the contemporary concern of Presbyterians for the former and indifference to the latter, "B" exclaims, "How we can have peace while this is our religion, I cannot tell. *Hoeret lateri lethalis arundo.*"[61] The Latin here is from Virgil's *Aeneid* (4.74) and can be translated as "the fatal arrow sticks in her side." This line is part of a description of Dido's sorrow at Aeneas's departure. In context, and in Dryden's translation, it reads as follows:

> Sick with desire, and seeking him she loves,
> From street to street the raving Dido roves,
> So when the watchful shepherd, from the blind,
> Wounds with a random shaft the careless hind,
> Distracted with her pain she flies the woods,
> Bounds o'er the lawn, and seeks the silent floods,
> With fruitless care; for still the fatal dart
> Sticks in her side, and rankles in her heart.[62]

Christianity as construed by Presbyterians, who do not differ significantly from Anglicans, is a fatal arrow, fired intentionally by ambitious clergy, that will destroy England unless there is a fundamental change. The religion must become one of the heart rather than of the head: "The seditious doctrine of the Presbyterians has been stuck so hard into people's heads and memories (I cannot say into their hearts;

---

[58] Hobbes (1990, 144).
[59] Hobbes (1990, 57, see also 90).
[60] Later in the work, 136, Hobbes again makes a distinction between "church philosophy" and "religion" and claims that the English Presbyterians, in attempting to outdo the Reformation of Luther and Calvin, "distracted their auditors into a great number of sects, as Brownists, Anabaptists, Independents, Fifth Monarchy men , Quakers and divers others, all commonly called by the name fanatics; insomuch as there was no so dangerous an enemy to the Presbyterians, as this brood of their own hatching." See also "B"'s statement on 172.
[61] Hobbes (1990, 57).
[62] Dryden (1847, 112). Notice in the first line of this passage the echo of Yeats' "Sailing to Byzantium," from which the title of this work is drawn.

for they understand nothing in it but that they may lawfully rebel), that I fear the commonwealth will never be cured."[63] Christianity must be limited to charity and belief in Christ.

This is not to say, though, that England will cease to be sick with desire, as we shall see in the conclusion.

We see here also an important corollary, not stated directly in *Leviathan*, to Hobbes's proposal that the sovereign must be authoritative in matters of biblical interpretation. This can only be effective if theology is no longer the central part of Christianity. If the core of Christianity turns out to be, as Hobbes says it is, faith that Jesus is the Christ, and that the duty of good Christians is, as "A" says, "a quiet waiting for the coming again of our blessed Saviour, and in the mean time a resolution to obey the King's laws," then the religious debates that predated the Civil War were really of no importance.[64] In fact the primary goal of all Hobbes's theological speculation, in *Leviathan* and elsewhere, is excising theology from religion, or at least relegating it to a matter of political indifference.

The suggestion that religion must become less about theology and more about inner conviction (with all the caveats outlined in Chapter 4) is hidden beneath a more complicated and circular set of arguments at the end of the first dialogue. "A" suggests that the universities will not be reformed until a monarch appears with the virtues of both Henry VII and Henry VIII. The former filled the state coffers, and the latter exercised "an early severity."[65] One problem with this suggestion from Hobbes's point of view is that it relies on a chance coincidence of personal attributes in some future king, rather than the institutional solution we find in *Leviathan* and *De Cive*. It is not characteristic of Hobbes to rely for a state's stability on the personal virtues of the sovereign. "B," in fact, takes this suggestion to mean that the king should ignore the university divines "till he have gotten ready money enough to levy and maintain a sufficient army and then to fall upon them and destroy them."[66] "A" dismisses this as a "horrible, unchristian, and inhuman" design, and says that the army should only be used "to suppress any rebellion, and to take from his enemies all hope of success, that they may not dare trouble him in the reformation of the Universities."[67] The strategy, then, seems to be that

---

[63] Hobbes (1990, 57).
[64] Hobbes (1990, 58).
[65] Hobbes (1990, 57).
[66] Hobbes (1990, 58).
[67] Hobbes (1990, 58).

the sovereign, once he can pay the army properly, can remove the offensive members of the university and replace them with more acceptable figures. This, though, seems to presuppose that the army's pay will render soldiers impervious to the words of ministers and the learned doctors in the universities. But this seems to contradict what "B" says in response to this proposal: "But what shall force the army? ... I am therefore of your opinion, both that men may be brought to a love of obedience by preachers and gentlemen that imbibe good principles in their youth at the Universities."[68] The army, then, is to enforce the reformation of the universities, but must first be brought to a love of obedience by the universities that are in need of reformation because they teach seditious doctrines.[69]

This cannot be what Hobbes had in mind. If we step back, we see that "B" initially understood "A" to be suggesting a direct method of reforming the clergy: "destroy them" with an army. "A" then suggested a less direct method: the army will serve as a deterrent while the sovereign presumably makes more acceptable university appointments. But this, too, would seem to be too direct given that the army is driven more by ideas, and good principles learned while young, than their pay. Hobbes's actual plan for the reformation of the universities must be still more subtle. The reformation he has in mind must originate entirely on the plane of ideas.

The most obvious way to accomplish this goal is through the establishment of a civil religion that would reinforce obedience to the crown by teaching that "the civil laws are God's laws."[70] As I have shown, though, Hobbes did not think it very likely that the theology he proposed in *Leviathan* would be taken seriously, let alone be adopted in its entirety by any particular sovereign. As I also have shown, Hobbes wanted to remove theology itself from the center of Christianity. Hobbes, in fact, faced a set of serious and practically irreversible obstacles to the

---

[68] Hobbes (1990, 59).
[69] Later in the work, 193, "B" points out a similarly close relationship between power and ideas:

> For they that keep an army and cannot master it, must be subject to it as much as he that keeps a lion in his house. The temper of all Parliaments, since the time of Queen Elizabeth, has been the same with the temper of this Parliament; and shall always be such as long as the Presbyterians and men of democratical principles have the like influence upon elections.

Holmes (1990, 138–9) touches on the need to convince the army before the army can force anyone else, but does not see this circularity.

[70] Hobbes (1990, 58).

establishment of a civil religion. As we see most clearly in *Behemoth*, the translation of the Bible into English and its wide dissemination among an increasingly literate public inevitably led to large numbers of sects that disagreed about just about every aspect of Christianity. The possibility of imposing an authoritative version of Christianity from the seat of government seemed very unlikely. If Hobbes was going to defuse the danger posed by religion, he had to work with the fragmentation of Christianity rather than against it.

The ideal solution would be the kind of Lockean toleration that can only be seen dimly in Hobbes's philosophy. The pre-condition for that toleration is lessening religious certainty among the devout. This is Hobbes's goal in wanting to reform the university; a goal he accomplished along with others such as Bacon, by altering what the grounds of certainty are. *Behemoth* is largely a portrait of the obstacles Hobbes faced; a society driven to violence by a wide array of incoherent and irrational long- and short-term motives, men who seemed equally willing to fight and die for a small amount of money or to save their eternal souls. The university of the future would have to make men more reasonable, if not entirely rational. In a different time and place, Hobbes might have thought that a small republic devoted to the gods and to virtue would have been the best solution. He recognized that belief was natural and ineradicable, as was the desire to be a part of a greater whole. The fact of Christianity interpreted through a Protestant lens, along with a complex and highly stratified society, led him to conceive of an entirely new political solution that would rely on transforming the entire culture through education, understood in the widest possible sense of the term.

Looking back, Hobbes's efforts seem aimed at the emancipation of the passions, or playing the passions off against each other.[71] While not wrong, however, this interpretation overlooks the extent to which Hobbes had to suppress or undermine what had been the extraordinarily powerful passion that is the desire to overcome death and achieve some kind of permanence. The image of a state of nature is often regarded, correctly, as a major part of Hobbes's educative strategy. Part of the advantage of presenting man this way is showing glory seekers as being quite insane given the lack of any overarching structure that would carry their glory beyond the present. Hobbes in *Behemoth* is engaged in a similarly reductionist project, which he knows is an abstraction from man's natural desire for transcendence. The reasonable man educated in

---

[71] This was part of Hirschaman's thought in *The Passions and the Interests* (1997).

Hobbes's rational university knows that those hopes are founded on dreams and illusions foisted on the uneducated by ambitious charlatans. What is certain is what we can see and feel, and the only kind of hedge against death is the acquisition of property and longevity achieved through health and safety.

To reiterate, Hobbes wants as much as possible to reduce the competing claims of those involved in the war to a concern for political power and domination, but he also indicates that underneath these power struggles is a desire for immortality of one kind or another. Both are probably simultaneously at work in a confused way for the actual actors, but Hobbes wants to downplay the importance of transcendent motives. If men's desires extend only to longevity and the honor that the state alone can provide, they are likely to be more obedient and peaceful. This is the shift in beliefs Hobbes wants to effect. The power of the mighty, we recall, is founded on the beliefs of the people.

GEORGE MONCK: THE PERFECT HOBBESIAN GENERAL

The men of the better sort Hobbes complains of wanted not only the form of government of the Greeks or Romans, or something like it, but also the great actions which were immortalized in the pages of Plutarch's *Lives*. These men wanted to be famous as much as they wanted a republic. The stilted prose of *Behemoth* is not calculated to inspire the same sorts of feelings. From Hobbes we learn that these aspiring democrats were susceptible to the same destabilizing impulse as their ancient forebears: the desire for rule, victory and domination that so often accompanies the desire for long-lasting fame.

The most important figure in the destruction of the monarchy, and the execution of the monarch, turned out to be Oliver Cromwell. Hobbes leaves no doubt that Cromwell's ultimate goal was always sovereignty. "A" tells us that taking Ireland was "one step more towards Cromwell's exaltation to the throne."[72] Fairfax laying down his command was "another step to the sovereign power." After the Dutch War, "Cromwell wanted now but one step to the end of his ambition, and that was to set his foot upon the neck of this Long Parliament," and, after Parliament dissolved themselves, they "surrendered their power to Cromwell that had given it to them."[73] This sovereignty, moreover, was

[72] Hobbes (1990, 163).
[73] Hobbes (1990, 163, 166, 179, 183).

George Monck: The Perfect Hobbesian General

to last until Cromwell's death and to pass to a successor named by him, which turned out to be his eldest son Richard.

Cromwell was not alone in wanting to replace the king. "B" sees clearly that if parliament wins the war, "they must be beholding for it to the valour, good conduct, or felicity of those to whom they give the command of their armies; especially to the general ... so that it will be in his power, either to take the government upon himself, or to place it where he himself thinks good."[74] This is no surprise, since, according to "A," "it is the desire of most men to bear rule; but few of them know what title one has to it more than another, besides the right of the sword."[75] Thus, we see that Cromwell had a competitor for power in General Lambert, and Richard Cromwell was dispossessed of his sovereignty by the machinations of both Lambert and Fleetwood.[76] These maneuvers, though, were not supported by any long-term plan: "For from the beginning of the rebellion, the method of ambition was constantly this: first to destroy, and then to consider what they should set up."[77]

The great exception to this rule was General George Monck who appears near the end of the work and clears the way for the Restoration. Monck had a plan, according to Hobbes, and did not have the ambition for rule or presumably fame that characterized Cromwell and many other figures in the work. Monck is the hero of the work as the last line of *Behemoth* attests: "You have told me little of the general till now in the end: but truly, I think the bringing of his little army entire out of Scotland up to London, was the greatest stratagem that is extant in history."[78] Monck is a model for Hobbes because his ambition runs only to stability, and yet he has the sort of courage we saw in Chapter 6 that Hobbes's state relies on. Monck, who never achieved the fame of Cromwell before him, or Marlborough after, exemplifies the medium-range self-interest that is not primarily concerned with immortal glory.

Monck was a general on the Royalist side of the Civil War.[79] When he was captured, parliament refused to exchange him for any number of prisoners, but the king supplied him with money in the Tower. After the execution of Charles, though, Monck pledged allegiance to Cromwell and served him loyally in Ireland and Scotland for the duration of the

---

[74] Hobbes (1990, 109).
[75] Hobbes (1990, 193).
[76] Hobbes (1990, 191–7).
[77] Hobbes (1990, 192).
[78] Hobbes (1990, 204).
[79] For Monck's biography, I have relied on Jamison (1975) and Guizot (1838).

Protectorship. After a bloody end to a siege that earned Monck a reputation as "the butcher of Dundee," he went on as governor to earn the respect and even affection of Scotland. Richard Cromwell was, in the meantime, forced from power by the army, and resigned the Protectorship, "A" says, "to nobody."[80] Monck then raised money from the Scots and led an army south to London without giving any hint about his ultimate intentions. Oliver Cromwell, before he died, had suspected Monck of having Royalist sympathies, but parliament had reason to believe he would support them. After demanding that the regular army withdraw from London, Monck "declared himself (with the city) for a free Parliament."[81] He forced the Long Parliament, with the previously secluded members, to formally dissolve itself and call new elections. The new parliament, as Monck suspected, was overwhelmingly Royalist, and the king was subsequently restored to the throne.

Through his recounting of the Civil War in *Behemoth*, Hobbes barely mentions Monck. The fact of his capture is entirely omitted, and there is only a cursory mention of his actions at Dundee.[82] The effect Hobbes intends here, as "B" suggests, is of Monck appearing unexpectedly from nowhere to restore order. *Behemoth* generally depicts man as power hungry and wholly self-interested. There are numerous suggestions that the leading generals both wanted and were capable of seizing control of the country. What is remarkable in this context is that Monck did not attempt to take the sovereignty for himself. In *the Elements of Law*, written long before the execution of Charles I, Hobbes had said that "if there be any man, who by the advantage of the reign of him that is dead, hath strength enough to hold the multitude in peace and obedience, he may lawfully, or rather is by the law of nature obliged so to do."[83] Monck, then, in Hobbes's eyes, might have been justified in establishing himself as a new Lord Protector for life. He had done well enough in Scotland. The republican party, preferring another Protector to the return of the king, which they feared was imminent, offered Monck sovereignty. Guizot records the following conversation on the matter:

"The people" said [Scott and Haslerig], "are always bad judges of what is best for themselves; and therefore, since a single person is necessary, there cannot be one fitter than yourself for the office; and in this we have good grounds to believe all the

---

[80] Hobbes (1990, 194).
[81] Hobbes (1990, 202).
[82] Hobbes (1990, 171) is the first mention of Monck.
[83] Hobbes (1999, 122).

George Monck: The Perfect Hobbesian General

good people of the nation will concur with us." Monk [sic] continued immovable. "I have the example of Cromwell," he said, "and I have reason to avoid the rock on which that family was split." They answered that Cromwell had usurped the power against the will of the army and the respectable classes; "you will, on the contrary, have their unanimous consent," said they, "and under what name and title you please to accept it." "We will give you 100,000 signatures," exclaimed Haslerig in his petulant manner. Monk persevered in rejecting with indifference the offer of fortunes which were too unreal to tempt him.[84]

That Monck did not attempt to claim sovereignty may have been due to his recognition that he was not, in fact, strong enough to control England, despite his success in Scotland. This alone sets him apart from the other actors in the work, who, as we have seen, were not adept at longer-term planning. Monck, it seems, understood that the peace and stability of the country depended on the return of the king.

Hobbes takes it for granted that Monck wanted to reestablish monarchy, and that in doing so he was following the will of the people: "The general knew very well his own and their forces ... and what generally city and country wished for, which was the restitution of the King: which to bring about, there needed no more but to come with his army (though not very great) to London."[85] In depicting Monck this way, Hobbes was following his source. Heath, who Hobbes says supplies the narrative of the war itself, makes only the following statement about Monck's motives:

According to the Parliament resolves to dissolve themselves, and being pressed by the General, whose well governed impatience of the Kings return, permitted not the least delay in that dangerous place, Writts were ordered to be issued out for Election of Members in the ensuing Parliament, in the name *Of the Keepers of the Liberty of England by Authority of Parliament.*[86]

It was not obvious, though, during Monck's march, that this was his aim. The Rump believed, or at least hoped, that his goal was securing their own position and eliminating Lambert as competitor for sovereignty. Neither was it clear to Clarendon, a contemporary observer, that Monck was aiming at a restoration of the king rather than his own aggrandizement. For Clarendon, Monck's dissimulation was really a cover for his own ambition:

---

[84] Guizot (1838, 231–2).
[85] Hobbes (1990, 199).
[86] Heath (1663, 754).

For without doubt he had not to this hour entertained any purpose or thought to serve [the king], but was really of the opinion he expressed in his paper, that it was a work impossible; and desired nothing but that he might see a commonwealth established, in such a model as Holland was, where he had been bred, and that himself might enjoy the authority and place which the Prince of Orange possessed in that government.[87]

For Clarendon too, Monck was simply forced by circumstances into restoring the king:

And at that time there is no question the general had not the least thought or purpose ever to contribute to the King's restoration, the hope whereof he believed to be desperate; and the disposition that did grow in him afterwards did arise from those accidents which fell out, and even obliged him to undertake that which proved so much to his profit and glory.[88]

What is striking in these passages is how well they would have fit in with the general tenor of Hobbes's *Behemoth*. Hobbes could have portrayed Monck as one more ambitious general who just happened to contribute to the restoration despite his real ambitions. Hobbes could then have drawn the lesson that without a solid education in Hobbesian political science, stability is only achieved by accident. This is no doubt one of the main messages of *Behemoth*, but Hobbes also wanted to portray Monck as a model to emulate. It turns out that the verdict of more recent historians is that Hobbes was correct about Monck's intentions.[89] Hobbes wants us to see that while many aristocrats and generals were short-sighted and enamored of the writings of Cicero and Aristotle, Monck understood the importance of stability, even at the possible expense of immortal fame.

From the point of view of an Alexander, Monck is not a particularly impressive figure, and it is true that historians have not in general been very fond of him. But from Hobbes's point of view, Monck really is a hero. From the point of view of those who think only of heaven and hell, or everlasting fame, Monck's concern for stability and his apparent lack of ambition for rule appears short-sighted, and perhaps even cowardly. But Hobbes has done everything he can in *Behemoth* to make everyone but Monck appear truly short-sighted. None of them, according to Hobbes, knew what was good for them. From this perspective, Monck comes to light as the most far-sighted character

---

[87] Hyde, Earl of Clarendon (2009, 413).
[88] Hyde, Earl of Clarendon (2009, 404).
[89] This is the verdict of Jamison, as well as Guizot's editor, Guizot (1838, 140).

in the work, and is, in fact, a model of what would come to be known as enlightened self-interest. Once immortality is no longer a reasonable option, the actions of someone like Monck appear eminently reasonable. This was Hobbes's goal in presenting Monck as the hero of *Behemoth*.

8

The Afterlife of Immortality

Hobbes was extraordinarily successful in his rhetorical strategy, a main goal of which was the manipulation of how individuals think about death and immortality. If he had been as successful as I argue he was, we would expect to find evidence of his influence in the deepest bedrock of liberal thought. A survey of political philosophy as a field today suggests as much. The thought of Thomas Hobbes is a popular research topic for political theorists of all types. Despite still sometimes being seen as one of the villains of the canon, there is a sense among a preponderance of scholars that Hobbes somehow helped to lay the foundations of liberalism and has had a deep impact on modern Western thought generally.

Grappling with Hobbes has for many become tantamount to grappling with the core of modernity. Everyone who studies Hobbes and his relation to modern liberalism, though, is confronted with an obvious problem. While one can point to liberal elements in Hobbes's thought, such as his stress on equality and the consent of the people, it is impossible to avoid the fact that Hobbes also champions absolute monarchy, and seems to have a bleak view of human nature that leaves little room for ideas such as human rights or the universal dignity of man. And while some see the illiberal aspects of Hobbes's thought as the effects of his historical situation, or excessive worry about man's propensity for violence, others, such as Carl Schmitt, see Hobbes's emphasis on absolute sovereignty as the real core of the modern state, which liberals refuse to acknowledge.[1]

---

[1] The best-known example of this view comes from Carl Schmitt (2007; 2008).

In this concluding chapter, I will argue that understanding Hobbes's attempt to diminish our perception of the prospects for immortality sheds important light into many of the paradoxes of modern liberalism.

EQUALITY OF MORTALITY

The new view of death and immortality that Hobbes wants to inculcate requires the widespread acceptance of equality. Glory must be diluted and made available to all in the form of dignity, as I will argue in the following section. Every man must also be able to discern for himself the best way to achieve salvation, and whether such a thing is possible at all. This negates the need for a clergy that serves as the sole conduit through which man can attain heaven. It even negates the need for a clergy that offers guidance on such matters. Everyone is on an equal footing with respect to knowledge about heaven and hell.

It is not so much man's equal capacity to kill that serves as the foundation of human equality but his equal vulnerability to death. Human beings are all equal primarily because they are all equally mortal. The wise man dies as the fool, and there is no remembrance of the wise any more than of the fool. Once man is made to feel this, he will be open to seeing peace as the good on which all can agree.

"All men," Hobbes says, "agree on this, that Peace is Good."[2] The reason all men agree that peace is good turns out to be the fact that they continually dispute the definition of good and evil, "Nay, the same man, in divers times, differs from himselfe; and one time praiseth, that is, calleth Good, what another time he dispraiseth, and calleth Evil."[3] It is these disagreements that plunge mankind into continual warfare in the state of nature. And "consequently" men all agree on the fundamental goodness of peace.

The argument as it stands here is jarring and in need of caveats that Hobbes does not supply. On its face, it cannot be true that universal disagreement about what is good results in universal agreement about it. Even less can it be true that all men agree that peace is good because they are willing to fight and die to defend their own views of good and evil.

It could be true that all men agree that peace is one among many goods, but that this particular good is frequently overridden. This seems to be the case in *On Man*, where Hobbes says that "the greatest of goods for each is

---

[2] Hobbes (2012, 242).
[3] Hobbes (2012, 242).

his own preservation" and that death is the "greatest of all evils."[4] He immediately qualifies the latter superlative, though, by claiming that extreme pain is in fact worse than death, "and may lead men to number death among the goods," which means that death is not always the greatest evil.[5] He does not qualify the former statement by suggesting there could be a goal higher than preservation, but we have seen elsewhere his acknowledgment that, in fact, for many there are more important goods. If peace and preservation are to be the highest goals, these goods must be deflated since they are clearly in conflict with peace. This is, as I have been arguing, what Hobbes is doing with regard to ideas of transcendence that have throughout history driven men to disregard peace in favor of violence. Also, because of the peculiar rhetorical strategy Hobbes employs, he does not spell this out and leaves his argument for the goodness of peace in the incomplete state in which we find it.

It is quite striking how little time Hobbes spends defending the premise that peace is good. The entire thrust of his political philosophy is the creation of a stable and peaceful state. It is true that his explicit concern tends to be civil war, but it would be hard to deny that Hobbes hoped for a more pacific world generally. He spends a great deal of time exploring the roots of man's tendency for violence, and deals at length with the nature of sovereignty, but all of this is done with the aim of promoting peace, the goodness of which is never treated with any degree of philosophic rigor. In so doing, Hobbes sidesteps one of the major topics of philosophic investigation of neo-Thomists such as Vittoria and Bellarmine, namely, just war theory. Hobbes was aware of these long-standing debates, but characteristically chose not to engage with them. By assuming the goodness of peace rather than arguing for it, Hobbes treats a controversial proposition as obvious and inculcates it through insinuation.[6]

The assertion that self-preservation is "the greatest of goods" also stands in sharp contrast to the very powerful statements Hobbes makes in the eleventh chapter of *Leviathan* about the lack of any absolute good for man: "[T]here is no such *Finis ultimus*, (utmost ayme,) nor *Summum Bonum*, (greatest Good,) as is spoken of in the Books of the old Morall Philosophers."[7] And yes, this ultimately plays into Hobbes's argument:

[4] Hobbes (1998a).
[5] Hobbes (1998a, 49).
[6] As Kateb (1989, 373) notes, "the theory says nothing about why staying alive is the highest good."
[7] Hobbes (2012, 150). In the Latin here, Hobbes specifies that he is speaking of the "vitae praesentis."

because there is nothing worth dying for, peace becomes the greatest good by default. The image of the natural state Hobbes presents in chapter 13 of *Leviathan* is perfectly suited to make this point. There is no memory outside human civilization. Nothing that is built will last. The gods can threaten physical punishment, but cannot promise the eternal life we read of in the gospel. There is only a constant threat of violent death, to which even the strongest is subject. This equal capacity to kill is, in Hobbes's system, the foundation of human equality, on which in turn he bases his argument that sovereignty ultimately derives from the consent of the ruled.

The sense of equality that exists in the state of nature is supposed to persist in civil society. By nature, men will always strive to excel others, and demand that others rate them as they rate themselves. Apart from those who take pleasure in conquest, however, there are those who "would be glad to be at ease within modest bounds."[8] The system Hobbes describes is meant to subdue the former into accepting the humility of the latter. I have argued that Hobbes does not think his system can, or even should be, fully realized. He does, though, expect to curb the danger posed by the most prideful and dangerous elements of society. Hobbes describes these prideful men in chapter 13 of *Leviathan* as those who take "pleasure in contemplating their own power in the acts of conquest, which they pursue farther than their security requires."[9] I have argued that this depiction is an abstraction that comes very close to the truth. Rather than attacking the longing for immortality as the source of political instability, Hobbes claims that a universal struggle for power, stemming from man's pride, is the root of the problem. As Hobbes knew, it is not always easy to distinguish between these two drives. Those who emerge as most powerful from the state of nature tend to devote enormous resources to monuments against time. This fact is almost never mentioned in Hobbes's political writings. In *The Whole Art of Rhetoric*, though, he acknowledges it: "The parts of *honour* are sacrifices, monuments, rewards, dedication of places, precedence, sepulchres, statues."[10]

The Hobbesian sovereign is not Minos, though, or a pharaoh. His subjects are not bound to dedicate their lives to him. He is the religious authority, but rather than being divine, he is a disposable vice-regent for an absent god. In order to focus man's attention on coercive power as the

---

[8] Hobbes (2012, 190).
[9] Hobbes (2012, 190).
[10] Hobbes (1845a, 429).

source of sovereignty he must import from the state of nature the sense that there is nothing in civil society greater and more permanent than the individual. There is no Athens he can join in perpetual union. In order to persuade, though, Hobbes must willfully ignore the monuments, literary, artistic and architectural, that have existed since the beginning of civilization and which the powerful have always sought to create as bulwarks against their own mortality. The buildings that are lacking in the state of nature are "commodious" or "*commoda*" in Latin, rather than monumental.[11] By deemphasizing this fundamental element of human civilization, Hobbes makes the individual feel most of all his isolation and vulnerability.

Under the sovereign, no one's desire for power or honor should be able to disturb the tranquility of the state. This feat cannot be accomplished simply through the overwhelming physical coercive power of the sovereign. The threat of violent death is simply not an effective check against those who long for immortality. The equalizing power cannot be a large police force. It must operate on the plane of ideas. If no one can be certain of their prospects for an eternal life in another world, the power of priests must diminish. If a man is seen as crazy or at least very foolish for risking his life to defend his honor in a duel, a powerful and perennial path to remembrance has been closed off. If Hobbes can be successful on this cultural level, every individual will be equally uncertain about whether there is anything beyond the life we have here and now. The recognition that everyone is subject to this fate may be a source of compassion. As Hobbes says, "To grieve because of another's evil, that is, to feel another's pain and to suffer with him, that is, to imagine that another's evil could happen to oneself, is called compassion."[12] In the state of nature, our equality is based on our equal ability to kill, but beneath this there is an equal vulnerability to the real finality of death.

MODERN ANXIETY

I have argued throughout this work that Hobbes recognized this desire for permanence as something inherent in man. He thought that many, or even most, people could be distracted from it in various ways but that it would ultimately persist in various ways for some. For many, the suppressed or

---

[11] Hobbes (2012, 192).
[12] Hobbes (1998a, 61).

muted quest for immortality would be experienced as anxiety-inducing loss, which was, however, preferable to interminable religious warfare.

This implies that Hobbes did not attempt a complete break with the culture in which he lived.[13] Nor did he think such a break was possible. This becomes especially apparent when we consider the complex way in which Hobbes both attacks and appropriates elements of Christianity. Those who criticized *Leviathan* in the seventeenth century for its atheism and its extreme heterodoxy were on the right track. There can be little doubt that Hobbes attacked and ridiculed many aspects of Christianity as it was practiced in his time. One of the striking facts about his political project, though, is the extent to which it incorporates on a deep level many of the core elements of Christianity. Peace, charity and even restless anxiety can all be seen as key Christian concepts.

Hobbes, like Francis Bacon, thought that philosophy should be primarily charitable. In language reminiscent of what we have seen in *De Corpore* and elsewhere, Bacon admonishes those who seek knowledge to do so "for the benefit and use of life," and urges them to "perfect and govern it in charity."[14] Hobbes too, despite what his detractors said about his negative view of human nature and his dangerous atheism, had as his goal the betterment of man's estate here on earth. This was not self-evidently the goal of all previous philosophers. Insofar as Christianity is a religion of peace and charity, Hobbes's critiques of Christian views of heaven and hell made the world more Christian.[15] Of course, though, this required the increase of the desire to live as long as possible here on earth.

Rousseau saw that Hobbes was largely responsible for a greater concern with longevity and an increased fear of death in man. As he says in *Emile*, "We believe that man has a lively love of his own preservation, and that is true, but we do not see that this love, the way we feel it, is in large part the work of man."[16] Although Hobbes did not want man to think constantly of death, or to live in constant fear, there is an underlying sense of restless anxiety that is connected to the awareness that this life is quite possibly all there is. Man reacts to this sense not by abandoning himself to despair, but with a feverish desire to make the most of this life. That is, he

---

[13] Hobbes was not, in my view, a proponent of the "radical Enlightenment" that Jonathan Israel describes. See Israel (2002).

[14] Bacon (1989, 16).

[15] To make this point clearer, we can compare Hobbes to Machiavelli, for whom peace was not self-evidently a worthy goal.

[16] Rousseau (1966, 96, my translation). For a lengthier argument on Rousseau's indictment of Hobbes's attempt to make man fear death more, see McClure (2008).

engages in a race against death that he cannot win. And because here and now may be as close as we will get to heaven, it is intolerable that another might have it better than we do. Hence the frantic attempt to outdo one's fellows in every possible way. Man, Hobbes says, is "famished even by future hunger."[17]

The feeling that there will never be enough, that life is unending restlessness with little prospect of satisfaction, did not characterize life in the ancient world. At the very least it was not as all-consuming as Hobbes presents it to be. A character such as Alcibiades in Thucydides may have been driven by a constant desire for power and success, but he had a clear goal.[18] Alcibiades knows that a man like him "shall as long as he liveth be envied ... but with posterity they shall have kindred claimed of them, though there be none, and his country will boast of him, not as of a stranger or one that had been a man of lewd life, but as their own citizen and one that achieved worthy or laudable acts."[19] There is something more indeterminate in the restless desire for power after power that Hobbes describes. This is an anxiety that cannot be sated.

Although it would take us too far afield to examine this claim in detail, there is more than a passing resemblance between the restlessness Hobbes describes in chapter 11 of *Leviathan* and the Christian concept of anxiety. In a typically Christian expression of this, Augustine, in the opening lines of his *Confessions*, says that "our heart is restless until it rests in you."[20] He links this sentiment to the fact that man "bear[s] his mortality with him."[21] The description of human nature in Hobbes, which has always fascinated readers who cannot help but admit that it is at least partially correct, may well be primarily a description of Christian man. At the very least, Hobbes seems to be drawing on this Christian sense of restlessness. For Hobbes, though, unlike Augustine, there is no certainty of an eventual resting place because it is not clear that there is a God. This makes the restlessness of modern man more acute.

---

[17] Hobbes (1998a, 40).
[18] Hobbes may well have been thinking of characters such as Alcibiades when, in the Latin *Leviathan*, he speaks of those who "for reasons of pride and glory would wish to conquer the whole world," Hobbes (2012, 191).
[19] Thucydides (1989, 386).
[20] Augustine (1998, 3).
[21] Augustine (1998, 3 (quoting 2 Corinthians 4:10)). We can also note here that for Kierkegaard, anxiety is a Christian concept. For him, anxiety is, "altogether different from fear and similar concepts that refer to something definite, whereas anxiety is freedom's actuality as the possibility of possibility." Kierkegaard (1980, 42).

Restlessness, though, is not the same as hopelessness. And hopelessness was not Hobbes's goal. Man can never really be entirely free of the desire to overcome death somehow, and so can never be in complete despair. Hobbes knows that those who can hope for nothing have nothing to lose, and are therefore extremely dangerous. This is the premise of his right to resistance. Man does not resist because he has a special right to do so. Men in despair are prone to viciousness. A nation of atheists may be in the same position as Moloch in Milton's *Paradise Lost*, who,

> now fiercer by despair.
> His trust was with th'Eternal to be deemed
> Equal in strength, and rather than be less
> Cared not to be at all; with that care lost
> Went all his fear: of God, or Hell, or worse
> He reck'd not.[22]

Kant later claimed that the Enlightenment represented man's emancipation from his self-imposed immaturity. The goal of Enlightenment was freedom for mankind. From another point of view, though, the Enlightenment replaced one kind of freedom with another. The promise of Christianity was, in fact, freedom from mortality. Belief in Christ meant that Christians would never die. This is the meaning of the traditionally eight-sided baptisteries attached to Christian cathedrals; seven sides for the seven days of the *seculum* and the eighth side for the emancipation from worldly time. In a simplified formulation, with Christianity, one was bound on earth, but free in the next world. With Enlightenment, one is free on earth, but cannot escape mortality. Christianity arguably offered a greater reward than was available in Judaism or in the ancient religions of Greece or Rome. The loss of such a reward was inevitably met with a greater inner-protest than, for example, the transition from paganism to Christianity. In Bede's *Ecclesiastical History of the English People* of 731, for example, the description (admittedly from a Christian point of view) of the conversion of an Anglo-Saxon tribe is telling. In this scene, one of the king's chief men says,

Your Majesty, when we compare the present life of man on earth with that time of which we have no knowledge, it seems to me like the swift flight of a single sparrow through the banqueting-hall where you are sitting with your thegns and counsellors. In the midst there is a comforting fire to warm the hall; outside the storms of winter rain or snow are raging. This sparrow flies swiftly through one door of the hall, and out through another. While he is inside, he is safe from

[22] Milton (2008, 51).

the winter storms; but after a few moments of comfort, he vanishes from sight into the wintry world from which he came. Even so, man appears on earth for a little while; but of what went before this life or of what follows, we know nothing. Therefore, if this new teaching has brought any more certain knowledge, it seems right that we should follow it.[23]

The move from limited knowledge of what happens after death to more knowledge, and greater possibilities, was attractive. The move in the other direction, from knowledge of the afterlife to ignorance of it, less so. Being promised eternal life, and then having that promise rescinded, could be deeply disquieting.

We recall that for Lucretius, the absence of the gods was comforting, because they could inflict no more punishments. For Christians, the absence of God was the equivalent of being in hell. Christians always had to wrestle with the prospect that their religion was not true. Faith has to be faith against great odds. This means the kind of restlessness Hobbes draws on was something that always existed just under the surface for many Christians, and which therefore was not alien. Accepting Hobbes's grim verdict about human nature and the nature of the universe has something of the character of accepting a truth one always dreaded might be true.[24] Christians, like Bede, were aware of the chaos and miasma that existed outside of their religion. Man had been used to living within ever-wider horizons, and Christianity offered perhaps the widest. What Hobbes offered was something narrower. The Enlightenment, in an extreme formulation, represents the opening of the widest possibilities on earth for mankind at the expense of closing off of other possibilities.

The fragmentation of Christianity into so many sects in Hobbes's day, along with the conflicting ethics of religion and honor made it, in his eyes, impossible to unite a political regime by any kind of cultural means that had ever been used before. Hobbes sought a settlement that he knew not everyone would find entirely fulfilling. He did not think man would go gently. Nor would Hobbes have been surprised to find man sick with desire and yearning to sail to Byzantium.

---

[23] Bede (1990, 129–30).
[24] As I pointed out in Chapter 3 as well, Hobbes suspected Aristotle of writing his *Metaphysics* in a way that would make it "consonant to, and corroborative of their Religion," Hobbes (2012, 1082). If Hobbes saw that Aristotle wrote his philosophy in order to fit somehow with his state's religion, and to alter it somewhat, it seems entirely possible that Hobbes would use the same strategy in his time.

DIGNITY AND DISENCHANTMENT

The desire to overcome death, Hobbes thought, was a permanent human aspiration. The ways in which this desire manifests itself, though, vary widely across time and place. Hobbes wanted to subdue the most dangerous aspects of this longing, those connected with honor and religion, and, as we have just seen, his emphasis on human equality was tied in part to that project. Could he know what new manifestations of the desire for immortality might arise once more traditional means had been called radically into question? Certainly he never raises this question explicitly. We can, though, discern the outlines of an answer by pointing out certain resonances between Hobbes's thought and more recent strands of thinking about modernity, and in particular the ideas of dignity and disenchantment. In this and the following section, I suggest that the longing for immortality remains in modernity, but is stifled and manifests itself in truncated ways. The concept of dignity, for those who are in favor of the modern turn, and disenchantment, for critics of modernity, are two powerful examples of this.

The disenchantment and sense of loss identified by many critics of modernity can be traced back at least in part to the darkening of traditional paths to immortality. I have argued throughout this work that Hobbes recognized this desire for permanence as something inherent in man. He thought that many, or even most, people could be distracted from it in various ways but that it would ultimately persist in various ways for some. For many, the suppressed or muted quest for immortality would be experienced as anxiety-inducing loss, which was, however, preferable to interminable religious warfare.

As mentioned above, what drove Hobbes was the vision of a more peaceful world. His intention was charitable. It could be that this intention itself became the impulse for a new way of understanding transcendence, unforeseen by Hobbes. If we cannot live on in heaven, or through the memory of our homeland, perhaps we can be a part of a universal human destiny. Consider the following passage from Kant's "Idea for a Universal History":

> If we assume a plan of nature, we have grounds for greater hopes. For such a plan opens up the comforting prospect of a future in which we are shown from afar how the human race eventually works its way upward to a situation in which all the germs implanted by nature can be developed fully, and in which man's destiny can be fulfilled here on earth.[25]

---

[25] Kant (2000, 52–3).

Kant's ideas about history can be seen as a further development of something nascent in Hobbes, which also represents a new manifestation of the desire for immortality. If we set aside the complexity of Kant's thought about the immortality of the soul, we can see in this passage the spirit that undergirds a great deal of subsequent thinking about man and politics, that man is in need of comfort because his destiny no longer lies beyond the earth. Neither does his destiny lie in any particular political regime. What gives meaning to mortality is the promise that there is a destiny for the human race to which we may contribute. We must see ourselves as part of this grand process and perhaps try to further it. Hobbes did not have this providential view of history, but he did work for progress toward a more rational political order that would benefit even the least of men.

So too can Kant's ideas about the importance of autonomy be seen as the extension of simple longevity into something almost spiritual. For Kant, and the vast majority of subsequent liberal thinkers, man as such deserves recognition. This recognition, at its heart, means being alive in the eyes of another.[26] The individual must be recognized for what he is here and now, because here and now may be all there is. There may be a future destiny for mankind, but one's own destiny is now, and one's hopes must be realized now. Taken to its extreme, one's life is a work of art that must be acknowledged now if it is to have any meaning. The longing for dignity, in short, may be a new expression of the now unfulfillable desire for immortality.

While this can, and is, seen by many as a positive development over the subjection to authority of past ages, others view the modern world as disenchanted, and mortality as fundamentally meaningless. Charles Taylor, for example, discussing Tocqueville, Kierkegaard and Nietzsche, notes that "[t]he worry has been repeatedly expressed that the individual lost something important along with the larger social and cosmic horizon of action. Some have written of this as the loss of a heroic dimension of life. People no longer have a sense of a higher purpose, of something worth dying for."[27] With the sense of loss Taylor describes, the absolute finality

---

[26] Cf. Kojève (2007, 211): man,

> exists as a human being only to the extent that he is *recognized*: recognition of a man by another is his very being ... in order to be *realized* as a human being, man must be able to risk his life for recognition. It is this risk of life (*Wagen des Lebens*) which is the genuine birth of man, if it is carried out as a result of the desire for recognition alone.

[27] Taylor (1991, 3–4).

of death becomes for many too horrible even to contemplate. Camus articulates this feeling well when he says that human existence "in its exalted and tragic forms, is only and can only be a prolonged protest against death, a violent accusation against the universal death penalty."[28]

It would be hard to deny that there is more than a passing resemblance between the kind of life Hobbes promotes and Nietzsche's description of the last man, who "lives longest," and believes that "[f]ormerly, all the world was mad."[29] Recall that for Hobbes, a madman was one who put his life in danger needlessly. Nietzsche plays on the widespread sense that the real trajectory of modernity has been a movement from error and superstition to truth and reason. The real cost of such transition, according to Nietzsche, has been that man can no longer strive for anything very great. He can no longer "*give birth to a dancing star.*" The last man is rather concerned above all with health and security: "'We have invented happiness,' say the last men, and they blink ... One has one's little pleasure for the day and one's little pleasure for the night: but one has regard for health."[30] The last men, living at the end of history, are tired: "One no longer becomes poor or rich: both require too much exertion. Who still wants to rule? Who obey? Both require too much exertion."[31]

Nietzsche, to simplify, thought that the drive to truth that was responsible for the modern predicament was in fact caused by an underlying and pervasive will to power.[32] In particular, it was an impulse to dominate on the part of Christians that, in a complex way, asserted itself and eventually manifested itself as liberal democracy.[33] Eventually, in what Nietzsche calls "a great ladder of religious cruelty," man in effect sacrificed his own God to this drive, and left himself with no hope of comfort or future bliss.[34] Discovering the truth meant rising above the horizons within which man had always found meaning, and coming to see them as

---

[28] Camus, *The Rebel*, quoted in Dallmayr (1969, 630).
[29] Nietzsche (1982, 129–30).
[30] Nietzsche (1982, 129–30).
[31] Nietzsche (1982, 130).
[32] Nietzsche (1989, 136): "[philosophers'] 'knowing' is *creating*, their creating is a legislation, their will to truth is – *will to power.*"
[33] Nietzsche (1989, 116): "the *democratic* movement is the heir of the Christian movement."
[34] Nietzsche (1989, 67): "Finally – what remained to be sacrificed? At long last, did one not have to sacrifice for once whatever is comforting, holy, healing; all hope, all faith in hidden harmony, in future blisses and justices? Didn't one have to sacrifice God himself and, from cruelty against oneself, worship the stone stupidity, gravity, fate, the nothing?"

groundless. The Christian belief in the immortal soul could be explained, and largely dispelled, by describing it as the product of a certain set of historical circumstances. For Nietzsche, and many others, those who engaged in this process were unaware of the ultimate grounds of their actions, and were themselves driven by forces they could not fully see or understand. Hobbes, who Nietzsche singles out as being responsible for the "mechanistic doltification of the world" and for "lowering the value of the concept of 'philosophy' for more than a century," was among this group.[35]

In Chapter 3, I argued that Hobbes was not driven primarily by a will to truth. He was agnostic about the truth of things we did not make ourselves and so took artistic license with his science in order to further his political project. One of the implicit arguments of this book has been that Hobbes knew exactly what he was doing and that both liberalism and the reactions against it we find in Nietzsche, Heidegger and others, owe a great debt to the intentional attempt by Hobbes to undermine the hope for immortality. In so doing, Hobbes had a specific political goal in mind that Nietzsche, and certainly Heidegger, do not take into account.[36] Seen from this perspective, it is in fact Nietzsche who is the dupe of Hobbes rather than Hobbes being the dupe of history. Nietzsche, like Taylor, does not consider the possibility that the disenchantment so many feel in the modern world was in fact a reaction Hobbes would have thought was a necessary evil.

Would the man who described life as a ceaseless desire for power after power that ends only in death have been surprised by Nietzsche's dissatisfaction with modern man? Would Nietzsche's description of man have been entirely novel to Hobbes? In fact, Hobbes had a model for something like the last man in Aristotle's *Rhetoric*. Hobbes may well have seen the depiction of small-souled old men in that work as a goal for his own project of cultural transformation. This description, which could almost have been uttered by Zarathustra in his indictment of the last man, is thus worth quoting at length. "Old men," Aristotle claims,

---

[35] Nietzsche (1989, 189).
[36] About the latter, Pippin (1999, 141), says,

> Nowhere does Heidegger seem sympathetic to the modern experience of an intense and well-motivated disappointment with the pre-modern tradition, the experience of long-entrenched and spectacular error (the Copernican issue being only the most notorious example), or with the political consequences of "methodologically unsecured" belief (the wars of religion so intertwined with the seventeenth century, rationalist excitement about security and universality).

are positive about nothing, and in everything they show an excessive lack of energy ... And neither their love nor their hatred is strong ... they love as if they would one day hate, and hate as if they would one day love. And they are little-minded [μικρόψυχοι, or "small-souled"], because they have been humbled by life; for they desire nothing great or uncommon, but only the necessaries of life ... And they are cowardly and inclined to anticipate evil ... they are chilled, whereas the young are hot, so that old age paves the way for cowardice, for fear is a kind of chill. And they are fond of life, especially in their last days ... And they are unduly selfish, for this also is littleness of mind. And they live not for the noble, but for the useful ... for the useful is a good for the individual, whereas the noble is good absolutely.[37]

Aristotle's small-souled man is fearful, concerned with what is useful, "there is more calculation than moral character" in his life, and he does not strive for anything great.[38] There are clearly important differences between this description and Hobbesian man, especially the constant striving for power that characterizes the latter. But Hobbes hopes to render that striving toothless and to direct it more to the mundane than the transcendent. In hindsight, this development appears as the ageing of man. Whether we look at it through Kant's – man's "emergence from his self-incurred immaturity" – or through Nietzsche's presentation of man at the end of history, after Hobbes, man appears older.[39]

The lack of a higher goal, though, in Hobbes's system, leaves a restless anxiety in Hobbesian man that we find in neither Aristotle's small-souled man, nor Nietzsche's last man (although perhaps in Nietzsche himself). Nietzsche urged man to "set a goal for himself" to "shoot the arrow of his longing beyond himself."[40] This entailed its own kind of restlessness, but one with a goal. Hobbes wanted to deny man such goals, and understood that "life is perpetual motion that, when it cannot progress in a straight line, is converted into circular motion."[41] What is restlessness if not circular motion with no goal? For Hobbes, history means primarily theological history, and in our time, one of his characters says, the only task left for man is "a quiet waiting for the coming again of our blessed Saviour."[42] Man, whose life is perpetual motion and perpetual striving, cannot help but experience a certain restlessness when it becomes clear that there is nothing for him to do but wait quietly for the end of days,

---

[37] Aristotle (2006, 251–3).
[38] Aristotle (2006, 255).
[39] Kant (2000, 54).
[40] Nietzsche (1982, 129).
[41] Hobbes (1998a, 54).
[42] Hobbes (1990, 58).

with no goal he himself can strive for. We saw in the introduction that some of the earliest critics of *Leviathan* noted its deeply disquieting effect, and that this was directly connected to Hobbes's attack on immortality.

In an insightful article on this topic, Jan Blits argues that "however much Hobbes expects modern science to contribute to man's happiness by increasing the commodities he may enjoy, Hobbesian fear proves to be not unlike what Kierkegaard, Heidegger, and others call anxiety (angst)."[43] This is because, Blits goes on, "[t]he core of man's being is his relation to the unalterably unknown. Thus, what at first seems to be existentialism's radical repudiation of the Enlightenment may be rather a distillation or culmination of its founding thought, for Enlightenment necessarily entails estrangement."[44] At least in the case of Hobbes, this estrangement was both fundamental to his project, and an intentional effect of his reconceptualization of man's possibilities.

Heidegger, for example, leveled perhaps the most scathing attack on the modern world. In *Being and Time*, he pinpointed the inability of *Dasein* to face its own mortality as the root of an inauthentic way of living.[45] In his later works, Heidegger claimed that the root of modernity's problems lay in what he called technology. Coincidentally, just as Hobbes spoke of "framing" the minds of his readers, and thus altering how they understood themselves and their possibilities, so he presents man as being trapped by the "frame" [*gestell*] of technology. As he conceives it, technology circumscribes thought, limiting it to rational calculation and quantification. This, Heidegger claims, has cut us off from the earth and the gods and leaves us either complacent and forgetful, or extremely anxious. This assessment is not too far from the instrumental reason Taylor speaks of or the mechanistic doltification for which Nietzsche blamed Hobbes.

The solution Heidegger put forth in *Being and Time* was what he called authenticity. The path to authenticity lay through a direct confrontation with our own mortality, and the experience of shock and wonder at the fact of our own existence. In later works, Heidegger extolled the "saving power" of poetry and spoke of the need for new gods. Through a more poetic way of living, we would establish, or reestablish, a connection with

---

[43] Blits (1989, 429).
[44] Blits (1989, 429).
[45] I take the view, that I cannot develop here, that although *Being in Time* seems to discuss man as such, there are good reasons to think that Heidegger is primarily concerned with modern man.

the earth and the gods. If seen from a high enough altitude, Heidegger's emphasis on the problem of mortality, and the importance of great works of art and poetry, along with the need for new gods, points to man's powerful, if now obscured, concern with overcoming death. Even the recognition that such an overcoming is impossible means that there has been a confrontation with the deep-seated need to do so. *Dasein*, like Hobbesian man, cannot easily bear the thought of its own mortality, and wants to persist. We have already noted, too, the vague similarity between Nietzsche and Kant on the possibility of some future historical destiny for man.[46]

One way or another, Kant, Heidegger and Nietzsche, as well as their innumerable followers, are all wrestling with the eclipse of traditional paths to immortality. As Robert Pippin claims, "Nietzsche and Heidegger fail to 'break free' of, or go beyond or behind modernity ... what they thought they had left behind simply reemerges."[47] The attempt by Hobbes to suppress or redirect the permanent desire for immortality, then, can be seen as one of the sources of both positive and negative reactions to modernity. If a key element of modernity was the undermining of previous visions of the afterlife, then modernity works against a permanent human aspiration that would inevitably reemerge in new and unexpected ways.

This goal of Hobbes's philosophy was not recognized by his contemporaries, but the Christian underpinning of much of the Enlightenment's attack on religion was recognized by others in hindsight. Another glance back at Nietzsche will be especially useful in showing this. In a well-known section of *The Gay Science*, he describes a madman who proclaims to "those who did not believe in God" that God was dead.[48] Despite apparently being atheists, the listeners do not take the madman's statement seriously. He is, after all, a madman. But from the point of view of the last men, formerly all the world was mad. Perhaps, then, this madman had some insight that was not yet available to his audience. In his interpretation of this passage, Heidegger claims that,

When unalloyed faith in God, as determined through the Church, dwindles away, when in particular the doctrine of faith, theology, in its role of serving as the normative explanation of that which is as a whole, is curtailed and thrust aside,

---

[46] Heidegger too saw a future destiny for the German *volk* with which Dasein could identify. The traditional idea of living on through one's state or nation is thus not alien to Heidegger's thought.
[47] Pippin (1999, 143).
[48] Nietzsche (1974, 181).

then the fundamental structuring, in keeping with which the fixing of goals, extending into the suprasensory, rules sensory, earthly life, is in no way shattered as well. Into the position of the vanished authority of God and of the teaching office of the Church steps the authority of conscience, obtrudes the authority of reason ... The flight from the world into the suprasensory is replaced by historical progress. The otherworldly goal of everlasting bliss is transformed into the earthly happiness of the greatest number.[49]

This seems to be what Nietzsche means when he says that "[m]odern philosophy, being an epistemological skepticism, is covertly or overtly, *anti-Christian* – although, to say this for the benefit of more refined ears, by no means anti-religious."[50]

Nietzsche, like Heidegger, does not seem to have recognized that this cultural transformation was an intended goal of early modern philosophy. He sees that "[s]ince Descartes ... all the philosophers seek to assassinate the old soul concept" but claims that what drove this attempt was an uncritical love of truth.[51] One of the arguments of this book, though, especially in Chapter 3, has been that Hobbes is far more ambivalent about the truth of scientific knowledge than many have taken him to be. There is a tremendous creativity in Hobbes's thought, and this is apparent in his scientific work *De Corpore* as much as anywhere else in his oeuvre.

A large part of the lasting infamy of *Leviathan* stems from its perceived negative, or bleak, view of human nature; of man as a grasping violent creature. But few careful readers of our time can come away without the impression of a strong charitable impulse on Hobbes's part, or the sense that, whether he was right or not, he thought real good would come from his philosophy. It would, I suspect, be going too far to suggest that Hobbes was a believer in the universal brotherhood of man. But it may be that insofar as this idea lay very deep in Christian culture, though obscured during the age of religious wars, Hobbes may have wanted to harness it to further his project.

Hobbes is not a theorist of dignity or recognition, but these core values of modern Western liberalism depend on the idea of equality, and Hobbes is a theorist of equality. It may, therefore, help to clarify these still obscure terms, dignity and recognition, if we trace them back to a possible origin in Hobbes. The importance of doing so becomes clear when we read from a contemporary scholar of dignity, that it is "the closest that we have to an

---

[49] Heidegger (1977, 64).
[50] Nietzsche (1989, 66).
[51] Nietzsche (1989, 66). On the philosophers' perennial searching for truth without knowing quite why see, for example, *Beyond Good and Evil* (1989, 9).

internationally accepted framework for the normative regulation of political life, and it is embedded in numerous constitutions, international conventions, and declarations."[52] The difficulty in defining the term dignity is a major concern of political theorists today, as is the connected issue of defining a system of rights in the absence of any specific definition of the good. By looking back to Hobbes, especially in light of what I have been arguing about the importance of equality to his thought on immortality, we may gain some insight.

Philip Pettit has put forward a well-known argument that Hobbes stands somehow at the origins of liberalism. For Pettit, Hobbes originated the notion that freedom could only mean freedom from physical coercion, including threats.[53] In so doing, Hobbes "was one of the earliest critics, and perhaps the most significant opponent, of the republican way of thinking about freedom and government."[54] In fact, Pettit goes on, this notion of freedom imperceptibly came to dominate liberal thought. When Rawls says, for example, that "liberty can be restricted only for the sake of liberty," he assumes, according to Pettit, that "law always represents a restriction on liberty, and reveals a conception of liberty that is directly continuous with that of Hobbes."[55]

Pettit does not, however, explore the reasons for this animus on Hobbes's part toward republicanism. At this point, the reason should be clear. Hobbes did not want citizens to believe their state had some independent reality of its own beyond the individual lives of its members. He did not want, as far as was possible, citizens to commit themselves to fighting to the death to defend their homeland. He wanted them to switch sides when the going got tough. There are limits to how successful such a strategy can be. Underlying this thought, though, we can see that Hobbes was an enemy of the very idea that one can be a part of a transcendent entity like a country or even a great family. Nothing that appears to confer life after death through devotion would exist in an ideal Hobbesian world. He would have been just as great an enemy of the idea that one could give one's life to the emperor as he was to traditional aristocracy or classical republicanism.

On the negative side, this means that, in an ideal Hobbesian state that not even Hobbes thinks can exist, there is no sense of shared meaning

---

[52] Rosen (2012, 1).
[53] Pettit (1997, 37).
[54] Pettit (2008, 1).
[55] Pettit (1997, 50).

conferred by living in a community with others, and no sense that one's death can have meaning in the continued existence of that community. The only significance of such a death is the complete disappearance of the deceased. On the positive side, the absence of an all-encompassing framework of meaning leaves one the freedom to find meaning where he will. Just as theories of religious toleration could only arise on the basis of an acknowledgement that the truth about religious matters is unknowable, the autonomy prized by modern liberalism comes at the expense of never being able to be fully a part of something like the city Pericles describes in the funeral oration.

Beneath the surface, this can be a chilling vision of life in a liberal system, and as we will see below, many have indeed found this aspect of it disturbing. It is in fact a common criticism of the West that liberalism is a soulless system, which, because it sees no meaning beyond the material world, is concerned only with material things and the preservation of the individual's material existence. From another point of view, though, the value Western states today place on human life probably stems less from an obsession with comfortable self-preservation, than from a very deep-rooted belief in the dignity of mankind. This longing for dignity may result from the fact that there is no shared sense of any real path beyond our mortality; that every individual is allowed, or, depending on one's point of view, forced to struggle with this fact.

We can also see the connection between Hobbes and modern ideas about dignity and recognition in one of the best-known statements on modern liberty, Isaiah Berlin's "Two Concepts of Liberty." Hobbes, for Berlin, is one of those responsible for the turn to negative freedom which is a hallmark of liberalism. Hobbes, though, according to Berlin, did not shy away from calling a spade a spade: "[H]e did not pretend that a sovereign does not enslave; he justified this slavery, but at least he did not have the effrontery to call it freedom."[56] Hobbes, in Berlin's terms, was an enemy of the concept of positive liberty, the idea that "the real self may be conceived as something wider than the individual ... as a social 'whole' of which the individual is an element or aspect: a tribe, a race, a Church, a State ... This entity is then identified as being the 'true' self."[57] But the view of man as little more than a slave who is provided with only a negative freedom from the state, which we do find in Hobbes, became the basis for a new ideal of autonomous man who creates his own ends

[56] Berlin (2000, 235).
[57] Berlin (2000, 204).

and should be allowed the space in which to pursue them. For Berlin, philosophers from Locke to Mill argue that

> there ought to exist a certain minimum area of personal freedom which must on no account be violated; for if it is overstepped, the individual will find himself in an area too narrow for even that minimum development of his natural faculties which alone makes it possible to pursue, and even to conceive, the various ends which men hold good or right or sacred.[58]

This view of man as being left on his own to draw his own conclusions about the meaning of life is, I have been arguing, one of Hobbes's goals. But for Hobbes, as for more recent liberal thinkers such as Berlin, this formulating and pursuing of one's own individual ends is almost necessarily silent about the possibility of immortality or transcendence; concepts with which the tribe, the Church and the total state had no such trouble. What Hobbes may or may not have been able to predict is that this development might have led, inadvertently, to a commitment to the concept mankind as a whole rather than to one's particular group.

And what was it that Hobbes wanted? No doubt he found his highest joy in philosophy. He was serious when he said that philosophy was not meant to be a matter of solitary contemplation but something of practical use to humanity. I have argued that Hobbes should be seen more as a sculptor than a scientist; his real work of art was shaping the thoughts of future generations. Hobbes wanted to live a long life, but he wanted even more to leave his philosophy as a monument to unageing intellect.

---

[58] Berlin (2000, 196).

Bibliography

Abizadeh, Arash (2011). "Hobbes on the Causes of War: A Disagreement Theory," *American Political Science Review* 101: 298–315.
Abosch, Yishaia (2009). "Hope, Fear, and the Mollification of the Vanquished in Hobbes's *Behemoth or the Long Parliament*," *Political Research Quarterly* 62: 16–28.
Ahrensdorf, Peter (2000). "The Fear of Death and the Longing for Immortality: Hobbes and Thucydides on Human Nature and the Problem of Anarchy," *The American Political Science Review* 94: 579–94.
Andrew, Donna T. (1980). "The Code of Honour and Its Critics: The Opposition to Duelling in England, 1700–1850," *Social History* 5: 409–34.
Ariès, Philippe (1991). *The Hour of Our Death*, transl. Helen Weaver. Oxford.
Aristophanes (2005). *Frogs*, transl. B.B. Rogers. Stilwell, KS.
Aristotle (1984). *Politics*, transl. Carnes Lord. Chicago.
    (2006). *Art of Rhetoric*, transl. J.H. Freese. Cambridge, MA.
Aubrey, John (1898). *"Brief Lives" chiefly of Contemporaries, set down by John Aubrey, between the Years 1669 & 1696*, ed. Andrew Clark. Oxford.
Augustine (1998). *Confessions*, transl. Henry Chadwick. Oxford.
    (2003). *City of God*, transl. Henry Bettenson. London and New York.
Bacon, Francis (1989). *The Great Instauration*. Wheeling.
    (2002a). *Essays, or Counsels, Civil and Moral*. London.
    (2002b). *The Great Instauration, in the Major Works*, ed. Brian Vickers. Oxford.
Bailey, Lloyd R. (1986). "Enigmatic Bible Passages: Gehenna: The Topography of Hell," *The Biblical Archeologist* 49: 187–91.
Baumgold, Deborah (1988). *Hobbes's Political Theory*. Cambridge.
    (1990). "Hobbes's Political Sensibility: The Menace of Political Ambition," in *Thomas Hobbes and Political Theory*, ed. Mary G. Dietz. Lawrence, KS.
Becker, Ernest (1997). *The Denial of Death*. New York.
Bede (1990). *Ecclesiastical History of the English People*, transl. Leo Sherley Price. London.
Beiner, Ronald (2011). *Civil Religion: A Dialogue in the History of Political Philosophy*. Cambridge.

Bejan, Teresa (2010). "Teaching the *Leviathan*: Thomas Hobbes on Education," *Oxford Review of Education* 36: 607–26.
Bellarmine, Robert (2012). *On Temporal and Spiritual Authority*. Indianapolis.
Berkowitz, Peter (2000). *Virtue and the Making of Modern Liberalism*. Princeton.
Berlin, Isaiah (2000). *The Proper Study of Mankind*, ed. Henry Hardy and Roger Hausheer. New York.
Berns, Laurence (1987). "Hobbes," in *History of Political Philosophy*, ed. Leo Strauss and Joseph Cropsey. Chicago.
Blits, Jan H. (1989). "Hobbesian Fear," *Political Theory* 17: 417–31.
Boyd, Richard (2001). "Thomas Hobbes and the Perils of Pluralism," *Journal of Politics* 63: 392–413.
Braddick, Michael (2009). *God's Fury, England's Fire*. London.
Bramhall, John (1842–1845). *The Works of the Most Reverend Father in God, John Bramhall*. 5 vols. Oxford.
  (1999). "Bramhall's Discourse on Liberty and Necessity," in *Hobbes and Bramhall on Liberty and Necessity*, ed. be Vere Chappell. Cambridge.
Bredekamp, Horst (2007). "Thomas Hobbes's Visual Strategies," in *The Cambridge Companion to Hobbes's Leviathan*, ed. Patricia Springborg. Cambridge.
Bunyan, John (1965). *The Pilgrim's Progress*. London.
Burns, Norman T. (1972). *Christian Mortalism from Tyndale to Milton*. Cambridge, MA.
Calvin, John (2008). *Institutes of the Christian Religion*, transl. Henry Beveridge. Peabody, MA.
Cantalupo, Charles (1991). *A Literary Leviathan: Thomas Hobbes's Masterpiece of Language*. Lewisburg, PA.
Chabot, Dana (June 1995). "Thomas Hobbes: Skeptical Moralist," *The American Political Science Review* 89:2, 401–10.
Coker, Christopher (2002). *Waging War Without Warriors? The Changing Culture of Military Conflict*. London.
Collins, Jeffrey R. (2005). *The Allegiance of Thomas Hobbes*. Oxford.
  (2007). "Silencing Thomas Hobbes: The Presbyterians," in *The Cambridge Companion to Hobbes's Leviathan*, ed. Patricia Springborg. Cambridge.
Cooke, Paul D. (1996). *Hobbes and Christianity: Reassessing the Bible in Leviathan*. New York.
Cooper, Julie (2007). "Thomas Hobbes on the Political Theorist's Vocation," *The Historical Journal* 50: 519–47.
  (2010). "Vainglory, Modesty, and Political Agency in the Political Theory of Thomas Hobbes," *The Review of Politics* 72: 241–69.
Cudworth, Ralph (1678). *The True Intellectual System of the Universe*. London.
Curley, Edwin (1992). "'I Durst Not Write So Boldly' or, How to Read Hobbes' Theological-Political Treatise," in *Hobbes e Spinoza, Atti del Convegno Internazionale, Urbino, 14–17 ottobre, 1988*, ed. Daniela Bostrenghi, intro. Emilia Giancotti. Napoli.
  (1996). "Calvin and Hobbes, or, Hobbes as an Orthodox Christian," *Journal of the History of Philosophy* 34: 257–71.

Dallmayr, Fred R. (August 1969). "Hobbes and Existentialism: Some Affinities," *The Journal of Politics* 31:3, 615–40.
Descartes, René (1995). "Meditations on First Philosophy," in *Selected Philosophical Writings*, transl. John Cottingham et al. Cambridge.
Dietz, Mary G. (1990). "Hobbes's Subject as Citizen," in *Thomas Hobbes and Political Theory*, ed. Mary G. Dietz. Lawrence, KS.
Dowell, John (1683). *The Leviathan Heretical, or, The Charge Exhibited in Parliament Against M. Hobbes Justified by the Refutation of a Book of his Entituled The Historical Narration of Heresie and the Punishments Thereof.* Oxford.
Dryden, John (1847). *The Works of John Dryden in Verse and Prose, Volume 2.* New York.
Dungey, Nicholas (2008). "Thomas Hobbes's Materialism, Language and the Possibility of Politics," *The Review of Politics* 70:2, 190–220.
Eisenach, Eldon J. (1981). *Two Worlds of Liberalism.* Chicago.
Elazer, Daniel J. (1992). "Hobbes Confronts Scripture," *Jewish Political Studies Review* 4: 3–24.
Eliot, T.S. (1975). "Tradition and the Individual Talent," in *Selected Prose of T.S. Eliot*, ed. Frank Kermode. New York.
Evrigenis, Ioannis (2014). *Images of Anarchy: The Rhetoric and Science of Hobbes's State of Nature.* Princeton.
Farr, James (1990). "Atomes of Scripture: Hobbes and the Politics of Biblical Interpretation," in *Thomas Hobbes and Political Theory*, ed. Mary G. Dietz. Lawrence, KS.
Faust, Drew Gilpin (2008). *This Republic of Suffering: Death and the American Civil War.* New York.
Flathman, Richard E. (1993). *Thomas Hobbes: Skepticism, Individuality and Chastened Politics.* London.
Freund, Julien (1980). "Le thème de la peur chez Hobbes," *Revue européenne des sciences sociales* 18:49, 13–32.
Frost, Samantha (2005). "Hobbes and the Matter of Self-Consciousness," *Political Theory* 33: 495–517.
Galston, William A. (1991). *Liberal Purposes: Goods, Virtues, and Diversity in the Liberal State.* Cambridge.
Garsten, Bryan (2006). *Saving Persuasion: A Defense of Rhetoric and Judgment.* Cambridge.
  (2010). "Religion and Representation in Hobbes," in *Leviathan*, ed. Ian Shapiro. New Haven, CT.
Gauthier, David P. (1969). *The Logic of Leviathan.* Oxford.
Gillespie, Michael (2006). "Where Did All the Evils Go?" in *Naming Evil, Judging Evil*, ed. Ruth Grant. Chicago.
Goldsmith, M.M. (1966). *Hobbes's Science of Politics.* New York.
Gray, Glenn J. (1998). *The Warriors: Reflections on Men in Battle.* Lincoln, NE.
Guizot, Francois (1838). *Memoirs of George Monck, Duke of Albermarle*, transl. J. Stuart Wortley. London.

Hamilton, Alistair (1999). *The Apocryphal Apocalypse: The Reception of the Second Book of Esdras (4 Ezra) from the Renaissance to the Enlightenment*. Oxford.
Hampton, Jean (1986). *Hobbes and the Social Contract Theory*. Cambridge.
Heath, James (1663). *A Brief Chronicle of the Civil Wars of England, Scotland and Ireland*. London.
Heidegger, Martin (1977). "The Word of Nietzsche 'God is Dead,'" in *The Question Concerning Technology and Other Essays*, transl. William Lovitt. New York.
Heraclitus (1996). *Fragments*, transl. T.M. Robinson. Toronto.
Hillier, H.C., and Basit Bilala Koshul (2015). *Muhammad Iqbal: Essays on the Reconstruction of Modern Muslim Thought*. Edinburgh.
Hirschaman, Albert O. (1997). *The Passions and the Interests*. Princeton.
Hobbes, Thomas (1839). *De Corpore in, English Works, Volume I*, ed. William Molesworth. London.
  (1840a). "An Answer to Bishop Bramhall's Book, called 'The Catching of the Leviathan.'" In *English Works IV*, ed. William Molesworth. London.
  (1840b). "Considerations upon the Reputation, Loyalty, Manners, and Religion, of Thomas Hobbes of Malmesbury, Written by Himself by Way of a Letter to a Learned Person," in *English Works IV*, ed. William Molesworth. London.
  (1840c). "*An Historical Narration Concerning Heresy, and the Punishment Thereof*" in English Works IV, ed. William Molesworth. London.
  (1845a). *The Whole Art of Rhetoric in English Works VI*, ed. William Molesworth. London.
  (1845b). "Six Lessons to the Savilian Professors of the Mathematics." In *English Works Volume VII*, ed. William Molesworth. London.
  (1973). *Critique du De Mundo de Thomas White*, ed. Jean Jacuot and Harold Whitmore Jones. Paris.
  (1976). *Thomas White's De Mundo Examined*, transl. Harold Whitmore Jones. London.
  (1990). *Behemoth, or, the Long Parliament*, ed. Ferdinand Tonnies. Chicago.
  (1994a). *Human Nature and De Corpore Politico*, ed. J.C.A. Gaskin.
  (1994b). *Leviathan*, ed. Edwin Curley. Indianapolis.
  (1994c). "Verse Autobiography," in *Leviathan*, ed. Edwin Curley. Indianapolis.
  (1996). *Leviathan*, ed. Richard Tuck. Cambridge.
  (1997). *A Dialogue between a Philosopher and a Student of the Common Laws of England*, ed. Joseph Cropsey. Chicago.
  (1998a). *Man and Citizen*, ed. Bernard Gert, transl. Charles T. Wood et al. Indianapolis.
  (1998b). *On the Citizen*, ed. Richard Tuck and Michael Silverthorne. Cambridge.
  (1999). *Human Nature and De Corpore Politico*. Oxford.
  (2004). *De Cive: The Latin Version*, ed. Howard Warrender. Oxford.
  (2007). *The Correspondence of Thomas Hobbes*, ed. Noel Malcolm. Oxford.
  (2012). *Leviathan*, ed. Noel Malcolm. Oxford.

Hoekstra, Kinch (2006). "The End of Philosophy: The Case of Hobbes," *Proceedings of the Aristotelian Society, New Series* 106: 25–62.
Holmes, Stephen (1990). "Political Psychology in Hobbes's *Behemoth*," in *Thomas Hobbes and Political Theory*, ed. Mary Dietz. Lawrence, KS.
Honey, Charles (2008). "Belief in Hell Dips, but Some Say They've Already Been There," http://pewforum.org/news/display.php?NewsID=16260.
Hood, F.C. (1964). *The Divine Politics of Thomas Hobbes*. Oxford.
Hyde, Edward, Earl of Clarendon (1676). "A Brief View and Survey of the Dangerous and Pernicious Errors to Church and State," in Mr. Hobbes's Book, Entitled *Leviathan*. Oxford.
  (2009). *The History of the Rebellion*, ed. Paul Seaward. Oxford.
Iqbal, Muhammad (2012). *The Reconstruction of Religious Thought in Islam*, ed. M. Saeed Sheikh. Stanford.
Israel, Jonathan (2002). *Radical Enlightenment: Philosophy and the Making of Modernity 1650–1750*. Oxford.
James, D.G. (1949). *The Life of Reason: Hobbes, Locke, Bolingbroke*. London.
Jamison Jr., Ted R. (1975). *George Monck and the Restoration: Victor without Bloodshed*. Fort Worth, TX.
Johnson Bagby, Laurie M. (2009). *Thomas Hobbes; Turning Point for Honor*. New York.
Johnston, David (1986). *The Rhetoric of Leviathan: Thomas Hobbes and the Politics of Cultural Transformation*. Princeton.
  (1989). "Hobbes's Mortalism," *History of Political Thought* 10: 647–63.
Kahn, Victoria (1985). *Rhetoric, Prudence, and Skepticism in the Renaissance*. Ithaca, NY.
  (1994). *Machiavellian Rhetoric: From the Counter-Reformation to Milton*. Princeton.
Kant, Immanuel (1991). *Political Writings*, ed. H.S. Reiss. Cambridge.
  (2000). "Idea for a Universal History," in *Political Writings*, ed. Hand Reiss, transl. H.B. Nisbet. Cambridge.
Kapust, Dan J. and Brandon P. Turner (2013). "Democratical Gentlemen and the Lust for Mastery: Status, Ambition and the Language of Liberty in Hobbes's Political Thought," *Political Theory* 41: 648–75.
Kateb, George (1989). "Hobbes and the Irrationality of Politics," *Political Theory* 17: 355–91.
Kavka, Gregory (1986). *Hobbesian Moral and Political Theory*. Princeton.
Kierkegaard, Soren (1980). *The Concept of Anxiety*, transl. Reidar Thomte. Princeton.
Kojève, Alexandre (2007). *Outline of a Phenomenology of Right*, transl. Bryan-Paul Frost and Robert Howse. Plymouth.
Krause, Sharon R. (2002). *Liberalism with Honor*. Cambridge, MA.
Kraynak, Robert P. (1982). "Hobbes's *Behemoth* and the Argument for Absolutism," *American Political Science Review* 76: 837–47.
  (1990). *History and Modernity in the Thought of Thomas Hobbes*. Ithaca.
  (1992). "The Idea of the Messiah in the Political Thought of Thomas Hobbes," *Jewish Political Science Review* 4:2, 115–38.
Kuhn, Thomas S. (1996). *The Structure of Scientific Revolutions*. Chicago.

Lamprecht, Sterling (1940). "Hobbes and Hobbism," *American Political Science Review* 34: 31–53.

Leijenhorst, Cees (2007). "Sense and Nonsense About Sense; Hobbes and the Aristotelians on Sense Perception and Imagination," in *The Cambridge Companion to Hobbes's Leviathan*, ed. Patricia Springborg. Cambridge.

Lloyd, S.A. (1992). *Ideals as Interests in Hobbes's Leviathan*. Cambridge.

(2009). *Morality in the Philosophy of Thomas Hobbes*. Cambridge.

Locke, John (1965). *On the Reasonableness of Christianity, As Delivered in the Scriptures*. Chicago.

Lott, Tommy L. (1982). "The Psychology of Self-Preservation in Hobbes," *Revue européenne des sciences sociales* 20:61, 37–55.

Lucretius (1992). *On the Nature of Things*, transl. W.H.D. Rose, ed. Jeffrey Henderson. Cambridge, MA.

Lund, William R. (1992). "Hobbes on Opinion, Private Judgment and Civil War," *History of Political Thought* 13: 51–72.

Luther, Martin (1962). *Martin Luther; Selections from His Writings*, ed. John Dillenberger. New York.

Luttwak, Edward (1995). "Toward Post-Heroic Warfare," *Foreign Affairs* 74: 109–22.

(1999). "From Vietnam to *Desert Fox*: Civil-Military Relations in Modern Democracies," *Survival* 41: 99–112.

Machiavelli, Niccolò (1996). *Discourses on Livy*, transl. Harvey Mansfield and Nathan Tarcov. Chicago.

Malcolm, Noel (2002). *Aspects of Hobbes*. Oxford.

(2012). *Leviathan, Introduction*. Oxford.

Mansfield, Harvey (2006). *Manliness*. New Haven, CT.

Mara, Gerald (1988). "Hobbes's Counsel to Sovereigns," *The Journal of Politics* 50: 390–411.

Marlowe, Christopher (1997). *The Jew of Malta*, ed. David Bevington. Manchester.

Martel, James R. (2007). *Subverting the Leviathan*. New York.

Martinich, A.P. (1992). *The Two Gods of Leviathan*. Cambridge.

(1999). *Hobbes: A Biography*. Cambridge.

McClure, Christopher S. (2008). "Stopping to Smell the Roses: Rousseau and Mortality in the Modern World," *Perspectives on Political Science* 37: 99–108.

(2011). "Hell and Anxiety in Hobbes's *Leviathan*," *Review of Politics* 73: 1–27.

(2014). "War, Madness and Death: The Paradox of Honor in Hobbes's *Leviathan*," *The Journal of Politics* 76: 114–25.

McGrath, Alister E. (2005). *Iustitia Dei: A History of the Christian Doctrine of Justification*. Cambridge.

Mill, John Stuart (1910). *The Letters of John Stuart Mill Volume 2*, ed. Hugh S.R. Elliot. New York.

Miller, Ted H. (2004). "The Uniqueness of *Leviathan*: Authorizing Poets, Philosopher, and Sovereigns," in *Leviathan after 350 Years*, ed. Tom Sorell and Luc Foisneau. Oxford.

(2011). *Mortal Gods: Science, Politics, and the Humanist Ambitions of Thomas Hobbes*. University Park, PA.
Milner, Benjamin (1988). "Hobbes: On Religion," *Political Theory* 16: 400–25.
Milton, John (2008). *Paradise Lost*, ed. William Kerrigan et al. New York.
Mintz, Samuel (1962). *The Hunting of Leviathan*. Cambridge.
Mitchell, Joshua (1996). *Not by Reason Alone*. Chicago.
Montaigne, Michel de (2003). *The Complete Essays*, transl. M.A. Screech. London.
Nietzsche, Friedrich (1974). *The Gay Science*, transl. Walter Kaufmann. New York.
  (1982). "Thus Spoke Zarathustra," in *The Portable Nietzsche*, ed., transl. Walter Kaufmann. New York.
  (1989). *Beyond Good and Evil*, transl. Walter Kaufmann. New York.
Oakeshott, Michael (1991). *Rationalism in Politics and Other Essays*. Indianapolis.
Orwin, Clifford (1997). *The Humanity of Thucydides*. Princeton.
Parkin, Jon (2007). *Taming the Leviathan: The Reception of the Political and Religious Ideas of Thomas Hobbes in England 1640–1700*. Cambridge.
Patrides, C.A. (1964). "Renaissance and Modern Views of Hell," *The Harvard Theological Review* 57: 217–36.
Peltonen, Markku (2001). "Francis Bacon, the Earl of Northampton, and the Jacobean Anti-Duelling Campaign," *The Historical Journal* 44: 1–28.
Pettit, Philip (1997). *Republicanism: A Theory of Freedom and Government*. Oxford.
  (2008). *Made with Words: Hobbes on Language, Mind and Politics*. Princeton.
Pindar (1997). *Nemian Odes, Isthmian Odes, Fragments*, transl. William H. Race. Cambridge, MA.
Pippin, Robert (1999). *Modernism as a Philosophical Problem*. Malden, MA.
Plutarch (1991). *Moralia X*, transl. Harold North Fowler. Cambridge, MA.
Pocock, John G.A. (1971). "Time, History and Eschatology in the Thought of Thomas Hobbes," in *Politics, Language and Time*. New York.
  (1973). "Time, History and Eschatology in the Thought of Thomas Hobbes," *Politics, Language and Time*. New York.
Polin, Raymond (1981). *Hobbes, Dieu, et les hommes*. Paris.
Prokhovnik, Raia (1991). *Rhetoric and Philosophy in Hobbes' Leviathan*. New York.
Robin, Corey (2004). *Fear: The History of a Political Idea*. Oxford.
Rosato, Sebastian (2003). "The Flawed Logic of Democratic Peace Theory," *The American Political Science Review* 97: 585–602.
Rosen, Michael (2012). *Dignity*. Cambridge, MA.
Rousseau, Jean-Jacques (1966). *Emile, ou, de l'education*. Paris.
Ryan, Alan (1983). "Hobbes, Toleration, and the Inner Life," in *The Nature of Political Theory*, ed. David Miller and Larry Siedentop. Oxford.
Schmitt, Carl (2007). *The Concept of the Political*, transl. George Schwab. Chicago.

(2008). *The Leviathan in the State Theory of Thomas Hobbes: Meaning and Failure of a Political Symbol*, transl. George Schwab. Chicago.
Scott, John T. (2003). "Godolphin and the Whale: Friendship and the Framing of Hobbes's *Leviathan*," in *Love and Friendship: Rethinking Politics and Affection in Modern Times*, ed. Eduardo A. Velasquez. New York.
Seery, John (1996). *Political Theory for Mortals; Shades of Justice, Images of Death*. Ithaca, NY.
Shakespeare, William (1997). "Henry V," in *The Riverside Shakespeare*. New York.
Shapin, Steven and Simon Schaffer (1989). *Leviathan and the Air-Pump: Hobbes, Boyle, and the Experimental Life*. Princeton.
Shklar, Judith (1989). "The Liberalism of Fear," in *Liberalism and the Moral Life*, ed. Nancy L. Rosenblum. Cambridge.
Shoemaker, Robert B. (2002). "The Taming of the Duel: Masculinity, Honour and Ritual Violence in London, 1660–1800," *The Historical Journal* 45: 525–45.
Skinner, Quentin (1996). *Reason and Rhetoric in the Philosophy of Hobbes*. Cambridge.
 (1997). *Reason and Rhetoric in the Philosophy of Hobbes*. New York.
Slomp, Gabriella (2000). *Thomas Hobbes and the Political Philosophy of Glory*. New York.
Sorell, Tom (1986). *Hobbes*. New York.
Spragens, Thomas (1973). *The Politics of Motion: The World of Thomas Hobbes*. London.
Springborg, Patricia (1975). "Leviathan and the Problem of Ecclesiastical Authority," *Political Theory* 3: 289–303.
Sreedhar, Susanne (2010). *Hobbes on Resistance; Defying the Leviathan*. Cambridge.
Stauffer, Devin (2007). "Reopening the Quarrel between the Ancients and the Moderns: Leo Strauss's Critique of Hobbes's 'New Political Science,'" *American Political Science Review* 101: 223–33.
Strauss, Leo (1959). *What is Political Philosophy?* Chicago.
 (1963). *The Political Philosophy of Hobbes; Its Basis and Its Genesis*, transl. Elsa M. Sinclair. Chicago.
 (1965). *Natural Right and History*. Chicago.
 (2011). *Hobbes's Critique of Religion and Related Writings*, transl., ed. Gabriel Bartlett and Svetozar Minkov. Chicago.
Strong, Tracy (1993). "How to Write Scripture: Words, Authority, and Politics in Thomas Hobbes," *Critical Inquiry* 20: 128–59.
Taylor, Charles (1991). *The Malaise of Modernity*. Toronto.
Teeter, Louis (1936). "The Dramatic Uses of Hobbes's Political Thought," *ELH* 3: 140–69.
Tenison, Thomas (1670). *The Creed of Mr. Thomas Hobbes Examined in a Feigned Conference between Him and a Student in Divinity*. London.
 (1695). *A Sermon Concerning the Folly of Atheism*. London.
Thomas, Keith (2010). *The Ends of Life*. Oxford.
Thucydides (1942). *Historiae I*. Oxford.
 (1989). *The Peloponnesian War*, transl. Thomas Hobbes. Chicago.

Tolstoy, Leo (2004). *The Death of Ivan Ilyich and Master and Man*, transl. Ann Pasternak Slater. New York.
Tuck, Richard (1990). "Hobbes and Locke on Toleration," in *Thomas Hobbes and Political Theory*, ed. Mary Dietz. Lawrence, KS.
  (1993). *Philosophy and Government 1572–1651*. Cambridge.
  (1998). "Hobbes and Education," in *Philosophers on Education: New Historical Perspectives*, ed. Amelie Oksenberg Rorty. New York.
Vaughan, Geoffrey, M. (2002). *Behemoth Teaches Leviathan*. New York.
Walker, D.P. (1964). *The Decline of Hell: Seventeenth-Century Discourses of Eternal Torment*. Chicago.
Walzer, Michael (1970). *Obligations: Essays on Disobedience, War, and Citizenship*. Cambridge, MA.
Warrender, Howard (1957). *The Political Philosophy of Hobbes: His Theory of Obligation*. Oxford.
Zagorin, Perez (2007). "Clarendon against *Leviathan*," in *The Cambridge Companion to Hobbes's Leviathan*, ed. Patricia Springborg. Cambridge.
  (2009). *Hobbes and the Law of Nature*. Princeton.
Zarka, Yves Charles. (1996). "First Philosophy and the Foundation of Knowledge," in *The Cambridge Companion to Hobbes*, ed. Tom Sorell. Cambridge.

Index

Abizadeh, Arash, 166
Abosch, Yishaia, 173
absolutism, 47
Adam, 69, 173
Adamite, 178
Ahrensdorf, Peter, 13, 24, 26, 27, 28, 31, 55, 149, 157
air pump, 72
Alcibiades, 13, 16, 206
Anabaptist, 178, 190
anarchy, 13, 16, 27, 159, 162
angels, 94, 124
Aquinas, Thomas, 21, 39, 40, 189
Ariès, Philippe, 11, 119, 168
Aristophanes, 65
Aristotle, 25, 28, 33, 34, 36–40, 41, 43, 44, 48, 50, 58, 61, 65, 66, 70, 71, 81, 86, 87, 155, 169, 175, 190, 198, 208, 212, 213
Atabalipa, 180
atheism, 5, 6, 7, 8, 52, 55, 89, 93, 94, 115, 137, 138, 205
Athelstan, 10
Athens, 13, 14, 16, 17, 19, 20, 21, 26, 80, 85, 101
Aubrey, John, 33
Augustine, 25, 111, 206

Bacon, Francis, 11, 38, 159, 193, 205
Bathurst, Ralph, 68
Baumgold, Deborah, 153, 165
Becker, Ernest, 15
Bede, 207, 208
Beiner, Ronald, 106, 177

Bejan, Teresa, 150
Bellarmine, Robert, 35, 104, 202
Berlin, Isaiah, 218, 219
Berns, Laurence, 55, 149
Blits, Jan, 135, 158, 214
Bolton, Robert, 129
Boyle, Robert, 72, 77, 131, 148
Bramhall, John, 51, 127, 135, 138, 139, 142, 143, 145
Brasidas, 13, 20
Bredekamp, Horst, 86, 120
Bunyan, John, 111
Burns, Norman T., 127, 128, 222

Calvin, John, 11, 98, 126, 127, 128, 190
Cambridge Platonists, 5
Camus, 4, 211
Cantalupo, Charles, 148
Cataline, 157, 169, 186
Cato, Elder, 10
Cavendish, William, 10
Chabot, Dana, 109
Charles I, 92, 106, 177, 178, 179, 183, 184, 188, 196
Cicero, 3, 37, 48, 186, 198
Coker, Christopher, 170
Collins, Jeffrey, 92, 137, 138, 139, 140
commodious living, 12, 13, 17, 160
conscience, 109, 116, 123, 130, 186, 216
consent, 47, 74, 107, 179, 197, 200, 203
Constantine, 36
Cooke, Paul, D., 136
Cooper, Julie, 10, 49, 156

232 Index

Copernicus, 64, 67
Corcyra, 13, 17, 18
Cromwell, Oliver, 174, 175, 194–9
Cromwell, Richard, 196
Cudworth, Robert, 5, 6, 7, 8, 51, 56
Curley, Edwin, 10, 50, 115, 120, 171
Cyrus, 85

Dallmayr, Fred, 4, 5, 211
Descartes, René, 74, 76, 133, 216
Dietz, Mary, 115, 156, 173, 223
Diodorus Siculus, 80
Dowell, John, 5, 47, 101
Dowland, John, 54
Dryden, John, 190
Dueling, 159–60
Dungey, Nicholas, 73, 74
Duppa, Brian, 47

Eisenach, Eldon J., 106
Elazer, Daniel J., 106
Eliot, T.S., 103
Empusa, 65, 70
Epicurean, 5, 7
equality, 29, 49, 82, 83, 156, 158, 165, 200, 201, 203, 204, 209, 216
Esdras, 'Ezra', 113, 114, 115
Euclid, 46
Evrigenis, Ioannis, 13, 28, 31, 46, 55

Farr, James, 115, 134
Faust, Drew Gilpin, 167
Fifth-Monarchy men, 178
Filmer, Robert, 47, 51
Flathman, Richard E., 5, 73
free will, 127, 138, 142

Galileo, 42, 64, 67
Garsten, Bryan, 56, 57, 88, 100, 148, 155
Gassendi, Pierre, 64
Gauthier, David, 61, 149
geometry, 38, 41, 43, 51, 63, 67, 71, 77, 79
Gillespie, Michael, 143
Godolphin, Sidney, 164, 167, 171
Goldsmith, M.M., 157
Guizot, Francois, 195, 196, 197, 198

Hamilton, Alistair, 113
Hammond, Henry, 47
Hampton, Jean, 149
Harrington, James, 47

Heath, James, 175, 176, 197
Heidegger, Martin, 13, 71, 212–16
Henry VIII, 106, 189, 191
Heraclitus, 76
Hirschaman, Albert O., 193
Hoekstra, Kinch, 30
Holmes, Stephen, 172, 173, 174, 192
Hood, F.C., 119, 120
Hyde, Edward, first Earl of Clarendon, 8, 28, 48, 51, 52, 55, 92–9, 100, 109, 139, 140, 197, 198

Iqbal, Muhammad, 12
Israel, Jonathan, 113, 205

James I, 106
Johnson Bagby, Laurie M., 148, 153, 163, 164, 167, 225
Johnston, David, 2, 4, 22, 23, 26, 27, 28, 30, 61, 62, 63, 64, 89, 125, 130, 148, 156, 163

Kahn, Victoria, 31, 59, 148
Kant, 12, 13, 207, 209, 210, 213, 215
Kapust, Dan, 186
Kateb, George, 149, 161, 162, 165, 202
Kavka, Gregory, 61, 149
Kepler, Johannes, 64
Kierkegaard, Soren, 206, 210, 214
Kojève, Alexandre, 210
Kraynak, Robert P., 106, 130, 166, 172, 173
Kuhn, Thomas, 62

Lamprecht, Sterling, 9
Lloyd, S.A., 148, 149, 151, 152
Locke, John, 16, 92, 98, 103, 138, 175, 219
Long Parliament, 35, 173, 194, 196
Lott, Timothy, 81
Lucretius, 5, 6, 208
Luther, Martin, 128, 133, 190
Luttwak, Edward, 170

Macauley, Thomas Babington, 53
Machiavelli, Niccolò, 25, 58, 59, 85, 157, 181, 205
Malcolm, Noel, 5, 6, 31, 40, 47, 58, 88, 91, 92, 97, 108, 138, 140, 145, 173
Malmesbury, 1, 9, 10, 34, 48, 57, 59
Mansfield, Harvey, 163, 164, 181
Marlowe, Christopher, 59

Index

Martel, James, 34, 35, 100
Martinich, A.P., 1, 9, 32, 45, 55, 56, 91, 119, 125, 126, 127, 134, 149
martyrs, 3, 96, 97, 98, 131, 182
materialism, 51, 73, 91, 94
McGrath, Alister E., 2
Merleau-Ponty, Maurice, 4
Mersenne, Marin, 64, 74
Mill, John Stuart, 12
Miller, Ted, 30, 31, 73, 75, 102, 140, 148
Milton, John, 59, 90, 91, 126, 127, 207
Mintz, Samuel, 17, 47, 48, 50, 52, 53, 56, 59, 127, 134, 136, 137, 138, 142, 156, 172
Mitchell, Joshua, 120, 121, 131
Monck, General George, 28, 172, 194–9
Montaigne, Michel de, 11
Montesquieu, 12
More, Henry, 66
mortalism, 126
Moses, 85, 93, 99, 107, 109, 112, 114

Namaan, 95, 96
natural law, 21, 66, 78, 140, 141
natural right, 79
Newton, Isaac, 138
Nicene Creed, 36
Nicias, 13
Nietzsche, Friedrich, 210–16

Oakeshott, Michael, 3, 23, 25, 54, 149
obligation, 81, 151, 152, 153, 161
Old Testament, 38, 102, 113
Orwin, Clifford, 16

Parkin, Jon, 9, 43, 46, 49, 51, 52, 66, 92, 93, 126, 134, 139, 142, 156
Patrides, C.A., 129
Pausanias, 20
Pelagian, 143
Peleau, Francois, 57, 58
Peltonen, Markku, 159
Pericles, 13, 14, 16, 19, 21, 26, 28, 80, 84, 85, 186, 218
Pettit, Philip, 133, 156, 217
Pindar, 117
Plato, 11, 37, 65, 70, 71, 101, 107, 160
Plutarch, 117, 194
Pocock, John G.A., 91, 119, 131
Polin, Raymond, 91
Prokhovnik, Raia, 35

Quaker, 178, 190
Quintilian, 3

resurrection, 111, 122, 123, 128, 135, 143, 144
Romulus, 85
Rousseau, Jean-Jacques, 205
Royalist, 47, 52, 92
Ryan, Alan, 110

Sartre, Jean-Paul, 4
Scargill, Daniel, 52
Schmitt, Carl, 154, 200
Scotus, John Duns, 39, 169, 181
Seery, John, 149
Seneca, 55
Shakespeare, William, 187
Shapin, Steven and Simon Schaffer, 71, 72
Shklar, Judith, 157
Skinner, Quentin, 3, 4, 31, 32, 54, 56, 130, 137, 148, 186
Slomp, Gabriella, 160, 166
Smith, Adam, 12
Socinian, 128
Socrates, 55, 57, 81, 160
Sorbière, Samuel, 5, 46, 59, 72
Sorell, Tom, 62, 134, 226
sovereignty, 38, 55, 86, 117, 147, 188, 194, 195, 196, 197, 200, 202, 203, 204
Sparta, 15, 20, 110
Spinoza, Benedict de, 103
Spragens, Thomas A., 25, 62, 175
Springborg, Patricia, 86, 120
Sreedhar, Susanne, 149
state of nature, 7, 13, 18, 19, 22, 27, 31, 39, 44, 51, 58, 82, 86, 141, 148, 157, 158, 168, 171, 193, 201, 203, 204
Stauffer, Devin, 91
Stoics, 11
Strauss, Leo, 4, 7, 23, 31, 54, 91, 120, 130, 136, 137, 154

Taylor, Charles, 210
Teeter, Louis, 59
Tenison, Thomas, 1, 47, 51, 93, 94, 138, 139
Tertullian, 25
Thucydides, 13–22, 31, 45, 50, 173, 175, 176, 206
Tillotson, John, 138

Tocqueville, Alexis de, 210
toleration, 13, 103, 104, 108, 117, 175, 193, 218
Tolstoy, Leo, 12
transubstantiation, 35, 100, 180
trinity, 102
Tuck, Richard, 74, 103, 130
Tyndale, William, 90, 127, 183

universities, 9, 37, 40, 52, 87, 169, 181, 187, 188, 189, 191, 192

vacuum, 72
Vaughan, Geoffrey, 70, 173, 174

Verdus, Francois du, 57
Verse Autobiography, 10, 50
Virgil, 190
Vitoria, Francisco de, 202

Wallis, John, 32, 51, 71, 72
Walzer, Michael, 148, 152, 155, 160
Warrender, Howard, 54, 119, 153
White, Thomas, 125, 167

Yeats, W.B., 190

Zagorin, Perez, 139, 151
Zarka, Charles Yves, 61, 62

Lightning Source UK Ltd.
Milton Keynes UK
UKOW01n2037261016
286235UK00002B/9/P